JACK THE RIPPER
End of a Legend

JACK THE RIPPER
End of a Legend

Calum Reuben Knight

ATHENA PRESS
LONDON

JACK THE RIPPER
End of a Legend
Copyright © Calum Reuben Knight 2005

All Rights Reserved

No part of this book may be reproduced in any form
by photocopying or by any electronic or mechanical means,
including information storage or retrieval systems,
without permission in writing from both the copyright
owner and the publisher of this book.

ISBN 1 84401 484 3

First Published 2005 by
ATHENA PRESS
Queen's House, 2 Holly Road
Twickenham TW1 4EG
United Kingdom

Printed for Athena Press

Preface

In the year 1888, two men and a woman conspired to murder six whores on the streets of England's capital city. They called themselves Jack the Ripper.

This is the story of who they were, and why they did it.

Contents

The Ghost of Mary Jane Kelly	13

Joseph, Mary and George

Mary Jane Kelly and Her Relatives	21
The Chief Mourner	23
George Hutchinson	26
Room Number 13, Millers Court, 26 Dorset Street, Whitechapel	29
The Providence Row Night Refuge and Shelter	33
The Likeness of Joseph Barnett	34
Murder Most Foul	36
The Murder of Emma Smith	38
The Last Days of a Billingsgate Fish Porter	39
George Yard Buildings	40
The Battle of George Yard Buildings	42
The Anagram	45
The Method	46
Bucks Row	48

Blood on Bucks Row	50
The Anagram	56
Number 29, Hanbury Street	58
Horror on Hanbury Street	61
Rings and Things	66
The Anagram	68
Scandal at Scotland Yard	69
The Scribe	72
Berner Street	77
Death in Dutfields Yard	80
The Statement of Matthew Packer	90
The Anagram	93
The Address of Jack the Ripper	94
Mitre Square	95
Mutilation in Mitre Square	97
The Anagram	103
Graffiti on Goulston Street	105
The Postcard	107
The Letter from Hell	109
Appointment with Death	111
Parting is Such Sweet Sorrow	113
The Plan	115

The Cast of Players	117
Mary Kelly, the Girl from Llymaryke	135
Mary Collier	137
The Anagram	138
The Police	140
A German Cousin – Julia	144
The Murder at Millers Court	146
Homeward Bound	149
Home Sweet Home	152
This Woman is Armed and Dangerous	155
A Cousin – Once Removed	162
Bad News	167
No News is Good News	169
The Inquest	170
Thou Shalt Not Bear False Witness	172
Attack is the Best Form of Defence	173
The Anagram – the Final Solution	174
The Man Who St-St-Stuttered	176
The Anagram – the Murder That Never Was	178
The Anagram – the Intended Solution	180

Homicide at Horsleydown	181
Killing on Castle Alley	183
The Package on Pinchin Street	185
Slaughter in Swallow Gardens	186
Savagery in Salamanca Place	191

George Buck

George Buck	195
The Search for George Buck	198
George Buck Died after November 1888	200
Census 1881	204
The Real George Buck	205
George Buck – the Invisible Killer	214

Mary Collier

The Search for Mary Collier	219
William and Mary	222
Philip Davies Collier	225
The French Connection	229
Wedding Bells	232
A Man Named Morganstone	235
A Man Named Joseph Flemming	239
The Wedding – the Witnesses	241
The Best Laid Schemes	244

Marie Thérèse Julien	247
The Franco-Prussian War	252
The Woman Who Never Was	261
Emily Julia Julien	264
The Victim – an Alternative Cousin German	266
Messrs Laurie & Marner	267
Marie Thérèse Julien (After the War)	269
The Second Time Around	275
The Last Will and Testament of Mary Rusher Collier	276
The Dying Days	280
Checklist – did Marie Thérèse Collier masquerade as Mary Jane Kelly?	287

Life… and Death

Joseph Barnett – the Anatomy of a Life	293
Philip Davies Collier… and Violet	303
Selina Ellen Sturman	304
Repent – for the End is Nigh	307
Jack the Ripper's Dead	313

8.30 A.M., FRIDAY, 9 NOVEMBER 1888,
DORSET STREET, WHITECHAPEL, LONDON

The Ghost of Mary Jane Kelly

Dorset Street glistened wet from the overnight rain.

Caroline Maxwell departed from the grim, forbidding building known as Crossinghams Lodging House and she ventured on to the thoroughfare which had the dubious distinction of being the most lawless street in the metropolis. Only the infamous Ratcliffe Highway laid claim to the same distinction.

Caroline Maxwell and her husband Henry worked at Crossinghams: she as a cleaner, and he as the lodging house deputy manager. Caroline had just finished the nightshift and, laden with bucket, brooms and mops, she was on her way home to number 14, Dorset Street.

Caroline was surprised to encounter Mary Jane Kelly, for it was unusual to find Mary Jane up and about at such an early hour. But there she was, standing outside the arched entrance way to Millers Court. Millers Court – a pleasant name in contradiction to the cluster of fearful, dirty tenements to which it alluded. These rooms were let individually to those lucky enough to be able to afford the luxury of such commodious premises.

Mary Jane Kelly resided in a ground floor room – room number 13.

"Why, Mary Jane! What brings you out so early?"

"Oh, Carrie, I do feel so ill. I have the horrors of drink on me, for I have been drinking for several days past."

Caroline noted that Mary Jane did look extremely poorly. "Have half a pint at Ringers. That'll soon make you feel better."

"I've already had one and I've brought it straight up." Mary Jane indicated a doubtful looking pool in the gutter.

"Well, you have my sympathy – I know how you feel. I must go. I have to get my husband some breakfast. I hope you soon feel better," and Caroline Maxwell proceeded on her way noting, as she did so, that Mary Jane was returning to the Court.

Caroline Maxwell quite liked Mary Jane Kelly. An "unfortunate" she may be, but life could be hard, particularly for a woman. And Mary Jane was a pleasant, attractive girl – and intelligent, not like most of her kind.

Once back home, Caroline deposited the tools of her trade and went out to shop in nearby Bishopsgate – just a few ingredients for her husband's breakfast.

When she returned to Dorset Street the time was just after nine o'clock. Caroline was pleased to see Mary Jane up and about.

Mary was standing at the corner of Dorset Street and Commercial Street, right outside the Britannia public house, otherwise known as Ringers, a reference to the landlord's name. She was wearing a dark dress, a black velvet bodice and a coloured scarf around her neck. Mary Jane was talking to a man, a stout man dressed as a market porter would dress. The man had his back to Caroline but she noted that he was about 5'5" in height, and she gained the impression that he was roughly thirty years of age.

Caroline Maxwell took no further notice. It was enough to know that Mary Jane was all right.

But Mary Jane Kelly was very far from all right. In fact, she was dead.

Mary Jane Kelly had been hacked into bloody pieces by a homicidal maniac known as Jack the Ripper. Moreover, the coroner was of the opinion that death had occurred at least five hours before Mary Jane had met, and had spoken to, Caroline Maxwell.

It was very odd.

One of the theories, advanced by the police, was to the effect that Caroline Maxwell had experienced a psychic manifestation; and this was a distinct possibility, for there had been a number of psychic manifestations on Dorset Street that morning: others claimed to have encountered the ghost of Mary Jane Kelly between the hours of 8 and 10 a.m. that long ago grey Friday morning, 9 November 1888.

The burial of the girl from Limerick took place at Leytonstone Catholic Cemetery, St Leonards, Shoreditch, on Monday, 19 November 1888, and a large crowd turned out to watch the procession as it wended its mournful way through the east London streets. Hands reached out to touch the oak and elm coffin affixed with a brass plate upon which was emblazoned the legend:

Marie Jeanette Kelly died 9 November 1888 aged 25 years.

It was a matter of some disappointment that none of Mary Jane Kelly's relatives could be contacted in order that they might attend the funeral for, although she came from a large family, none of them could be traced in time. Indeed, they were never traced. All of the mourners were, at best, casual friends of the dead woman. Only the chief mourner claimed an acquaintance with the deceased longer than one year. He had known her, he claimed, for nearly twenty months.

The sad mourners drifted away and drowned their sorrows in the nearby Birbeck Tavern, leaving one man to mourn alone: her common-law husband, Joseph Barnett.

If funerals can be said to be a success, it was a successful funeral.

Later, the memory of the ceremony would be slightly tarnished by an onlooker who claimed that one man had stayed behind after the others had departed and, thinking himself unobserved, had spat venomously into the still open grave. It's a sad world when people allege such things.

No stone was erected. Mary Jane's friends were not rich people.

The years went by. The earth grew cold and hard. Not a friend, not a relative visited the lonely grave. This was death and desolation.

The girl from Limerick was forgotten.

But not by one man: a man named John Morrison. On 3 December 1986, moved by the sad death of this beautiful young woman; acting in good faith and with generosity of spirit; at his own expense, he erected a memorial stone. The inscription thereon reads:

> *Marie Jeanette Kelly*
> *Age 25*
> *The Prima Donna of Spitalfields*
> *And Last known Victim of*
> *Jack the Ripper*
> *Murdered Fri. Nov. 9th, 1888*
> *Do not stop to stand and stare*
> *Unless to utter fervent prayer*
> *(Mary Magdalene intercede)*
>
> *Dedicated by John Morrison*
> *Dec. 3rd, 1986*

It must be the strangest memorial stone in the world. For the body that lies in this grave is not that of Mary Jane Kelly.

And the inscription commemorates one of the bloodiest killers in the annals of recorded crime:

Dark Angel of Death... Jill the Ripper.

Marie Jeanette Kelly's gravestone
from Peter Underwood's *Jack the Ripper: One Hundred Years of Mystery*

Joseph, Mary and George

Mary Jane Kelly and Her Relatives

Mary Jane Kelly was born circa 1862, in Limerick, Ireland. Whilst still a child she, together with her family, moved to Wales. In Caernarvonshire, or Carmarthenshire, they began a new life. Mary's father, John, obtained work in an iron foundry where he attained the status of foreman or gaffer. The family comprised of John and his wife, six or seven sons and two daughters. Only one name has survived – a brother named Henry who, in the year 1888, was serving with the Second Battalion, Scots Guards, then (in November) enjoying a tour of Ireland. Henry, for some reason, was known amongst his comrades, as Johnto (or Jonto).

The unnamed sister (whether older or younger is not stated) followed her aunt's profession travelling from market place to market place with materials. Mary Jane was very fond of this sister (presumed reciprocated but never stated) who, we are assured, was a respectable woman.

During her formative years Mary Jane apparently enjoyed the benefit of a good education and the family were considered fairly well off.

At the age of just sixteen years, Mary married a collier named Davis or Davies but, tragically, after only two or three years, her husband was killed in an explosion. Unable or unwilling to accept assistance from her, or his, immediate family, Mary Jane, possibly suffering from depression, went to live with a female cousin in Cardiff. This cousin, whose name has not been passed down, made her living from prostitution and Mary Jane was persuaded to follow the same sordid path. Joseph Barnett blamed this cousin for Mary Jane's downfall and, as he told newspaper reporters, "I often told her so".

And Mary Jane had a female relative on the London stage.

And Mary Jane had a young son aged, in 1888, six or seven years.

Mary Jane Kelly removed to the West End of London circa 1884 and there she entertained clients in a high-class brothel. She attracted many men, one of whom persuaded her to accompany him to France, and in Paris she frequently rode around in a carriage.

It was said that after this experience, she took to calling herself Marie Jeanette (though Joseph Barnett insisted that her real name was indeed Marie) but she rejected the idea of living abroad on a permanent basis and, after a time, she returned to London though she continued to make occasional trips to Paris. Possibly her depression had worsened for, this time, she went not to the West End but to the East End; and not just to the East End but to the worst place in the East End: the notorious Ratcliffe Highway.

It was an inexplicable descent that could only end in disaster and, perhaps, she had developed a death wish for she had been known to speak of suicide. On Good Friday, 8 April 1887, she met a man in Commercial Street, Whitechapel. She could not have known it then, but this man was destined to be the chief mourner at her funeral. His name was Joseph Barnett.

There was an immediate mutual attraction and the entranced pair quickly decided to live together. No sooner decided than done. Mary and Joseph took lodgings in George Street the very next day. They would reside at two more addresses before making their final, fateful and, for Mary Jane, fatal move. In February or March 1888, Joseph and Mary took up residence in room number 13, Millers Court.

For all of this information we are indebted to Joseph Barnett. Only the move to Millers Court can be verified.

Mary Jane Kelly has never been traced.

Nor have any of her relatives.

The Chief Mourner

> Whilst we conventional Social Democrats were wasting our time on education, agitation and organisation, some independent genius has taken the matter in hand and, by simply murdering and disembowelling four women, converted the proprietary press to an inept sort of communism.
>
> George Bernard Shaw, in a letter to
> *The Star*, September 24 1888

The chief mourner at the funeral of Mary Jane Kelly was her common-law husband – a man named Joseph Barnett. It was Joseph Barnett who had identified the "unrecognisable" body of Mary Jane. "I know her," he said, "by her hair and her eyes." Joseph Barnett had another unique distinction. Joseph Barnett was Jack the Ripper.

It becomes immediately necessary to qualify that statement. Joseph Barnett styled himself Jack the Ripper and Joseph Barnett signed himself Jack the Ripper. In fact, Joseph Barnett was the leader of a team of three – himself, a woman he named Mary Jane Kelly (Mary J Kelly is an anagram of Mary Jekyll) and a man he named George Hutchinson (G Hutchinson is an anagram of No Such Thing).

Both Mary and George were assigned these *noms de guerre* in order that their true identities would be hidden. Had he felt able to tell the complete truth, Joseph Barnett would, probably, have preferred to title himself, "The Anagram Assassin" for, although Joseph Barnett was a killer, it was, in actual deed, war veteran, Mary Jane Kelly who had the distinction of being "The Ripper".

Joseph Barnett had designed an anagrammatic construction using street names as the basis for his message. The design for the anagram would be comprised of these street names:

George Yard
Bucks Row
Hanbury Street
Berner Street
Mitre Square
Millers Court

It will become necessary, as the anagram resolves, to decide whether Joseph wished the inclusion of additional information, but in the beginning it is certain that he first ensured that he secured his own name then the names of his accomplices. He didn't have to look far. He was aware that Hanbury Street contained an anagrammatic construction of Barnett, but perhaps the easiest choice was George Yard buildings, and "George" and "(M)ary" can be clearly seen in George Yard. (The letter M is taken from (M)illers Court whilst the D from Yar(d) will be carried forward to be utilised later.)

To decipher the anagram it will be necessary to uncover the real surnames of George and Mary and, having done that, to subtract these names, and the name of Joseph Barnett. The residual letters will then reveal, with a little imagination, the message from Jack the Ripper.

In constructing the anagram Joseph Barnett had to:

a) Restrict his activities to the Whitechapel area, for his interest was confined to that region, and to no other.
b) Keep to a particular format whilst keeping a close watch on accumulation of "letter debt".
c) Keep the message as short and succinct as circumstances would allow, else the message would be obliterated under the weight of its own construction.
d) Keep the level of murders to manageable proportions, else he risked inevitable detection.
e) Utilise his own address – Millers Court – for the final murder and "kill" Mary Jane Kelly in the process.

The message would, of necessity, require to be adjusted according to the availability of essential letters, which would be dictated by the self-imposed strictures.

George Hutchinson

At 6 p.m. on Monday, 12 November 1888, (four to five hours after the inquest into the death of Mary Jane Kelly had closed) a man calling himself George Hutchinson strolled confidently into Commercial Street police station. George described himself as a casual labourer and he gave as his address The Victoria Workingmen's Home, Commercial Street.

George, it transpired, had had an unusual experience. He had come face to face with Jack the Ripper and had lived to tell the tale.

It was obvious to the police that George Hutchinson was anxious that the fiend be apprehended. Why else would he have come?

This is George Hutchinson's actual statement:

About 2 a.m. 9th, I was coming by Thrawl Street, Commercial Street, and just before I got to Flower & Dean Street, I met the murdered woman, Kelly, and she said to me: "Hutchinson, will you lend me sixpence?"

I said: "I can't. I have spent all my money going down to Romford."

She said: "Good morning. I must go and find some money."

She went away towards Thrawl Street.

A man coming in the opposite direction to Kelly tapped her on the shoulder and said something to her. They both burst out laughing.

I heard her say: "Alright," to him.

And the man said: "You will be alright for what I have told you."

He then placed his right hand around her shoulders. He also had a kind of a small parcel in his left hand with a kind of strap round it.

I stood against the lamp of The Queen's Head public house, and watched him. They both then came past me and the man hung down his head with his hat over his eyes.

I stooped down and looked him in the face.

He looked at me stern.

They both went into Dorset Street. I followed them. They both stood at the corner of the Court for about three minutes. He said something to her.

She said: "Alright my dear. Come along. You will be comfortable".

He then placed his arm on her shoulder and gave her a kiss. She said she had lost her handkerchief.

He then pulled his handkerchief, a red one, out, and gave it to her. They both then went up the Court together.

I then went to the Court to see if I could see them but could not.

I stood there for about three quarters of an hour to see if they came out. They did not, so I went away.

DESCRIPTION:

Age: 31 to 35 years.
Height: 5'6".
Complexion: Pale.
Dark hair, dark eyes and eyelashes.
Slight moustache curled up each end.
Dress: Long, dark coat. Collar and cuffs trimmed with astrakhan. Dark jacket. Light waistcoat. Dark trousers. Dark felt hat turned down in the middle (sic). Button boots and gaiters with white buttons. White linen collar. Black tie with horseshoe pin.
Respectable appearance. Very surly looking.

What a stroke of luck!

A dream witness!

But G HUTCHINSON is an anagram of NO SUCH THING.

And, if George was "NO SUCH THING", then who was the man who had strolled into Commercial Street police station and claimed to have encountered Jack the Ripper?

27

Commercial Street

Metropolitan Police.

H Division.
12th November 1888

No. 8.

Special Report.

Re Murder

At 6 pm 12th George Hutchinson of the Victoria Home Commercial Street came to this Station and made the following statement.

About 2 am 9th I was coming by Thrawl Street Commercial Street and just before I got to Flower and Dean Street I met the murdered woman Kelly, and she said to me Hutchinson will you lend me sixpence. I said I cant I have spent all my money going down to Romford. she said good morning I must go and find some money. she went away toward Thrawl Street. a man coming in the opposite direction to Kelly tapped her on the shoulder and said something to her they both burst out laughing. I heard her say alright to him. and the man said you will be alright. for what I have told you. he then placed his right hand around her shoulders. He also had a kind of a small parcel in his left hand with a kind of a strap round it. I stood against the lamp of the Queens Head Public House and watched him. They both then came past me and the man hid down his head with his hat over his eyes. I stooped down and looked him in the face. He looked at me.

George Hutchinson

Room Number 13, Millers Court, 26 Dorset Street, Whitechapel

According to the landlord, John McCarthy, Joseph and Mary Jane took up residence in Millers Court, Dorset Street, around February or March 1888; a fact confirmed by Joseph Barnett at the inquest into the death of Mary Jane Kelly. Millers Court was chosen by Joseph, as the ideal location for Murder Headquarters.

Dorset Street lay in the shadow of Hawksmoor's Christchurch and ran in an east-west line between Crispin Street and Commercial Street. On the western side of Crispin Street, overlooking Dorset Street, stood The Providence Row Night Refuge and Shelter, with a statue of the Virgin Mary atop the central doorway, gazing down the most dangerous street in London, which rejoiced in the soubriquet "Do as you please street".

Today, the Virgin Mary gazes down a benign service road, flanked by a multi-storey car park on the south side and the extended Spitalfields Market on the north side. It is a road that bears no name.

On the eastern side of Commercial Street stood, and still stands today, Christchurch. The church does not stand directly opposite to Dorset Street, that honour goes to Brushfield Street, but the ancient burial ground with its low wall and high railings does. So too does the drinking fountain erected in 1860 and inscribed: "Erected by the Metropolitan Free Drinking Fountains Association, 1860". But, when last tested, there was no free water available. This view too was a familiar sight to the wretches that inhabited Dorset Street in the year 1888.

Dorset Street was laid out in the seventeenth century. It was then known as Datchett Street and was, no doubt, a salubrious address but, well before the year 1888, it had become a fearful, lawless place and was considered, if one discounts its arch-rival, the notorious Ratcliffe Highway, the most dangerous street in London. It comes then as something of a surprise to discover that the length of Dorset Street can be walked in just 120 paces.

In spite of the brevity of its length, Dorset Street was packed with a seething mass of humanity (estimated at 1,200 souls) for here were the rat-infested dosshouses that catered exclusively to the homeless and hopeless.

The street enjoyed the advantage of three public houses all situated on the north side, where the market extension is today. The Britannia, managed by Walter and Matilda Ringer (the census for the year 1891 records that Matilda is a widow) at the Commercial Street corner, the centrally located Blue Coat Boy, and The Horn of Plenty which stood at the corner with Crispin Street.

Number 26 Dorset Street was situated on the north side of the road, just thirty-five paces from the Commercial Street end. Millers Court was built at the rear of these premises.

The Court was first constructed under the name Millers Rents, circa 1845. The original complex comprised of six tenement houses and these were numbered, 1, 2, 3, 4, 5, 6. To facilitate access to these tenements a covered alleyway had been constructed (a break in the old line of kerb stones indicates the exact spot).

This situation remained unchanged until circa 1860 when Millers Rents became Millers Court though the actual accommodation, as far as can be ascertained, remained unaltered.

Circa 1885, new buildings were erected within the complex and the census for the year 1891 records that the abodes were numbered 2, 3, 5, 6, 7, 8, 11, 12, 13 and provided living accommodation for forty-one souls overall. Room number 13 was the first room on the right as one emerged through the arched tunnel which itself was approximately fifteen foot in length and four foot wide.

(It is unlikely that the 1891 census reflects accurately the number of persons who lived in Millers Court. Room number 13 alone indicates the presence of six souls comprising three different families! It seems likely that there were many people who did not wish to cooperate with the authorities and not too many census takers prepared to argue with their individual points of view.

Neither does this census reflect the situation that existed in the year 1888, since one witness (Elizabeth Prater) at the inquest into the death of Mary Jane Kelly, gave her address as Room number 20 Millers Court; a room number which doesn't exist in the later 1891 census.)

The derelict wash-house, Old Castle Street

Rooms were let individually and, certainly by the year 1888, were collectively known as McCarthy's Rents after the landlord, John McCarthy, who also had a chandlers shop next door at number 27.

A cold-water tap had been generously provided and this was situated in the small open area in the middle of the complex.

Room number 13 was approximately twelve foot by twelve foot. Directly opposite the door was a fireplace surmounted by a picture which is sometimes described as "The Fisherman's Widow", other times as "The Fisherman's Wife".

Two windows, side by side, overlooked the open area where the cold-water tap was situated, and they served to illuminate the drab interior. The furnishings, as far as can be ascertained, consisted of a wooden chair, a bed, two small tables, a wardrobe and a cupboard which contained cooking utensils and chinaware. There was also a bucket.

The floor was bereft of covering and the bare boards were filthy. No curtains covered the windows, though ragged material hung across the grimy panes as an acceptable alternative. There was patterned wallpaper on the walls, so overlaid with dirt that the pattern could not be deciphered.

Almost certainly, a privy was situated somewhere within the complex which would have catered for the needs of all the inhabitants.

The cold water tap would have been considered sufficient for daily ablutions but for those requiring the luxury of a bath, a public wash house stood on Castle Alley and had stood on Castle Alley since the year 1846.

The edifice of the wash-house (converted into a library circa 2001) stands on the same spot today though Castle Alley is now called Old Castle Street.

Room number 13, Millers Court, was the accommodation that Joseph Barnett was referring to when, at the inquest into the death of Mary Jane Kelly, he said: "We led a comfortable life there."

The Providence Row Night Refuge and Shelter

The Providence Row Night Refuge and Shelter was opened in the year 1868, as a refuge for the homeless.

The building stood, and stands today (no longer used as a shelter) at number 50, Crispin Street.

Stephen Knight, in his book entitled, *Jack the Ripper: The Final Solution*, asserts that Mary Jane Kelly was given refuge by the nuns of Providence Row and that she (Kelly) lived at the shelter for some time, though Stephen Knight provided no proof of this assertion.

The refuge was operated by the nuns of the Order of the Sisters of Mercy and, in the year 1973, an elderly nun was interviewed by BBC television. She said she had been a novice at the refuge in the year 1915 and, whilst there, she had been told by an old Sister who had worked at the refuge at the time of the Jack the Ripper murders: "If it had not been for the Kelly woman then none of the murders would have happened."

The Likeness of Joseph Barnett

The pictures hereunder both purport to be a likeness of Joseph Barnett: both drawn in the same month, same year, i.e. November 1888.

The top picture shows a man of approximately thirty years. (Joseph Barnett was thirty years of age in November 1888, though a newspaper reporter recorded that he looked about twenty-six.) The drawing was made at the inquest into the death of Mary Jane Kelly whilst Joseph was on the witness stand; 12 November 1888.

The lower picture shows a much heavier man with an impressive moustache and sideburns and he appears to be expensively clothed. But the most startling change is that Joseph Barnett appears to have aged twenty-five to thirty years within the space of a few days.

On what basis the *Illustrated Police News* hired their staff is not known but accuracy does not appear to have been a prime requisite and they obviously erred in their identification of Joseph Barnett, else they captioned the picture incorrectly.

The top picture is a likeness of Joseph Barnett.

It is not known who is depicted in the lower picture.

Murder Most Foul

> In May of the year 1887, began a series of mysterious crimes, which for barbarity and almost superhuman cunning have rarely been equalled and, certainly, never surpassed.

Thus does Elliot O'Donnell begin Chapter X of his 1926 book, entitled *Great Thames Mysteries*.

If Elliott O'Donnell was correct he was talking about four, or possibly five, murders, which encompassed a period of five years, from May 1887 to June 1902.

One evening in the early part of May in the year 1887, two working-class men were taking the air by the ferry at Rainham, Essex.

Their attention was drawn to a large, canvas-covered bundle, tied with rope, which was floating on the surface of the water. Curious, they dragged it to the bank and, after a tentative examination, they decided to enlist the aid of the local constabulary, who conveyed the bundle to the nearby Phoenix Inn for a more detailed examination.

The bundle was unwrapped and was found to contain a human torso.

This torso was forensically examined and, the opinion was expressed, that the remains were of a female aged about twenty-eight years. Neither the canvas nor the rope which had bound the bundle yielded a clue, and the identity of the unfortunate victim could not be ascertained.

On 8 June 1887, near Temple Stairs in the heart of London, another grisly bundle was dragged from the murky water of the Thames. This was found to contain two of the limbs which had been severed from the Rainham torso, and forensic examination of these appendages indicated that they had been removed with a degree of medical skill, though this opinion did not advance the investigation of the case.

In the month of July 1887, a labourer at Regents Canal, Chalk Farm, recovered another bundle from the water and this was found to contain the two missing limbs.

The head remained in absentia and, indeed, it was never recovered.

On 13 August 1887, an inquest into the death of the deceased was held at Crowndale Hall, Camden Town presided over by D G Danford Thomas, coroner for central Middlesex.

At the inquest, Dr Thomas Bond, acting under instructions from the Home Office, indicated that he had measured the several pieces of the dismembered corpse and had reached the conclusion that the deceased had, in life, been a well-nourished young woman, around 5'4" in height, and that she had never born a child. Dr Bond further concluded that whilst some degree of medical skill had been shown, he was in no doubt that the deceased had been unlawfully killed.

The verdict: murder by person or persons unknown.

If the police thought that they had heard the last of this killer (or killers) they were mistaken.

The Murder of Emma Smith

Emma Elizabeth Smith was a 45-year-old widow who resided in a common lodging house at number 18, George Street, Spitalfields. She had by all accounts known better times and her accent still retained a quality of refinement. Emma's clothes, however, were little better than rags and she had become an "unfortunate" (a Victorian euphemism for a prostitute).

Emma Smith ventured out sometime in the early evening of Easter Monday, 2 April 1888, in search of a jolly time, but it was not to be. Emma did enjoy a few drinks in various local hostelries but she was not considered to be badly intoxicated.

Returning homeward along Whitechapel Road, Emma was approaching St Mary's Church when she was alarmed to see, coming towards her, three drunken and abusive men. Fearful for her safety, Emma took avoiding action by crossing the road and turning left into Osborn Street. But the men pursued her and they caught up with her near to the corner with Wentworth Street. They attacked Emma Smith, beating her so badly about the head that her right ear was nearly torn off. The beasts then inflicted massive internal injuries on the poor helpless creature, by ramming a stick so hard into her vagina that her peritoneum was ruptured. They left her lying on the pavement, unconscious.

Emma Smith recovered sufficiently to stagger back home and from there she was removed to the London Hospital where she later died of her injuries.

It is not suggested here that Emma Smith was a Jack the Ripper victim, but the murder acted as a springboard for the main event.

The curtain was about to rise.

Mary, Joseph and George were standing in the wings… awaiting their cue.

The Last Days of a Billingsgate Fish Porter

It happened in July, 1888. The argument had been noisy and, some would have said, a little theatrical.

Precisely why the normally imperturbable Joseph Barnett had sworn at the foreman was something of a mystery but there it was: it was done and could not be undone.

Joseph Barnett was summarily dismissed from a job he had held for roughly fifteen years. This event took place approximately two weeks prior to the George Yard murder of Martha Tabram.

Joseph Barnett had contrived to be sacked for the simple reason that it would be less suspicious than resigning, and a good deal less suspicious than requesting temporary leave of absence. Joseph needed more free time in his new role as Jack the Ripper, and he needed this free time during the early hours when he was ordinarily required to be at Billingsgate market.

The objective had been achieved. Joseph Barnett was no longer a Billingsgate porter. He was full time, Jack the Ripper. The year was 1888. Eighteen years would pass before Joseph would be reinstated in his old job, in the year 1906, and by that time he would be forty-eight years old and grey-haired.

George Yard Buildings

> *I've got no time to tell you how*
> *I came to be a killer*
> *But you should know*
> *As time will show*
> *That I'm Society's pillar*
>
> Joseph Barnett, 1888

George Yard buildings stood, unsurprisingly, in George Yard. A grim Gothic structure, it was a "model dwelling" which housed respectable people of the working class. (George Yard is now named Gunthorpe Street. George Yard buildings stood at the northern end of George Yard on its western side.)

Turning into the entranceway, there was a flight of wide stone stairs, which ascended to the next level where there was a generous landing. The gas-jets which illuminated the staircase were turned out every night at eleven o'clock, after which time George Yard buildings was plunged into forbidding near darkness.

It was bank holiday Monday, 6 August 1888. Alfred Crow, a cab driver, returned to his lodgings at number 35, George Yard buildings, at 3.30 a.m. and, when he reached the first floor landing, he could see sufficiently to make out a dark shape lying on the stone floor, which he took to be a vagrant; a not unusual occurrence.

Adopting a live and let live philosophy, Alfred Crow retired to his bed where he slept the remainder of the night, undisturbed.

A labourer, John Reeves, arose early that morning, for he had to be at his place of employment. He left his room, number 37, and descended the stairs. It was 4.45 a.m. and the sky was beginning to lighten.

On the first floor landing, Reeves was somewhat disconcerted to behold the body of a woman, lying on her back, in a lake of blood. He rushed excitedly into the street to find a policeman.

The woman's name was Martha Tabram (otherwise known as Turner) and she was dead. In life Martha had been middle-aged. Had she been erect she would have stood 5'3" in height. Standing or lying down Martha was undeniably fat. It was, at first, considered that sexual molestation had occurred, but this was later discounted. But the most astonishing thing about the murder of Martha Tabram was that she had been stabbed thirty-nine times.

All of the wounds, bar one, had apparently been inflicted with a single weapon, possibly a scalpel. The exception was a wound to the breastbone, made with heavier force and a longer knife, possibly a bayonet or a dagger. In addition, there was heavy bruising and swelling to the victim's neck and lower jaw. It appeared that she had been pinned down and butchered.

Time of death was estimated at between 2 a.m. and 3 a.m.

Mrs Frances Hewitt, manageress of George Yard buildings had, in the early hours, been awakened by a piercing cry of: "*Help, murder!*" Frances Hewitt sensibly went back to sleep. No one else had heard a sound though it seems likely that there were those who were reluctant to admit that they had cowered in their bed.

George Yard today

The Battle of George Yard Buildings

Martha Tabram had spent the evening of bank holiday Monday, 6 August 1888, with her friend, Mary Ann Connolly, otherwise known, delightfully, as Pearly Poll. Together, in their round of the local hostelries, they had picked up with a couple of soldiers, a corporal and a private. Not rank conscious, Martha had agreed to entertain the private.

Martha then spent some time balancing on top of a dustbin in Green Dragon Place with her amorous soldier on top of her, whilst Pearly Poll performed a similar feat of acrobatic agility and daring with her corporal in the inaptly named Angel Alley.

Pearly Poll had possibly fallen into the dustbin and been unable to extricate herself, for Martha had lost contact with her friend. Nonetheless, it had been a pleasant way to spend the bank holiday and, no doubt, both Martha and Pearly Poll were a few pence richer. Undaunted by the absence of her erstwhile companion, Martha emerged from Green Dragon Place and turned right onto Whitechapel High Street no doubt hopeful of further light relief.

Whether she was glad to encounter Mary Jane Kelly, standing outside The White Hart public house next to the covered entrance to George Yard (now Gunthorpe Street) is not known, for Mary Jane had something of a reputation for being aloof. It must have been a pleasant surprise, then, to be greeted with such enthusiasm.

It transpired that Mary Jane had the loan of a room in George Yard buildings where she was required to entertain two men, both of whom had money.

Would Martha help her out?

Even though the hour was late, it was obvious that the bank holiday rush was not yet over, and the chance to experience a sexual encounter without the hazard of a dustbin lid handle bruising her bottom appealed to the sensitive Martha.

Mary Jane Kelly and Martha Tabram commenced walking

toward the entrance of George Yard, heading for Target Zero: the first floor landing of George Yard buildings, just 200 yards away.

Two men emerged from the dark shadows further along Whitechapel High Street and they too moved towards the entranceway to George Yard, but they did not walk together. The taller of the two men walked on the right-hand side of the narrow street known as George Yard and immediately behind the two women at a distance of thirty yards. The shorter man stayed on the left-hand side of the street and a little to the rear.

A witness, had there been a witness, would have seen two women, apparently enjoying each other's company, and two men who, obviously, were not together.

As the two women neared the grim Gothic entranceway to George Yard buildings, both men perceptibly increased their pace until the gap between them and the two females had narrowed to just twenty yards.

Mary Jane and Martha enter George Yard buildings: both men are now walking quickly.

George Hutchinson enters George Yard buildings, moving fast. Joseph Barnett crosses the street and moves in behind George.

The two women are on the first floor landing of George Yard buildings – Target Zero.

Mary Jane is "looking for her key". Martha Tabram waits patiently.

If Martha sees the figure of a man entering George Yard buildings and moving quickly up the dark stairway, she will not be alarmed. This is a place where people live. And, aren't they here for the purpose of entertaining two men? And yes, here comes the second one.

George Hutchinson seizes Martha Tabram by the throat and yanks her off of her feet, propelling her backwards.

Martha kicks out wildly, desperately trying to free herself. Mary Jane Kelly moves forward with the scalpel and tries to get in a telling blow but with four people on the landing, space is restricted. Martha Tabram succeeds in kicking Mary Jane and sends her reeling back.

Mary Jane's feet get mixed up with her skirt, she overbalances and, Mary Jane is down!

The better positioned Joseph Barnett decides to intervene. He raises the dagger and smashes it into the chest of the struggling woman, piercing her heart. George lets the dying woman fall to the floor.

Martha Tabram's legs are only twitching now and the maddened Mary Jane scrambles to her feet and hurls herself upon the nearly dead body. Kneeling astride her victim, Mary Jane commences a furious avalanche of blows upon the bleeding tormented flesh.

George moves away. His job is done.

A minute later, drenched in perspiration, liberally spattered with blood, panting for air, Mary Jane Kelly discontinues her murderous assault.

Martha Tabram is dead.

One blow, the first, was struck by Joseph Barnett; thirty-eight were struck by the berserk Mary Jane Kelly.

Martha Tabram had clearly lost the battle of George Yard buildings but it was a dishevelled and blood-stained trio that made their way home, to Murder Headquarters, just four minutes walk away.

Turn left out of George Yard buildings, left onto Wentworth Street, then right onto George Street, left onto Flower and Dean Street, right onto Commercial Street. They can see Dorset Street now, just a minute away.

They have learned a lesson… they must improve their technique.

The farce that was The Battle of George Yard buildings must never happen again.

The anagram is begun.

The Anagram

When Joseph Barnett originally conceived the anagram, he wanted to use street names and street names only but, as the message progressed, it became obvious that he would have to use additional peripheral information else the message could not be finished. It will become necessary later to decide the exact ingredients of the anagram, but the "pure" ingredients are:

GEORGE YARD
BUCKS ROW
HANBURY STREET
BERNER STREET
MITRE SQUARE
MILLERS COURT

After the murder of Martha Tabram at George Yard, the name GEORGE, and three letters of mARY have been secured. The missing letter M will be taken from Millers Court so that MARY can be completed and the extraneous letter D will be carried forward. The undernoted "pure" ingredients are carried over to the next murder:

D
BUCKS ROW
HANBURY STREET
BERNER STREET
MITRE SQUARE
ILLERS COURT

The message, after the murder of Martha Tabram is:

George.
Mary.

The Method

The murder of Martha Tabram was popular with those who suffered from the affliction of morbid curiosity. The desire to view the bloodstained flagstones brought out the crowds who clustered excitedly around George Yard buildings. Sadly however, the newspaper reviews were only lukewarm.

It was disappointing. If the media took little notice of this murder then what was the guarantee that they would take notice of the next or subsequent murders? Quite apart from anything else, the killing of Martha Tabram had not been as straightforward as had been anticipated and the trio had been liberally spattered with blood, particularly Mary Jane. To add insult to injury, the police and the press seemed convinced that Martha Tabram had been killed by a soldier. Even now they were holding an identity parade at the Tower of London so that Mary Ann Connolly could review the troops.

There would need to be a major change of policy. Blood control was of paramount importance, and the murders should have a more distinctive appearance. There was no point in taking risks if others were accorded the credit.

They would need to consult an "expert" and for that they only had to look as far as front-line nurse, veteran of a war zone; the ferocious Mary Jane Kelly.

Mary Jane had always claimed that she could conduct a post mortem in the street, in the near dark and, in record time. Joseph Barnett had always been doubtful of this claim but maybe it was time to find out. They could hardly do worse than the George Yard fiasco.

Rehearsals would begin immediately with Mary Jane Kelly playing the part of the victim. George would continue in the same role but, in future, he must hold the victim higher in the throat and partially around the lower mandible to prevent her from screaming, and to keep from having his fingers cut off.

He would need to wrest her backwards; pulling the head back and exposing the throat to Joseph Barnett's knife. Mary Jane Kelly explained the direction that blood would spout from a severed carotid artery and George and Joseph must rehearse where they should stand in relation to the victim so as to avoid being saturated with her blood.

A post-mortem would be conducted immediately by Mary Jane Kelly.

Mary Jane didn't need any rehearsals.

The "lucky" Mary "Polly" Ann Nicholls would be the first beneficiary of the improved technique.

Bucks Row

> *I'm not a butcher*
> *I'm not a yid*
> *Nor yet a foreign skipper*
> *But I'm your own light-hearted friend*
> *Yours Truly*
> *Jack the Ripper*

Joseph Barnett, 1888

Bucks Row (now Durward Street) ran in an east-west line from Brady Street to Bakers Row (now Vallance Road).

From Brady Street the road was narrow until, after 200 yards, one came to the imposing edifice of the Board School (a school run by a Board of Governors) after which the road doubled in width and continued on its way to Bakers Row.

This narrative is only concerned with the narrow section, from the eastern end of Bucks Row beginning at Brady Street, to the Board School.

This section was part residential and part commercial. There was a public house at the southern corner with Brady Street, named The Roebuck (demolished in 1995) then a line of terraced houses which housed, for the most part, the respectable working class. The terraced houses ceased at the point where Mr Brown's Stables, with its gateway onto Bucks Row, began – just before reaching the Board School. The northern side of Bucks Row was mainly commercial; warehouses, stables and sundry other commercial enterprises.

It was the gateway of Mr Brown's Stables that Joseph Barnett designated Target Zero.

(It is difficult to discern the advantage of this location today. The buildings that stood on the narrow section of Bucks Row were razed to the ground in the 1980s. This section was completely rebuilt in 1996/97 and is unrecognisable from the

1888 version, with one exception. The Board School still stands. It has been converted into apartments.)

It was 3.40 a.m., Friday, 31 August 1888. George Cross was on his way to work, at Spitalfields Market. From Brady Street, he turned into Bucks Row. The lighting in the street was poor and George was a little apprehensive as he made his way along the dark, deserted street.

George had nearly reached the Board School when, in the gateway leading to Mr Brown's Stables, he noticed a dark shape lying in front of the gates.

Curious, in spite of his apprehension, George Cross decided to investigate, for the dark shape might be something of value and, as he did so, another man, John Paul, arrived on the scene.

They conferred together over the dark shape and they both agreed. This wasn't anything either of them wanted to take home.

"You can have my share mate!"

But George Cross declined the generous offer. And both men, badly shaken, rushed away to find a policeman.

The dark shape was the dead body of a woman.

Her throat had been cut from ear to ear.

Blood on Bucks Row

It was shortly after midnight on Friday, 31 August 1888 when Mary Ann "Polly" Nichols stumbled out of Ye Frying Pan and into the fire.

(Ye Frying Pan was a public house which stood in Brick Lane.

The building is there today with the words "Ye Frying Pan" inset into the upper brickwork. It is currently an Indian restaurant.)

There was, in fact, no fire but Polly would get burned, for her compass was set on collision course with the anagram. Target Zero had already been chosen for a death. Fate had decreed that that death would be the death of Polly Nichols.

The 43-year-old drunken prostitute, proudly wearing her new hat, had found her way to a dosshouse in Thrawl Street the night prior to her death and she was allowed to sit in the kitchen of that establishment warming herself until being evicted for lacking the necessary funds with which to rent a bed for the night. Not that Polly was unduly bothered.

Defiantly, she asserted her independence.

"I'll soon get me doss money. Look what a jolly bonnet I've got now."

How Polly spent the rest of that night and the following day has not been recorded but the next evening she found her way safely to Ye Frying Pan, at which establishment she consumed a generous quantity of alcohol before departing in high spirits.

Emily Holland (described as an elderly, married woman) had spent the evening at Shadwell Dock, where she had enjoyed a particularly voracious fire which had destroyed a large part of that area. Presumably her elderly husband did not accompany her, for he is not recorded as having encountered Polly Nichols at the corner of Osborn Street and Whitechapel High Street, at 2.30 in the morning, as did his wife. Emily remembered the time, for the clock of St Mary's, just across the street, tolled the half hour. It was Polly Nichol's "death knell".

Strangely, Polly declined Emily's offer to share her doss, fierce independence or drunken obstinacy overcoming her. It was an offer she should not have refused, and the last Emily Holland ever saw of the sad Polly Nichols was her lonely figure flapping eastward towards Whitechapel Road.

Fifteen minutes later Polly arrived at the corner of Whitechapel Road and Cambridge Road where stood The Blind Beggar public house.

(The Blind Beggar stands on the same spot today, but it is not the building of 1888. Today's building is dated 1894.)

It was outside The Blind Beggar that Polly Nichols met the "Grim Reaper" in the shape of a beautiful woman. The time was a quarter to three.

None of the local prostitutes really liked Mary Jane Kelly. She was known to be standoffish and everyone knew that her really close friends were not of the sorority. Also, she was notorious for having a vicious temper and Polly, drunk though she was, was a little wary as Mary Jane approached her. But Mary Jane was smiling and Polly was too inebriated, and too flattered, to detect that it was the smile on the face of the tiger.

At first, Polly Nichols declined Mary Jane's offer to share her bed just as she had declined Emily Holland's offer. But Mary was more persuasive (though some would have said, "insistent") and Polly would be foolish to risk offending the lovely Mary Jane. Polly's friends would be so envious when she told them.

The fact that Mary Jane wanted to return home, to Millers Court, via Bucks Row, was no problem; indeed it was a marginally shorter journey.

Mary Jane Kelly and Polly Nichols walked west along Whitechapel Road until they reached Brady Street where they turned right, heading north: Millers Court for one, eternity for the other.

The two men, who observed the women from a vantage point on the other side of Cambridge Road, were in no hurry.

From The Blind Beggar to the eastern end of Bucks Row is just 260 yards but the staggering Polly Nichols could only progress at a funereal pace, which, under the circumstances, was appropriate.

It wasn't until the two women had turned into Brady Street that the two men moved to follow them. They walked slowly, but even so, as the men themselves turned into Brady Street, the two women were still twenty yards from The Roebuck at the corner with Bucks Row. The men waited until Mary Jane and Polly Nicholls had disappeared from view.

They strolled across to The Roebuck, and turned into Bucks Row. The street was deserted except for the two women now eighty yards ahead. Only a few flickering gaslights served to illuminate Bucks Row. From one of the terraced houses came the sound of a baby crying. But this wasn't a night reserved for new life. It was a night reserved for death.

George stayed on the left-hand side of the street ambling slowly behind the two women. Joseph moved to the right-hand side of the street, keeping a little to the rear of the procession.

Mary Jane Kelly and Polly Nichols are just thirty paces away from the gateway of Mr Brown's Stables. Mary Jane looks back. Joseph and George are there, just fifty paces away and closing. Joseph Barnett looks back. George Hutchinson looks back. The street is empty.

George is moving faster now. Joseph follows.

The women are just ten stumbling paces from Target Zero.

Joseph Barnett looks back.

George Hutchinson looks back.

All clear.

Five paces to Target Zero.

George moves in for the kill.

Joseph crosses the street. He reaches into his pocket for the knife.

Both men closing fast. Not too late to abort. Not too late. Not too...

Mary Jane Kelly and Polly Nichols reach Target Zero. Mary Jane Kelly stands away from Polly and reaches in her bodice for the scalpel. Polly stumbles and nearly falls.

Too late to abort now!

The powerful George Hutchinson seizes Polly Nichols by the throat, wrenching her off her feet and dragging her backwards to the ground.

Polly's throat invites Joseph Barnett's knife.

Joseph cuts once.

He gets it wrong! The knife has cut a jagged wound down instead of across.

And again. This time Joseph nearly cuts off Polly's head.

The industrious Mary Jane Kelly begins her investigation into the cause of death.

Joseph and George move away. Their job is done. Just stand guard until the post mortem examination is completed.

Somewhere, far off in the lonely distance, a dog barks. Nearer, a different sound; a ripping sound; a sound not unusual in this part of Bucks Row for, just along the street, is Barber's horse slaughter house.

Mary Jane Kelly must have felt quite at home as she disembowelled the late Mary Ann "Polly" Nichols. After a minute Mary Jane stands up.

The three move away, and continue their interrupted journey westward; twenty yards to the Board School, around to the other side of the building then exit immediately to the right into Woods Buildings; over the railway bridge and out, single file, through the narrow covered archway, emerging onto Whitechapel Road.

(The archway is still there today, practically next to the Grave Maurice public house, and so reminiscent of the archway that once surmounted the entrance to Millers Court.)

The trio strolled triumphantly west, along Whitechapel Road, itself leading onto Whitechapel High Street, the men either side of Mary Jane Kelly.

Right onto Osborn Street, itself leading onto Brick Lane, then left along Fashion Street and onto Commercial Street immediately opposite Whites Row. One half minute now from Murder Headquarters, just across the road.

The time: twenty minutes after three o'clock, George Cross and John Paul are just leaving home.

The method had been a complete success.

The trio relaxed in room number 13 and refreshed themselves with tea. Afterwards George wended his way homeward. In the unlikely event that George should be stopped and questioned, he had the perfect alibi. George had spent the entire evening with his friends, Joseph and Mary.

Mary Ann "Polly" Nichols lay dead in the street. Her fine, jolly bonnet lay in the gutter beside her.

But Polly would have been pleased if she had known the useful contribution her death had made to the anagram.

Woods Buildings today

The Anagram

These are the "pure" ingredients carried forward following the George Yard murder of Martha Tabram:

```
D
BUCKS ROW
HANBURY STREET
BERNER STREET
MITRE SQUARE
ILLERS COURT
```

Joseph Barnett's anagram was as *tight* as he could possibly make it.

That is to say, the anagram is not simply a mass of letters to be rearranged in any order. Each murder site was chosen on individual merit and Bucks Row, with only eight letters, assumes particular significance for this reason. SROW was relatively easy. The murders were a protest against prostitution, therefore SROW was needed to construct the word WHORES. BUCK was such a difficult construction that it could only be a name and, after due consideration, it was decided that BUCK was George's name though, of course, it could be Mary's name. It will be assumed here that George Hutchinson was, in fact, George Buck.

In order to complete the word WHORES, an H and an E will be subtracted from Hanbury Street.

The undernoted "pure" letters are carried over to the next murder:

```
D
ANBURY STRET
BERNER STREET
MITRE SQUARE
ILLERS COURT
```

The message, after the murder of Mary "Polly" Ann Nicholls is:

George Buck
Mary
Whores

Number 29, Hanbury Street

> *Up and down the Goddam town*
> *The coppers try to find me*
> *But I aint a man yet to drown*
> *In Thames or drink or sea*
>
> Joseph Barnett, 1888

Hanbury Street (once Browns Lane): a long, busy thoroughfare comprising residential houses, shops, restaurants and pubs: carved a crooked east-west line from Commercial Street in the west to Bakers Row (now Vallance Road) in the east.

(Today, Hanbury Street terminates at a footpath leading to Old Montague Street.)

Several other thoroughfares intersect with Hanbury Street: the busiest being that with Brick Lane.

Number 29, Hanbury Street, was on the northern side of the thoroughfare, approximately fifty yards west from the corner with Brick Lane.

(Number 29, along with most of the other buildings that once stood on the north side of Hanbury Street, between Commercial Street and Brick Lane, has been demolished. Only a blank, brick wall stands where once stood number 29. The south side of that part of Hanbury Street, however, boasts many buildings familiar to Jack the Ripper. Numbers 28 and 30 are immediately opposite to the site.)

In the year 1888, number 29 was a four-storey building which boasted a cats' meat shop on the ground floor. Succulent tit-bits were served from the front room.

The remainder of the premises comprised of living accommodation occupied, for the most part, by market workers. Men, women and children who resided there, in the latter part of the year 1888, numbered around twenty souls.

There were two front doors, side-by-side, sited on the left-hand side of the building, both of which opened directly onto Hanbury Street. The one on the right served the ground floor only and was otherwise kept locked against intruders. The front door on the extreme left-hand side of number 29 was invariably unlocked. This was a common entrance and intended for use by the residents of the house only.

Entering through this front door, on the right, was a cellar door and, beyond that, a staircase leading to the first-floor level.

Straight ahead was a through passageway which ran the depth of the building. At the end of this passageway was a door, and this too was kept unlocked. Anyone exiting through this rear door encountered two stone steps which led down to a small enclosed back yard. (20' x 15'). The enclosure consisted of a wooden fence which was approximately 5'9" high.

Within the area of the yard was a privy and a cold water tap. Anyone entering the yard had virtually only one exit route and that was the reverse of the route of entry. In other words the back yard of number 29, Hanbury Street was a trap.

The yard was often used by prostitutes to entertain clients but, although it was secluded, it was dependent for privacy on darkness since it was overlooked by the back windows of number 29 and the adjacent properties. A fornicator might be embarrassed if discovered by an outraged resident, or be doused with a bucket of cold water, or worse.

It follows then that a murderer would avoid the backyard of number 29, Hanbury Street, particularly during the hours of daylight.

This was obviously not a place that would be attractive to Jack the Ripper for, in addition to its other disadvantages, it was less than 400 yards from Millers Court: Murder Headquarters.

At approximately ten minutes to six[1] on Saturday, 8 September 1888, John Davies, a market porter who was resident at number 29, Hanbury Street, ventured into the backyard.

By the fence, on the left-hand side of the yard, her head reposing in the recess between the stone steps and the wooden

---

[1]The Almanac for the year 1888 records that, on Saturday 8 September sunrise was at 05.26 hours. *British Almanac and Companion*, The Stationers' Company, 1888.

palings, was the body of a woman. She lay on her back. Her throat was cut to the vertebra: her bloody entrails trailed across her right shoulder.

She was dead.

Horror on Hanbury Street

Annie Chapman, otherwise known as Dark Annie, was a 47-year-old prostitute and, at half past one, on the morning of Saturday, 8 September 1888, she was slightly the worse for drink, though she was not considered to be drunk.

The man who voiced that judgement was Timothy Donovan, deputy manager of Crossinghams Lodging House, which was situated at number 35, Dorset Street, opposite to Millers Court. He had made this observation at the inquest into her death.

It was at 1.45 a.m. that Donovan, becoming aware that Annie Chapman had loitered overlong in his kitchen, requested her lodging money.

"I have no money at present."

"You can find money for beer but not for your lodgings," Donovan admonished, "well... you know the rules."

Annie knew the rules very well. No money meant the misery of the cold, dark, cheerless streets.

She loitered in the street doorway for a few minutes, chatting to John Evans, the nightwatchman at Crossinghams, reluctant to take that final irrevocable step into the darkness. But, with a resignation born of repeated failure, she walked to her death. Her misery was soon to end.

George Buck was staying overnight in room number 13, Millers Court.

George had his own accommodation, and it was unusual, and uncomfortable, for him to stay overnight in that tiny room, but the Hanbury Street murder necessitated an early start and it was essential that the operation be precisely coordinated.

At the same moment that Annie Chapman was being evicted from Crossinghams Lodging House, her three assassins were abed, just a few yards away, at Murder Headquarters.

Precisely how Dark Annie spent the next few hours is not known but, since she did not return to Crossinghams nor to any other lodging house, it seems reasonable to hypothesise that she did not earn sufficient money to make such a return possible, a good indication that the last few hours of her life were as miserable, cold and empty as had been the majority of her forty-seven years.

Mary, Joseph and George arose early on the morning of Saturday, 8 September 1888 – very early. It was just four o'clock. The close proximity of Murder Headquarters to the Target Area made a night-time foray difficult: there were just too many whores on the streets – whores who would know and recognise Mary and Joseph. An early morning start gave the best opportunity for success. The killers wanted just one loose stray. After a rudimentary breakfast it was time to begin.

At 4.35, George Hutchinson left room number 13. He walked out of the Court and turned left onto Dorset Street, turned left again at The Britannia and walked north along Commercial Street. At The Golden Heart public house, George turned right. He was on Hanbury Street. The journey had taken him just three minutes. He proceeded to stroll east, towards Brick Lane.

At 4.45, Mary and Joseph left room number 13, Millers Court. Mary Jane has taken the precaution of bringing a shopping bag with her but she won't be doing any shopping. Left onto Dorset Street then, at the corner with Commercial Street, they crossed over the road toward Christchurch, then turned right at The Ten Bells, along Church Street (now Fournier Street), then left onto Brick Lane, arriving at the crossroads with Hanbury Street, just fifty yards east from number 29. The more circuitous journey had taken them just five minutes.

Looking to their left, they saw, standing on the northern side of Hanbury Street, a familiar figure. It was George and he was talking to a woman.

Joseph and Mary both knew who the woman was. It was Dark Annie Chapman.

Mrs Elizabeth Long, wife of a cart minder named James Long, left her home and proceeded on her way to Spitalfields Market. She walked north along Brick Lane, then turned left. It was approximately five o'clock as she walked west along Hanbury Street. Mrs Long observed a man and a woman standing talking on the pavement near to number 29. The woman was facing toward Mrs Long and Mrs Long would later identify her as having been Annie Chapman.

The man had his back to Mrs Long, so that she did not see his face. She did however, hear him speak. He said:

"Will you?"

Annie Chapman replied, "Yes."

Mrs Long paid them no further heed.

She (Mrs Long) only saw his back. At no time did she see his face. She would not be able to identify him. She gained the impression that he was over forty years of age and a little taller than Annie Chapman (Annie was about 5'1"). Mrs Long thought the man was wearing a dark coat and a deerstalker hat and, his overall appearance was, she considered, "shabby genteel". Complexion dark: a foreigner perhaps.

The sky was beginning to register light as George walked, with Annie, those few paces to the door of number 29. The early morning workers were beginning to make their appearance on Hanbury Street.

As George and Annie entered through the communal front door of number 29, Joseph and Mary were just fifty paces to the east and moving casually toward the Target Area.

As they entered through the front door and into the passageway, George and Dark Annie were just exiting through the back door, and out into the yard. The time: 5.05 a.m.

George and Annie are in the backyard, Target Zero. Annie stands with her back to the wall of the house, between the two stone steps and the wooden fence which separates this yard from the one next door, number 27.

Annie tries to relax.

The man looks a little rough. I do hope he'll be gentle with me.

George seizes Annie by the throat with his right hand. With his left hand he grabs a handful of her clothing and wrenches her forward, away from the wall. Now he has a clearance of five feet from the wall. He puts his leg behind hers, and forces her over backwards.

Albert Cadosch, a carpenter, lived at number 27, Hanbury Street, next door to number 29. On the morning of the murder he arose at approximately five o'clock and went into the backyard of number 27 in order to visit the privy. Returning, he heard voices which appeared to be coming from the backyard of number 29 but he could not discern any words. Almost immediately after, he heard a sound like a heavy object hitting the fence which separated number 27 from number 29. A woman's voice exclaimed, *"No! No!"* Not afflicted overly by curiosity, Albert Cadosch did not investigate.

Annie Chapman hits the fence as she is propelled forcibly backwards by the powerful George Buck. He changes the grip on her throat, Annie exclaims *"No! No!"* before George seizes her again, reversing his hand to allow room for the knife. He is kneeling over her struggling body, pinning her down as Joseph Barnett, followed immediately by Mary Jane Kelly, enter the arena. The knife is already in Joseph's hand as he kneels, his left knee against the lower of the two stone steps. It's an easy cut. Plenty of time. The knife slices once across Annie's throat, from left to right. He nearly severs Annie Chapman's head.

Mary Jane Kelly lifts Annie Chapman's skirts.

Joseph moves back. George releases his grip, gets up and steps over the body. Both George and Joseph retreat back, into the passageway. Anyone wanting to go into the backyard just now will have to deal with two abusive men.

The Ripper steps back from her victim and places a few bloody trophies into her shopping bag. She emerges into the passageway. Her face is flushed and she smiles at Joseph and George.

The time is ten past five – just sixteen minutes from sunrise!

Emerging onto Hanbury Street, Joseph and Mary turn right. George turns left. They will all return to Murder Headquarters for a quick wash and groom.

Refreshed, they are enjoying a beer in the Ten Bells when they hear of the horrible murder on Hanbury Street.

They will stroll down there later – just to see what all the fuss is about.

The Ten Bells (present-day exterior)

Rings and Things

Before leaving Hanbury Street it is worth considering the injuries to Annie Chapman and the way in which her dead body was "anointed".

George Buck had seized Annie high in the throat and under the chin, evidenced by the abrasions and bruising to that area.

Joseph Barnett had cut her throat from left to right, severing the left carotid artery.

The abdominal injuries had been inflicted immediately after death, by Mary Jane Kelly. Mary had sliced open the abdomen and then eviscerated the unfortunate victim.

She had laid the small intestine across the victim's right shoulder and part of her stomach on her left shoulder.

She had then removed the uterus, the bladder and parts of the vagina and she took these away, presumably in a bag carried specifically for that purpose.

Two, or possibly three, brass rings were wrenched from the dead woman's fingers and, either these were removed from the crime scene or they were laid at the feet of the victim: depending on whose account is considered the most credible.

It is not disputed that a piece of muslin and two combs were laid at Annie's feet and these appear to have been placed in a deliberate pattern. Part of an envelope which contained a few pills had been taken from her pocket and deposited by her head.

Reporters were quick to converge on 29, Hanbury Street, and the early edition of the *Pall Mall Gazette* stated categorically that the "missing" rings had indeed been placed at Annie's feet.

The *Daily Telegraph* asserted that, in addition to the rings, there were also included a number of coins, and that these items were laid out in a neat row.

The late Stephen Knight in his book, *Jack the Ripper: The Final Solution*, considered that Jack the Ripper was a Mason and that the ritual associated with the murder of Annie Chapman lent weight to his theory.

Philip Sugden in the first edition of his book, *The Complete History of Jack the Ripper*, gives us this categoric assurance: "The truth was very different. Neither rings nor farthings were found at Annie's feet and hers was certainly not a ritualised Masonic killing."

Maybe so, but Joseph Barnett was a Master Mason, and the reason for making up the story is considerably less obvious than the reason for denying it.

The Anagram

These are the "pure" letters carried forward following the Bucks Row murder of Mary "Polly" Ann Nicholls.

    D
    ANBURY STRET
    BERNER STREET
    MITRE SQUARE
    ILLERS COURT

The Hanbury Street murder of Annie Chapman enabled Joseph Barnett to secure his own name – BARNETT. The residual letters, UYSR, are probably part of "Yours Truly" but, for the time being, these letters will be carried forward.

The undernoted "pure" letters are carried forward to the next murder:

    D
    UYSR
    BERNER STREET
    MITRE SQUARE
    ILLERS COURT

The message, after the murder of Annie Chapman is:

    Barnett
    George Buck
    Mary
    Whores

Scandal at Scotland Yard

On Tuesday, 11 September 1888, a left arm was recovered from the Thames at Pimlico.

Forensic examination indicated that this arm had been wrenched from its owner, indicating a lack of skill but a formidable degree of strength.

A few days later, in the grounds of The Blind Asylum, Lambeth, another left arm was discovered, though this latter discovery was thought by the police to be a hoax perpetrated by medical students: albeit that The Blind Asylum seems an unlikely place to perpetrate a hoax which was dependent, for its effect, on visual appreciation.

In the early afternoon of Tuesday, 2 October 1888, Fred Wildborn, a carpenter employed by Messrs J Grover & Sons (Builders) of Pimlico: groped his way through the labyrinthine basement tunnels of the embryonic New Scotland Yard, the future headquarters of the Metropolitan Police.

Messrs J Grover & Sons were contractors for part of the work in progress and Fred Wildborn, as their employee, kept his tools on the premises though perhaps "secreted" is a better word, for there were many workmen on the site and Fred hid his tools to guard them from possible theft.

The huge basement with its network of tunnels was on two separate levels and Fred chose the deepest level in which to hide his possessions. The area was a haven of comparative peace when compared to the clamour above. It was also dark and gloomy with only an occasional shaft of light for illumination. Fred groped his way to the remotest corner and retrieved his tools. He noticed a large bundle. He'd seen it before; the day earlier, but it had failed to excite his interest and he had thought nothing of it. This time he reported the matter to his superior, Mr Bronn (Assistant Works Manager) and he and Mr Bronn investigated the contents of the mysterious find. They soon discovered that the contents were not to their liking and quickly rushed to the nearest police station, from whence reinforcements were rushed to New Scotland Yard.

The bundle was found to contain a female torso and this was taken to the mortuary in Millbank Street for further examination.

The torso was examined by the same Dr Thomas Bond, who had given evidence at the inquest relating to the Rainham Torso Murder, in his capacity as surgeon to "A" Division of the Metropolitan Police, and Dr Charles Hibberd of The Westminster Hospital.

Initially, they noted that the torso had been wrapped in three quarters of a yard of a woman's black broche silk dress with a flounce, 3" wide at the bottom, and, in addition, there was a bloodstained newspaper which proved to be a copy of *The Echo*.

After examining the torso, Dr Bond exclaimed, "I have an arm that will fit it." It proved to be so. For the left arm that had been fished from the Thames at Pimlico, 11 September fitted the female torso found in the basement of New Scotland Yard.

After further examination, the doctors concluded that, in life, the woman had been young, well nourished, 5'8" to 5'9" tall, had fair skin and dark hair and had not been of the working class. From the state of decomposition, they concluded that she had died circa 20 August 1888.

The identity of the victim could not be ascertained and neither could the cause of death be established.

On 17 October 1888, an enterprising Central News reporter named Waring, acting with the consent of the police, decided to walk his dog in the New Scotland Yard basement in the hope that a new lead might be established. It was to prove all too embarrassingly easy.

In the vicinity of the original discovery, the dog unearthed further human remains most notably a leg complete with foot; and these remains were found to match with the torso and the arm that then reposed in the mortuary.

The leg and foot were, of course, in an advanced state of decomposition and forensic examination divulged no new evidence that shed any light on either the cause of death or the identity of the victim.

Neither could it be established how the murderer, or murderers, gained access to the premises since during the week the site was a hive of activity and at weekends, it was securely locked and guarded by a watchman.

It seemed likely that the murderer was a workman who had openly walked in during the working week and deposited the remains in the basement. There was, of course, a leg, an arm and a head still missing, not to mention a spare left arm from The Blind Asylum, still awaiting a claimant!

The Times, 16 October 1888, reported that a person walking along Cannon Row by the side of New Scotland Yard, on the Saturday evening immediately prior to the discovery of the torso by Fred Wildborn, had seen three men standing by a wheelbarrow upon which reposed a bundle.

One of the men, it was reported, had scaled the perimeter fence that surrounded the building site and the other two men had passed the bundle up to their compatriot!

The inquest into the death of the New Scotland Yard victim recorded a verdict of: murder by a person or persons unknown.

The Scribe

On the evening of Tuesday, 25 September 1888, Joseph Barnett sat at the table in Murder Headquarters and composed a letter, a letter which would launch Jack the Ripper. It had been seven weeks since Martha Tabram had been murdered at George Yard buildings and seventeen days since Annie Chapman had been slaughtered on Hanbury Street. In just four days time Joseph is due to embark on his most dangerous mission yet. The double murders of 29 to the 30 September.

Nonetheless he is supremely confident: "How can they catch me now." The "Dear Boss" salutation is carefully chosen. He will need it for the anagram. But the "Dear Boss" salutation would haunt him for a long time to come.

25 Sept. 1888

Dear Boss

I keep on hearing the police have caught me but they wont fix me just yet. I have laughed when they look so clever and talk about being on the right track. That joke about Leather Apron gave me real fits. I am down on whores and I shant quit ripping them till I do get buckled. Grand work the last job was. I gave the lady no time to squeal. How can they catch me now, I love my work and want to start again. You will soon hear of me with my funny little games. I saved some of the proper red stuff in a ginger beer bottle after the last job to write with but it went thick like glue and I cant use it, red ink is fit enough I hope ha ha. The next job I do I shall clip the ladys ears off and send to the police officers just for jolly wouldn't you. Keep this letter back till I do a bit more work then give it out straight, My knife's so nice and sharp I want to get to work right away if I get a chance.
Good luck.
Yours truly

Jack the Ripper
Dont mind me giving the trade name

Joseph read the letter three times then, satisfied, he addressed the envelope:

The Boss
Central News Office
London City

Joseph Barnett folded the letter twice and placed it in the envelope. He changed his mind about sealing it. He was meeting with George tomorrow. He'd let George read it first.

It was quiet in The Prospect of Whitby but then it always was Wednesday nights.

George read the letter twice and pulled reflectively at his lower lip. He passed it back to Joseph Barnett.

"What's 'buckled' mean?"

"Buck led."

George smiled. "You must think I need the publicity."

"They'll just think it's a slang term. Otherwise?"

"I like Jack the Ripper. It's got a nice flavour."

"Marie's idea."

"But you've dated it the 25th."

"So?"

"So it's the 26th today. You've missed the last post. It won't go now till the 27th. Looks a bit odd that's all."

Joseph pondered the situation. "Got a pencil?"

George fished around in his pockets and handed Joseph Barnett a crayon. "That's all I've got."

And so... Joseph Barnett added a footnote in crayon:

Wasnt good enough to post this before I got all the red ink off my hands curse it. No luck yet. They say I'm a doctor now, ha ha.

The letter was postmarked London, EC Sep. 27 88.

The letter was forwarded to Scotland Yard on Saturday, 29 September 1888: just hours before the murder of Liz Stride in Dutfields Yard.

25. Sept. 1888.

Dear Boss,
    I keep on hearing the police have caught me. but they wont fix me just yet. I have laughed when they look so clever and talk about being on the right track. That joke about Leather Apron gave me real fits. I am down on whores and I shant quit ripping them till I do get buckled. Grand work the last job was, I gave the lady no time to squeal. How can they catch me now. I love my work and want to start again. You will soon hear of me with my funny little games. I saved some of the proper red stuff in a ginger beer bottle over the last job to write with but it went thick like glue and I cant use it. Red ink is fit enough I hope <u>ha.ha</u>. The next job I do I shall clip the ladys ears off and send to the

Photo of the "Dear Boss" letter (front)

police officers just for jolly wouldnt you. Keep this letter back till I do a bit more work. then give it out straight. My knife's so nice and sharp I want to get to work right away if I get a chance. Good luck.

        yours truly
          Jack the Ripper

Dont mind me giving the trade name

wasnt good enough to post this before I got all the red ink off my hands curse it No luck yet. They say I am a doctor now ha ha

Photo of the "Dear Boss" letter (back)

"Dear Boss" letter envelope

Berner Street

> *Eight little whores, with no hope of Heaven*
> *Gladstone may save one, then there'll be seven*
> *Seven little whores, begging for a shilling*
> *One stays in Heneage Court, then there's a killing*
>
> Joseph Barnett, 1888

On the south side of Commercial Road lay Berner Street (today named, oddly, "Henriques Street, formerly Berner Street".) Berner Street ran in a north-south line, for a distance of approximately 260 yards from the southern side of Commercial Road, to Ellen Street in the south, where the road ended.

Today, Henriques Street ends at Boyd Street. Several streets intersected with Berner Street, the most important being the crossroads with Fairclough Street at the approximate midway point.

On the western side of Berner Street and just north of the Fairclough Street intersection was, in the year 1888, an enclosed yard which was known to the local inhabitants as Dutfields Yard. This name was a reference to Arthur Dutfield, a master wheelwright who ran a van and cart builders from the premises but who lived at number 282, Commercial Road. In fact, Arthur Dutfield had vacated Dutfields Yard a few weeks previously and had moved his business two streets away, to Pinchin Street, so that strictly speaking, the name was no longer apposite.

The two high wooden gates which guarded the narrow entranceway to Dutfields Yard were, however, still adorned with the legend: "W Hindley, sack manufacturer & A Dutfield, van & cart builder".

Through the gateway, one entered a twenty-foot long corridor formed by the walls of the two buildings which flanked the entrance to Dutfields Yard. Facing into the yard, a private house, number 42, was to the left and number 40 was to the right.

Number 40, Berner Street, was a two-storey building which housed the premises of the International Workingmen's Educational Club: a socialist club – an arm of the Jewish League. Also housed within its precincts was a printing firm which published a Yiddish radical weekly; *Der Arbeter Fraint* (The Worker's Friend).

Past the corridor formed by these two buildings, entry was afforded into a more generous area which housed Hindley's sack manufacturing business. Also within this area were stables which were not, in the latter part of 1888, fully utilised.

The main door to the International Workingmen's Educational Club fronted directly onto Berner Street but this was often kept locked in favour of the side, or kitchen door which was located on the south wall of the premises some twelve feet inside the area known as Dutfields Yard. Entry and exit to and from the club was made possible by reason of the fact that the gates leading into the yard were commonly left open, even at night; though they might be closed when all the club members had gone home.

The corridor leading into Dutfields Yard was bereft of direct illumination and, in consequence, was extremely dark at night, but the members of the club had no fear, for they had not encountered nor been involved in any unpleasantness within the yard's confines and therefore saw no reason to provide additional lighting. Moreover, Berner Street was not a notorious area for vice, and prostitutes were infrequently seen in the immediate vicinity, in consequence of which Dutfields Yard was not used for nefarious activity.

Louis Diemschutz was the steward of the International Workingmen's Educational Club and he lived on the premises with his wife who assisted him in the running of the club. Louis was, in addition, a market trader and every Saturday ordinarily he sold his wares from a stall set up at Crystal Palace.

At 1 a.m., Sunday, 30 September 1888, he returned from Crystal Palace with the intention of depositing his unsold stock on the club premises. He entered the gateway leading into Dutfields Yard – or rather, his horse did – for Louis Diemschutz was in charge of a horse and cart and it was customary for the horse to go first.

However, on this occasion, the horse objected to this procedure and shied violently to the left. Mr Diemschutz dismounted from the cart and entered the yard.

On his right, against the south wall of the club, lay a dark bundle. Unable, in the near darkness, to properly identify its nature, Louis poked at it with his whip, and then, still uncertain he struck a match.

The flame revealed something not ordinarily to be found in Dutfields Yard.

The bundle was the dead body of a woman. Her throat had been cut.

Death in Dutfields Yard

The night of Saturday, 29 and Sunday, 30 September was reserved for double murder.

The experts concluded that Jack the Ripper had been interrupted before he could begin his mutilation of the Berner Street victim and, maddened with frustrated blood lust, had rushed to Mitre Square where he savagely attacked, killed and mutilated Catherine Eddowes. This is not correct. Joseph Barnett was not a psychopath nor was he, in the accepted sense, a sexual deviant. He was simply complaining about the state of the streets, albeit in a somewhat unconventional manner.

The double murder then, was not a spur of the moment decision, and the primary reason why the Berner Street victim was not "ripped" was because Mary Jane Kelly was not present, and she was not present because Joseph Barnett had decreed that it was too dangerous for her to loiter at Target Zero. Her job that night was to set up a victim at Mitre Square and await reinforcements.

Joseph Barnett had targeted (for the anagram) not just Berner Street but Dutfields Yard. It was an enterprise replete with danger and he considered that the risk of being detected was unusually high. In the event that this should occur, flight, or worse fight, would be the only choices. Mary Jane, with her long skirts, would prove a hindrance should that eventuality take place. She would have to be content with the victim she procured at Mitre Square.

There were more sightings of Jack the Ripper on Berner Street than at all of the other murder sites put together and, whilst none of them can be proven, they can be utilised to paint an interesting picture, albeit incomplete.

On Saturday nights, the International Workingmen's Educational Club was given over to free discussion, and the subject under discussion on Saturday evening, 29 September was entitled, "Why Jews Should Be Socialists".

Although the evening was wet and cold, the meeting was generously attended, there being a crowd close to 100 present.

The meeting came to an end at approximately midnight when most of the members departed homeward. Twenty or thirty, however, stayed behind and the rest of the evening was given over to music, singing and persiflage.

Joseph Barnett departed from Murder Headquarters at approximately 8.45 p.m. and headed south in the direction of St George's-in-the-East. He was attired in a cutaway jacket, dark trousers and a fore-and-aft hat. Under his arm was a parcel wrapped in newspaper.

Joseph was headed for a 9 p.m. meeting with George Buck. This took place at The Old Rose public house, opposite Hawksmoor's Church, St George's-in-the-East and just 500 yards south of Berner Street. (Both of these buildings survive today, embattled survivors of a bygone age.)

Joseph had anticipated a scarcity of available victims in the Target Area. The first part of the operation would be devoted to luring a prostitute within striking range of Dutfields Yard and keeping her in the area until the most propitious moment for her execution presented itself. Joseph Barnett had observed the activity that took place at The International Workingmen's Educational Club over the last few weeks, from a window seat in The Gun Deck beer house, just across the street from the Target Area.

The best time to strike, he considered, would probably be between 12.30 and 1 a.m. The side door of the club presented the biggest danger. If anyone should leave the premises when the operation was in progress there would be no warning of their approach. Such an interruption would necessitate immediate departure from the scene. It was for this reason that Mary Jane was not in attendance.

Joseph and George left The Old Rose together at approximately 9.30, separating after they had crossed over St George's Street. They then headed north along Cannon Street Road, then turned left onto Cable Street.

They strolled north up Berner Street, George on the left-hand side of the road, Joseph on the right-hand side. They both observed Dutfields Yard. The gates were open. There was no apparent obstacle to the operation proceeding as planned.

They walked to the northern end of Berner Street and turned

right onto Commercial Road. They surveyed the street. At a distance of less than 200 yards stood a woman. Neither Joseph or George knew her. Her name was Elizabeth Stride and she was in the wrong place at the wrong time. It was ten o'clock.

Liz Stride, otherwise known as Long Liz, was a short woman with a long face and a scarcity of front teeth, which afforded her the alternative nickname, Mother Gumm.

George strolled east along Commercial Road toward Liz Stride, whilst Joseph Barnett crossed over the road and observed the pick-up.

After a brief conversation George and Liz Stride linked arms and sauntered east. They crossed over Commercial Road, and turned left onto Settles Street.

Joseph walked slowly to the corner with Commercial Road and Settles Street and saw George and Liz walking north on the right-hand side of the road.

When they reached the Bricklayer's Arms public house, number 34, Settles Street (on the corner with Fordham Street – currently Hussains Cash and Carry) they turned into the doorway and disappeared from sight. The time: 10.10.

It was drizzling with rain.

Nearly one hour later at eleven o'clock, Joseph Barnett observed the pair emerging from the Bricklayer's Arms and begin walking south along Settles Street. A sudden downpour caused them to take shelter in a doorway.

James Best and John Gardner, two drunken labourers, seemingly oblivious of the rain, jeer at the couple in the doorway.

"That's Leather Apron getting round you!" And, laughing loudly at their jest they strolled away. Joseph Barnett smiled, a grim smile. George too, was amused at the irony of the situation. It is not recorded what Liz Stride thought.

James Best and John Gardner gave evidence at the inquest into the death of Elizabeth Stride. They were certain that the woman was Stride. This is the description they gave of the man:

5'5" tall.
Black moustache.
Weak, sandy eyelashes.
Morning suit and billycock hat. Definitely English.

At 11.10, the rain eased, and George and Liz Stride continued south along Settles Street then turned right onto Commercial Road.

They crossed over Commercial Road, continuing westward, crossing over Berner Street, continuing until they reached The Castle public house on the corner with Goodmans Stile. They entered the pub. The time was 11.25.

After a quick drink, George and Liz departed from The Castle and walked east toward Berner Street. The time was 11.35.

At approximately 11.45, William Marshall was taking the air at his front doorway at number 64, Berner Street. He noticed a man and a woman on the opposite pavement. They were standing opposite to number 58, just three houses to the north of his own premises.

Marshall saw the man kiss the woman and heard him remark: "You would say anything but your prayers," which made the woman laugh.

The couple stood around chatting for a further fifteen minutes, though Marshall took little notice of them.

Around midnight (at, or about, midnight, the majority of club members were exiting from the International Workingmen's Educational Club) the two began to stroll south, towards Ellen Street; away from the direction of Dutfields Yard, which was situated just seventy yards to the north of number 64. They walked past Marshall who noted that they appeared to be perfectly sober.

William Marshall later identified the woman as having been Liz Stride.

This is the description William Marshall gave of the man:

Middle-aged.
5'6" tall.
Stout.
Decently dressed in a black cutaway coat (jacket).
Dark trousers.
A cap with a small peak (like a sailor would wear). No gloves.
Carried nothing in his hands.

Although Marshall did not see, or did not note, the man's face, he nonetheless considered that he was not of the labouring class, placing him as someone who worked in a clerical capacity. Marshall considered the man to be educated and mild speaking.

George and Joseph are now aware that the meeting of the International Workingmen's Educational Club was ended and that therefore most of the club members had departed, or were making preparation to depart.

Joseph Barnett bought himself a beer in the Gun Deck and took a window seat where he could observe Dutfields Yard.

At fifteen minutes to midnight, club member William West, together with his brother, left the International Workingmen's Educational Club via the Berner Street door. Joseph Barnett watched them leave.

At 12.30, George returned to the Target Area bringing the victim with him.

Working to a prearranged plan, George, observing the approach of a policeman, excuses himself and enters the Gun Deck, leaving Liz Stride outside. Without acknowledging George, Joseph leaves the Gun Deck and propositions Liz Stride.

At approximately 12.31, PC Smith, number 452H, sees a man and a woman standing on the eastern side of Berner Street, talking. The couple are sited diagonally opposite to Dutfields Yard.

PC Smith would later identify the woman as having been Liz Stride.

This is the description PC Smith gave of the man:

Approximately 28 years of age.
5'7" to 5'8" tall.
Took little notice of his face but observed that he had a small dark moustache and had a dark complexion.
The man was respectably attired in a black diagonal cutaway coat (jacket), white collar and tie.
A hard, felt deerstalker hat, in a dark hue.

PC Smith overheard no conversation but considered the couple to be sober.

The man carried a newspaper parcel with approximate dimensions, 18" long, 6" to 8" broad.

At approximately 12.40, Joseph Lave, a printer and photographer visiting London from America, exited from the side door of number 40, Berner Street, to take a breath of fresh air. He walked as far as the gates which were open onto Berner Street, and proceeded back into the club. He noticed nothing unusual and certainly there was the distinct absence of a dead body reposing in Dutfields Yard.

At approximately 12.45, Maurice Eagle, the club chairman, entered the club via the side door in Dutfields Yard. He neither saw nor heard anything unusual.

Joseph Barnett, having been informed by Liz Stride that his attentions were unwelcome, returned to the Gun Deck. There he opened the parcel and removed an overcoat and a battered hat. He passed the overcoat to George. George puts the coat on, notwithstanding the fact that it is too long for him. Should George require to explain the sudden acquisition of the garment, he will say he took it as security against a debt which will itself explain his lone visit to the Gun Deck. George and Liz walk slowly southward.

At approximately 12.47, James Brown, a dock labourer of number 35, Fairclough Street, observed a man and a woman standing talking at the eastern corner of Berner Street and Fairclough Street.

The woman faced the man, her back to the wall. The man was bent over the woman, his arm resting against the wall. Brown heard the woman say:

"Not tonight. Some other night."

Brown was *fairly* sure that the woman was Elizabeth Stride.

James Brown gave this description of the man:

5'7" tall (the man was bent over which made estimation difficult).
Dark overcoat that nearly reached his heels.
No other information.

Joseph contrived to meet Liz and George in the street. Liz Stride is surprised to note that this is the same man who propositioned her a few minutes earlier. Joseph repaid the "debt" to George, in cash, and took back possession of the coat. He walked away and donned the coat and the American style hat. The time: 12.48.

George has manoeuvred Liz Stride to a position just outside the entrance to Dutfields Yard. Joseph Barnett stands in the shadows opposite.

It's now or never.

George is unable to convince Liz Stride that it is a good idea to enter Dutfields Yard and no amount of cajoling will budge her.

George decides to resort to force.

He pulls Liz Stride away from the wall and tries to propel her into the Yard but succeeds only in knocking her off of her feet.

(If the only objective is to kill Liz Stride then George and Joseph will kill her now, but it isn't. She must be killed in Dutfields Yard.)

At approximately 12.49, a man named Israel Schwartz, of 22, Ellen Street, turned into Berner Street from Commercial Road. Mr Schwartz spoke little or no English but he understood the language of violence. As he walked south on the right-hand side of the thoroughfare, he saw, fifty yards ahead, a man throw a woman to the ground.

The woman did not scream but emitted a series of squealing sounds as though in some distress. (Possibly George had punched her in the solar plexus and Liz Stride was striving to get some air into her lungs.)

Israel Schwartz did not wish to be involved in violence and still less in a matter which was probably domestic in origin.

He continued walking in the same direction; south, but crossed over to the left-hand side of the street. As he neared the warring pair, the altercation increased in volume and Schwartz stopped in his tracks and turned, uncertain what, if anything, to do next.

As he did so, a match flared in a doorway situated opposite to Dutfields Yard, and a man moved out and confronted him; a man lighting a clay pipe, but a man who, to Israel Schwartz, exuded menace.

At the same instant a voice shouted "*Lipski!*"

Schwartz was uncertain which of the two men uttered the cry, or warning.

("Lipski" had become a pejorative term for all Jews following the brutal murder of the exotically named Miriam Angel by one Israel Lipski, a Polish Jew, in the year 1887. It was a crime for which Lipski had been executed. The Murder Squad simply used the name to shout a warning to one another.)

Demoralised, Schwartz turned and resumed his journey south. A quick look over his shoulder. *The man is following.*

Totally unnerved, Israel Schwartz started to run and run. He didn't stop until he'd reached the railway arch on Cable Street a quarter of a mile away.

Israel Schwartz later identified the woman as having been Liz Stride.

This is the description Israel Schwartz gave of the two men:

The man who threw the woman to the ground:

Age; 30 years.
Height; 5'5".
Hair; Dark.
Small brown moustache.
Full face.
Broad shoulders.
Dark jacket and trousers.
Black cap with peak.
The man carried nothing in his hands.

The man in the doorway:

Age: 35 years.
Height: 5'11".
Hair and moustache, both brown.
Dark overcoat.
Old black hard felt hat with a wide brim.
Clay pipe in his hand.

As Israel Schwarz began to run, Joseph Barnett crossed over the street and he and George seized Liz Stride and dragged her into the dark confines of Dutfields Yard. As George held her lower mandible and head, Joseph quickly cut her throat. The cut failed to totally sever the carotid artery but was, nonetheless, sufficient to cause death. The poor quality of the work can be attributed to inadequate lighting and undue haste.

Exit left from Dutfields Yard. To turn right would be foolhardy: that was the direction in which the frightened Jew had fled – and he could return with a policeman.

Turn left onto Sander Street toward Backchurch Lane where they'd head north toward Mitre Square. From the direction of Commercial Road, they could hear the sound of a horse and cart: a horse and cart headed for Dutfields Yard.

The Murder Squad had succeeded; or had they? Success or failure had to be measured against the anagram. Had Target Zero been achieved, or had Joseph and George been forced to flee before they could reach Target Zero? What was Target Zero? Dutfields Yard? Berner Street? The International Workingmen's Educational Club? Forty, Berner Street? Number (No) Forty (Four O)? All of these or any combination?

The International Workingmen's Educational Club seemed unlikely for it had not been achieved but, nonetheless, it might have been a frustrated attempt and could not be ignored. Possibly Joseph and George had intended hurling the dead body of Liz Stride through the open side door of the club, leaving her corpse half in and half out, and then could legitimately have claimed the International Workingmen's Educational Club and Dutfields Yard.

But Berner Street was a problem; all those EEEs and RRRs. How could they be dispersed? Unless Berner Street contained a name and, if it did contain a name, it could only be the true name of Mary Jane Kelly.

The suspicion began to grow into conviction.

Somewhere within the words "Dutfields Yard" and/or "Berner Street" was contained an anagrammatic construction of Mary Jane Kelly's real surname. But how to prove it?

Bricklayer's Arms, 1997

The Statement of Matthew Packer

Matthew Packer was a greengrocer and fruiterer whose premises (including living accommodation) were situated at number 44 Berner Street, just fifteen yards south of Dutfields Yard, on the same side of the road. He lived at this address with his wife, and was known as an intelligent, respectable, hard-working man.

Matthew Packer's statement was not incorporated into the main story for the reason that Matthew Packer's version of events is in contradiction of the police version of events, insofar as those events relate to the taking of his statement.

Following the murder of Elizabeth Stride, in Dutfields Yard, the police interviewed everyone who resided on Berner Street including, of course, Matthew Packer. The undernoted report was written by Sergeant Stephen White of H Division on 4 October 1888 (his notebook, containing the original material, has been lost):

About 09.00 hours (30 September) I called at number 44, Berner Street, and I saw Matthew Packer, fruiterer, in a small way of business. I asked him what time he closed his shop on the previous night. He replied:

"Half past twelve, in consequence of the rain it was no good for me to keep open."

I asked him if he saw anything of a man, or woman, going into Dutfields Yard or saw anyone standing about the street around the time he was closing his shop. He replied:

"No, I saw no one standing about, neither did I see anyone go up the yard. I never saw anything suspicious nor heard the slightest noise and knew nothing about the murder till I heard of it this morning".

I also saw Mrs Packer, Sarah Harrison and Harry Douglas, residing in the same house but none of them could give the slightest information respecting the matter.

On 2 October (two days after Sergeant White had interviewed Packer, and two days before Sergeant White wrote his report respecting that interview) Matthew Packer was telling a different story to two private detectives who were conducting their own enquiry on behalf of the Mile End Vigilance Committee.

Matthew Packer began his revelations by first stating that, although a plain-clothes policeman had come to the shop the day after the murder, he had confined his activities to looking around the premises including the backyard. His comment regarding the interview conducted by Sergeant White was, the astonishing:

"The police? No, they haven't asked me a word about it yet."

It is presumed, but not stated, that Mrs Packer, Sarah Harrison and Harry Douglas agreed that they too were not interviewed by Sergeant White.

There is no way of resolving these contradictory statements except to say that Matthew Packer later exhibited a tendency to embroider his story according to his audience, but the substance of his account, which never varied, indicates that Packer observed a killer intent upon keeping a prospective victim in a specific area awaiting a suitable moment to strike and, for that reason, the account is intriguing, One thing is not disputed – Matthew Packer did have a ringside seat.

This then is Matthew Packer's statement:

> I'd been out with my barrow during the afternoon/evening of Saturday, 29 September but I hadn't done much business on account of the rain, so I returned home and took a hand serving in the shop.
>
> Some time between 23.30 hours and midnight a man and a woman walked up Berner Street from the direction of Ellen Street (from the south) and stopped to look at the fruit (Matthew Packer later identified the woman as having been Liz Stride).
>
> They looked for a minute or two then the man said: "I say, old man, how do you sell your fruit?"
>
> I said, "Sixpence a pound the black 'uns sir and four pence a pound the white 'uns."
>
> The man turned to the woman and said: "Which will you have my dear, black or white? You shall have whichever you like best."
>
> The woman chose the black grapes, and the man said to me: "Give us half a pound of the black ones then."

91

I put the grapes in a bag, handed them to the man and took the money. The couple stood near my window for a minute or two then they crossed over the road and stood directly opposite my shop (which vantage point afforded a clear view of Dutfields Yard).

After they'd been stood there for some time I said to my wife: "Them people must be a couple of fools for standing outside in the rain, eating grapes, when they could just as well have found shelter."

They were still stood there when I shut up shop and went to bed, shortly after midnight.

This is Matthew Packer's description of the man:

28 to 35 years of age.

Medium height, about 5'7" stout, square built, with a dark complexion.

Long black coat and black soft felt hat (or wide awake, or yankee hat).

A clerical worker. Sounded educated. A loud, rough voice and a quick, commanding, decisive way of speaking.

He was clean-shaven and had an alert look.

The post-mortem examination of the stomach contents of the Berner Street victim failed to discover the presence of grape skins, but perhaps Mother Gumm preferred only the juice. And stories abound of a grape stalk clutched in the victim's hand and/or grape skins/seeds in the area where the body reposed.

The Anagram

These are the "pure" letters carried forward following the Hanbury Street murder of Annie Chapman:

```
D
UYSR
BERNER STREET
MITRE SQUARE
ILLERS COURT
```

Berner Street was obviously not a "pure" target. Other information had to be added to this target, but what was this other information?

It seemed certain that the Berner Street murder was the "sweeper". The last target chosen by Joseph Barnett, and designed to "round off" the anagram.

The way in which Liz Stride had been manoeuvred into position suggested that Target Zero was Dutfields Yard. Was the required information, Dutfields Yard, Berner Street? Perhaps.

But, there was another possibility: that Target Zero was The International Workingmen's Educational Club: that Joseph Barnett had intended that the body of Liz Stride be thrown through the doorway of the club, but had been thwarted in this endeavour by the arrival of Louis Diemschutz.

There was, of course, something wrong with this idea. The number of letters would almost certainly cause the anagram to collapse under the weight of its own construction. But there was no way to be sure.

After the murder of Liz Stride in Dutfields Yard, the anagram remains unchanged.

The Address of Jack the Ripper

It is doubtful that Joseph Barnett ever left the East End during his sojourn as Jack the Ripper, so that correspondence from such far away places as Liverpool and Glasgow could scarcely have been *posted* by him, but certainly one letter, from Liverpool, was *written* by Joseph Barnett and was probably forwarded to a confederate for onward transmission.

It was addressed to the Central News Agency. The letter was posted 29/30 September 1888, the receipt of which was timed to coincide with the Berner Street and Mitre Square murders.

This is the content of the letter:

Prince William Street, Liverpool

What fools the police are. I even give the name of the street where I am living.

Yours Truly,

Jack the Ripper

There is no Prince William Street in Liverpool.
Prince William Street is an anagram.
It translates as:

Tip. We are in Millers Ct.

Joseph Barnett constructed this anagram late in September. Feeling that he was perhaps cheating by using the word TIP but failing to find a better construction, he legitimised its use by composing a postcard which utilised the word TIP, a postcard he composed on the night of the double murders and posted the following day.

Mitre Square

> *Six little whores, glad to be alive*
> *One sidles up to Jack, then there are five*
> *Four and whore rhyme aright, so do three and me*
> *I'll set the town alight ere there are two*

> Joseph Barnett, 1888

Mitre Square encompasses an area approximately thirty yards by thirty-five yards. It was, and is, situated on the eastern edge of the City of London and therefore falls just outside the jurisdiction of the Metropolitan Police.

There were, and are, three points of entry/exit.

On the south-eastern side of King's Street (now Creechurch Lane) was, and is, an area enclosed on three sides, named St James's Place (now Creechurch Place) and known colloquially, in the year 1888, as The Orange Market.

On the south-eastern side of The Orange Market was a narrow, covered, unlit passageway (widened now) which gave access to the north-western side of Mitre Square. This passageway was named Mitre Passage.

Another covered passageway led directly from Duke Street (now Duke's Place) into Mitre Square and this was illuminated, at night, by one poor light at its Duke Street end.

(This passageway, named Church Passage, was widened in the year 1986; the covering was demolished and the renovated entry re-named St James's Passage.)

The main point of entry to Mitre Square was, and is, afforded direct from Mitre Street. This was a carriageway and there was illumination, albeit poor, adjacent to this point.

The Square was surrounded by buildings, mostly warehouses, which crouched over the tiny area like huge predatory monsters and, by night, it was a lonely and intimidating place to be.

It did not however have a bad reputation: quite the reverse in fact.

By day Mitre Square was a bustling arena of noisome commerce, and by night, though poorly lit with a feeling of peculiar isolation, it was not associated with prostitution or crime. Only the over-imaginative traveller need avoid Mitre Square.

The few private houses that fronted Mitre Square (on Mitre Street) were dilapidated and unoccupied; save one. Number 3, which was inhabited, ironically, by city policeman PC Richard Pearce, number 922, and his family.

Police Constable Pearce retired to his bed at half past midnight and was asleep when duty constable, Edward Watkins, number 881, entered Mitre Square from Mitre Street at 1.30 a.m. It was quiet. All was well.

It was 1.45 when PC Watkins returned to the Square. All was still quiet but all was no longer well. He shone his torch into the blackness that cloaked the southernmost corner of Mitre Square. The light of the beam illuminated the latest, and the worst yet, of Jack the Ripper's handiwork.

Catherine Eddowes lay on her back, her feet pointing into the centre of the Square. Her clothes had been pulled up above her waist. Her throat had been cut and her bowels were protruding through massive wounds inflicted to her abdomen. Her face had been slashed.

The surrounding area was a sticky red lake of still oozing blood.

Police Constable Watkins, had he wished to make a closer examination, would have ascertained that Catherine Eddowes had, in addition, been relieved of her womb and one of her kidneys.

Communication to Major Henry Smith, Acting Commissioner, City of London Police.

Old Boss,

Have you seen the Devle with his mikerscope and scalpul a-looking at a kidney with a slide cocked up.

Mutilation in Mitre Square

At three minutes to one o'clock, Joseph and George departed from Dutfields Yard, headed for Mitre Square and their appointment with Mary Jane Kelly. They were running late.

But on reflection this seemed unlikely. If Mary Jane was waiting at Mitre Square, how would she know how to react if things went wrong?

And, if they had gone wrong, how could she alibi Joseph and George if she was standing anonymously in Mitre Square?

More likely then Mary Jane was waiting in room number 13, Millers Court, awaiting the return of Joseph, bearing the good news that he had succeeded in ridding the world of another whore.

So Joseph Barnett left George to make his own way to Mitre Square and to select the next victim en route, whilst he (Joseph) walked back to Murder Headquarters to change his clothes and to pick up Mary Jane Kelly. It was a journey of just 1,000 yards. He walked it comfortably in just ten minutes.

Joseph Lawende, a commercial traveller of 79, Fenchurch Street, departed from the Imperial Club, 16–17 Duke Street, at approximately 1.30. Lawende was in the company of two friends; Joseph Hiram Levy, a butcher, and Harry Lewis, a furniture dealer.

These three exited left from the club and were proceeding down Duke Street when they saw a man and a woman standing at the corner of Church Passage, which led into Mitre Square. Levy was of the opinion that the man was about three inches taller than the woman, whilst Lewis was unable to offer any consideration whatsoever regarding the pair. Joseph Lawende was nearest to the couple and noticed a little more.

This is the description Lawende gave regarding the couple:

> I did not see the woman's face and am therefore unable to identify her as having been Catherine Eddowes. The woman was short. (Catherine Eddowes was about 5'0" tall.) She wore a black

jacket and a bonnet. She stood facing the man, her back towards me. One hand rested on the man's chest. There was no quarrel in progress, indeed the couple appeared to be conversing, but very quietly.

The man was aged approximately 30 years and was about 5'7" to 5'8" in height. He had a fair moustache and a fair complexion and was of medium build. He wore a loose jacket, pepper and salt pattern, with a grey cloth cap with peak and a reddish neckerchief. He had the appearance of a sailor.

If encountered again, I would not be able to recognize the man.

Lawende was shown the clothes that Catherine Eddowes had worn that night and he expressed the opinion that they were identical to the clothes he had seen adorning the woman who had stood at the corner of Church Passage, on the night in question.

(There is no way of ascertaining who Lawende saw that night but, if the man was Joseph Barnett, then the woman was more likely to have been Mary Jane Kelly, which means Lawende saw them at the time they were waiting for George to arrive with a victim. There is a certain intimacy about these two: the woman's hand on the man's chest: the quiet conversation and, if the woman was only 5'0" tall then Barnett would have been not two or three inches taller but a considerable seven or eight inches. In addition, Joseph Barnett must have known Catherine Eddowes and she him, for she had lodged frequently on Dorset Street. Unlikely then that Joseph Barnett would have made the pick-up.)

Catherine Eddowes had a secret. She knew, or suspected that she knew, the identity of Jack the Ripper, and was excited by the prospect of receiving a considerable sum in the way of reward money.

This information from the *East London Observer*, 13 October 1888.

Our reporter interviewed the Casual Ward Superintendent of Mile End, who was acquainted with the Mitre Square victim, who said:

I asked her, "Where have you been?" for I had not seen her in some time.

"I have been to Kent, hopping," she replied, "But I have returned to get the reward offered for the arrest and conviction of Jack the Ripper, for I think I know who he is."

"Well mind he don't get you," I said.

"No fear of that," replied Kate Eddowes.

If this statement is true, and Catherine Eddowes knew, or suspected that she knew the identity of Jack the Ripper, then Kate did not confide the basis of her suspicion to her friend, John Kelly and, it is most probable that she made up the story in order to dramatise herself.

Some writers have postulated the theory that Catherine Eddowes knew too much and was lured to Mitre Square so that she might be silenced. It is certainly an intriguing idea, for Catherine Eddowes had dossed in the room fronting Dorset Street, at number 26, and this room backed onto the partition wall of room number 13, Millers Court. Had she picked up scraps of information from overheard conversations and put two and two together?

Persuasive as the idea is, it doesn't stand up to close examination for, if Catherine Eddowes was murdered according to a plan devised by Jack the Ripper, then it was a plan that relied on 99 per cent luck for its success.

Catherine Eddowes had just returned from Maidstone, in the county of Kent. She had been hopeful of securing work, hop-picking, with her common-law husband, John Kelly, the day prior to her demise.

It had proven to be an unsuccessful endeavour due, no doubt, to the fact that the season was almost over and the couple had been forced to return from their foray earlier than anticipated – wiser, but certainly not richer.

They assessed their plight on some street corner and it was decided that the best course of action would be to go their separate ways until their financial situation improved. With the cunning of the professional alcoholic, Catherine Eddowes had ensured that she had sufficient funds to finance another binge and, having ensured the disappearance, albeit temporary, of her ardent swain, she embarked upon a tour of the local hostelries with the intention of drinking herself into oblivion.

It was an unqualified success, as police constable Louis Robinson, number 931, would be able to testify. At 8.30 on the evening of Saturday, 29 September 1888, PC Robinson scraped the inebriated, inert, but still breathing body of Catherine Eddowes from the shop doorway of number 29, Aldgate High Street.

Robinson, with assistance, managed to convey the drunken carcass of the hapless creature to Bishopsgate police station, where it was considered appropriate to install her in a cell until such time as she was able to demonstrate that she was in a fit state to look after herself.

It fell to police constable George Hutt, number 968, to make that decision, for it was he who took over as duty officer of Bishopsgate police station at 9.45 that evening.

PC Hutt visited the prisoner several times and, at 12.50, 30 September 1888, he adjudged that she was sufficiently able to find her own way home: a decision not altogether disassociated from the fact that the public houses were, for the most part, closed.

"What time is it?" asked Catherine Eddowes.

"Too late for you to get any more drink," replied Hutt.

"Well," she insisted, "what time is that?"

"Just on one o'clock."

"I'll get a good hiding when I get home."

"Serve you right."

Upon being discharged Catherine Eddowes, who had, on admittance, given her name as "Nothing", gave her name as Mary Ann Kelly. (It should be remembered that Catherine was consorting with John Kelly. Nonetheless, it is something of a coincidence.)

Catherine Eddowes left Bishopsgate police station, and headed south in the direction of Mitre Square, just ten minutes' walk away.

Her last recorded words, addressed to Hutt, were: "Goodnight Old Cock."

At the same time that Catherine Eddowes was being released from Bishopsgate police station, Joseph and George were leaving Dutfields Yard and the dead, or dying, Liz Stride behind them.

As Joseph headed for Millers Court and the pick-up with Mary Jane, George took his time and strolled west along Commercial Road. The shrill, distant sound of a police whistle from behind him caused George to turn right into Church Lane.

After a stop-over in Church Lane, where he loitered briefly to wipe his hands, George resumed his journey up Church Lane and turned left onto Whitechapel High Street which itself led onto Aldgate High Street. There was no hurry. Joseph and Mary would not be in position until 1.30.

If it had been Catherine Eddowes' intention to return home, she would have headed due east after her departure from the police station, towards the familiar doss area of Flower & Dean Street and Thrawl Street. Such was not her intention, for she headed south along Bishopsgate, past Liverpool Street station, then turned left onto Houndsditch. Catherine was seeking a replenishment of funds to enable her to purchase more liquid refreshment.

How lucky she was to stumble into the arms of George Buck at the corner of Aldgate High Street and Houndsditch, for George knew of a public house open till dawn, and not far away – just as far as Mitre Square. Only 200 yards to heaven, which, as it happened, was a literal truth... to those who believe.

George watched and waited as three men emerged from Duke Street and crossed over Aldgate High Street towards Minories. But Lawende, Lewis and Levy were deep in conversation and they were looking to their right as they crossed Aldgate. George waited thirty seconds before deciding it was all clear. It was time to steer the drunken whore into Mitre Square.

An immediate right into Duke Street and George and the shambling ruin that was Catherine Eddowes approached the entrance that led into Church Passage, past the couple embracing at the corner, and now heading into the forbidding near darkness of Mitre Square.

Joseph and Mary fell into step just twenty yards behind George and Catherine, towards the south corner of Mitre Square now just fifty yards away. Fifty yards to darkness and death, Target Zero, the place that for years to come would be known as Ripper's Corner.

101

George seized Catherine Eddowes by the throat and forced her to the ground. He brutally pulled back her head and Joseph Barnett cut her throat with one bloody sweep of his knife. He slashed Catherine's face as Mary Jane greedily lifted the victim's skirt.

Joseph and George moved away. Joseph to Mitre Street, George to Mitre Passage where he could also observe Church Passage.

Deprived of the kill on Berner Street, Mary Jane was thirsty for blood. She excelled herself as she removed Catherine Eddowes' womb and one of her kidneys. She was stuffing the gory trophies into the bag when Joseph Barnett signalled that it was time to depart. Clutching the bloody bag in her right hand, she moved towards Church Passage.

Mary Jane pressed her bloody left hand against her mouth. She could taste the blood. She licked her lips in anticipation.

What a wonderful rehearsal for the grand finale...the murder and mutilation of her hated cousin in room number 13, Millers Court.

(Because it would be necessary to mutilate the features of victim number six, in order to disguise the fact that number six was not Mary Jane Kelly, it was deemed advisable to cut the face of Catherine Eddowes, so that the disfigurement of victim number six would not be seen as a singular occurrence.)

The Anagram

These are the "pure" letters carried forward following the Hanbury Street murder of Annie Chapman but not including the Berner Street murder of Liz Stride:

D
UYSR
BERNER STREET
MITRE SQUARE
ILLERS COURT

Mitre Square was primarily to add the word MASTER to the anagram. This leaves the letters QUIRE and it will be assumed here that these letters are needed for "require". Accordingly an R and an E will be subtracted from Berner Street. The letter D is still being carried over from George Yard and therefore this letter D will be utilised to make the word REQUIRED.

The undernoted "pure" letters are carried over to the next round:

UYSR
BNER STREET
ILLERS COURT

The message after the murder of Catherine Eddowes but not including the murder of Liz Stride is:

Barnett, Master
George Buck
Mary
Whores
Required

At this juncture we can guess that the word MASON and, almost certainly, YOURS TRULY are needed for the anagram. There is no letter M in the remaining "pure" letters, neither is there an A. There is only one Y (two are needed) and only one O, (two are needed) and consideration should be given as to where these missing letters will be obtained.

One piece of information will assist. Joseph Barnett, at the inquest into the death of Mary Jane Kelly, gave his address – at the time of his living with Mary Kelly – as room number 13, Millers Court.

But, crucially, we need to know the real surname of Mary Jane Kelly.

Graffiti on Goulston Street

Whilst Mary Jane Kelly was busy mutilating the unfortunate Catherine Eddowes, Joseph and George were standing guard: Joseph at the Mitre Street entrance to the Square and George at or about the Duke Street entrance.

It was Joseph Barnett, observing the approach of PC Watkins, who signalled Mary Jane that they should depart from the Square immediately. These two exited through Church Passage into Duke Street whilst George departed via the Orange Market.

They met as they converged on Houndsditch. Into Gravel Lane, then onto Middlesex Street (Petticoat Lane) and into New Goulston Street and left onto Goulston Street. It was here that they stopped and one of them, probably Mary Jane, wrote a message in chalk, on the black dado of the wall at the entranceway of Wentworth Model Dwellings:

> *The Juwes are*
> *The men That*
> *Will not*
> *be Blamed*
> *for nothing.*

But that is *not* how it happened.

When Joseph and Mary left Millers Court and proceeded to Mitre Square they followed the same route by which they later returned. So Mary Jane wrote the Goulston Street message on the way to Mitre Square *not on the way back.*

On the way back she dropped the piece of material she had torn from Catherine Eddowes' apron, now saturated with blood and faecal matter, in the doorway of Wentworth Model Dwellings, in order to signpost the message she had written forty minutes earlier.

But what does the message mean? It may contain an anagram but if so, almost certainly its interpretation requires esoteric knowledge. But the message was probably simply an expression of anti-Semitism.

This, from *The Complete History of Jack the Ripper* by Philip Sugden:

> Advocates of the Masonic conspiracy theory cite "Juwes" as proof that the murderer was a Freemason. This assertion is based upon an erroneous belief, promulgated by Stephen Knight, Melvyn Fairclough and others, that "Juwes" was a Masonic term by which Jubela, Jubelo and Jubelum were collectively known. In fact this was simply not the case. By 1888 the three murderers of Hiram Abiff had not been part of British Masonic ritual for more than seventy years, and although they had survived in American ritual in neither country had they ever been called, officially or colloquially, the "Juwes". "It is a mystery", wrote Paul Begg, one of the most dependable modern students of the case, "why anyone ever thought that 'Juwes' was a Masonic word."

The Postcard

2 a.m., Sunday, 30 September 1888

They sat there in the small dark room listening to the activity outside.

The City of London police had poured into Dorset Street in force two minutes earlier, as Joseph Barnett was washing his hands at the outside tap. He'd been lucky to get back inside room number 13 before they'd charged into Millers Court.

"There's blood here, sir." The shouted information was not good news for the three fugitives.

Major Henry Smith, the acting commissioner for the City of London police, moved towards the sink. "Where?"

"Here in the sink."

They listened and they waited for the knock on the door.

But the police never called. They barged about in all directions, shouting and cursing then, as suddenly as they had come, they departed.

The City of London police had strayed out of their territory but they'd come the closest yet to catching Jack the Ripper.

It was five minutes before Mary Jane broke the silence.

"I'm cold."

Joseph Barnett stood up. "I'll light the fire. You'd better stay here tonight, George."

George smiled in the near darkness. "Honoured I'm sure."

They slept fitfully and rose an hour before dawn. After a desultory breakfast George departed.

It was later that same afternoon that Joseph Barnett decided to write a postcard. It was a calculated move but the postcard gives the deliberate impression that it was written in haste.

I wasnt codding dear old Boss when I gave you the tip You'll hear about saucy Jackys work tomorrow Double ev-ent this time number one squealed a bit Couldn't finish straight off had not time to get ears for police Thanks for keeping last letter back till I got to work again.

Jack the Ripper

Joseph Barnett addressed the card to *Central News Office, London City EC.*

He retrieved Catherine Eddowes kidney from Mary Jane, smeared both sides of the card with her blood and allowed it to dry.

The postcard was posted Sunday evening, 30 September 1888, and bears the post-mark, London E R9 Oc 1 88.

It is interesting to note that "number one squealed a bit", when compared with the statement of Israel Schwartz.

The Letter from Hell

George Lusk lived at number 1, Alderney Road, Mile End, and George was the chairman of the Mile End Vigilance Committee.

On the afternoon of Tuesday, 16 October 1888, sixteen days after the murder of Catherine Eddowes, George Lusk was the recipient of a small package, wrapped with brown paper.

Inside the wrapping was a small cardboard box and inside the box was a letter from Jack the Ripper together with half a kidney which had evidently been partially preserved in spirits of wine.

The letter, written in jagged, stabbing strokes, reads:

From hell Mr Lusk Sor I send you half the Kidne I took from one women prasarved it for you tother piece I fried and ate it was very nise I may send you the bloody knif that took it out if you only wate a whil longer

signed

Catch me when you can

Mishter Lusk

Whether or not the organ section was actually a part of Catherine Eddowes' missing left kidney has never been established, so the grisly package could have been sent by a hoaxer.

The strange misspellings might indicate a hidden message within the letter but there is no letter J and only one letter B. It is not impossible to take out key words, such as "whore", "kill", "murder", and build around such words. The problem lies in the fact that it is too easy, so that a message, if there is a message, is obliterated under the weight of too many alternatives. (Too many alternatives that do not include the name, Jack the Ripper.)

The writer hadn't finished with George Lusk. A few days later, George received a postcard. It read:

Say Boss, you seem rare frightened. Guess I like to give you fits, but I cant stop long enough to let you box of toys play copper games with me but hope to see you when I dont hurry too much.

Goodbye Boss

If this postcard is from the same man, his spelling has improved considerably.

(I have not seen the actual postcard, if indeed it still exists. Much of the original correspondence has been lost or stolen.)

NEWSFLASH

From our foreign correspondent, Wednesday 24 October 1888:

It is with deep regret that we announce the death of Mary Jane Kelly's mother, Marie Catherine, who passed away today at 3.30 p.m., after a short illness.

Her husband, John, comforted her in her last hours.

Notice of the funeral arrangements will be made as soon as possible though, at this time, it is considered doubtful that Mary Jane Kelly will be able to attend, due to a prior engagement.

Appointment with Death

It is recorded that, following the Mitre Square murder of Catherine Eddowes, Mary Jane Kelly disappeared from her usual haunts.

Most particularly she ceased to be in attendance at the Britannia public house on Fish Street Hill, which stood just 100 yards from Billingsgate Market, and only fifteen yards from The Monument.

(A Britannia public house stands on part of the site today but it is not the building familiar to Mary Jane Kelly. The side door of the present pub is in the position previously occupied by the front door of the old building.)

Seemingly she was very popular in this establishment which she visited frequently in the evenings, until the night of the double murders when she ceased to attend altogether. Her long absence notwithstanding, it was the management, staff and friends of this public house who sent a wreath to Mary Jane's funeral.

The distance from Millers Court to Fish Street Hill is just under one mile, and Mary Jane preferred to travel to the Britannia most evenings, for it was there, away from Dorset Street, where she could relax and be herself for a few hours each day.

Mary Jane's absence from her usual haunts, has been attributed to her fear of Jack the Ripper but, of course, this is not so.

Mary Jane was busy making an appointment with death, an appointment which would end with the murder and mutilation of her hated cousin in room number 13, Millers Court, 9 November 1888. Almost certainly it was this cousin who was an actress on the London stage.

"I have a female relative who is an actress on the London stage." (Mary Jane Kelly to Lizzie Allbrook.)

And almost certainly this cousin was appearing in a current (1888) West End (or provincial) production.

Joseph Barnett said of this cousin: "Marie lived a bad life with her cousin who was, as I often told her, the cause of her downfall."

This cousin will be invested with a name. Henceforth she will be known as Emily: cousin Emily.

It is hypothesised that Emily had done Mary Jane a terrible wrong: a wrong that had forever blighted her life and filled her with a terrible desire for vengeance.

What this wrong might have been can only be conjectured but it seems likely that it involved Mary Jane's husband.

It is certain that Mary Jane was the wronged and Emily the wrongdoer and both perceived themselves thus, for only the wronged can carry the olive branch with any certainty of success, whilst the wrongdoer is almost certain to be rebuffed.

Mary Jane was certain that she would not be rebuffed and she had gradually insinuated Emily in the false belief that all was forgiven and forgotten. Emily would be surprised but pleased that the unpleasantness appeared to be over and, she would be anxious that the restoration of goodwill be maintained.

This process had probably commenced at around the time that Joseph and Mary had moved to Millers Court, but it intensified in the month of October 1888, immediately following the murder of Catherine Eddowes in Mitre Square.

The process reached its culmination during the weekend of 27 to the 28 October 1888, when Emily accepted the appointment with death. Her death.

The appointment was predicated on a solid foundation of greed and lust – two vices guaranteed to appeal to the mercenary side of Emily's nature. Whatever the invitation was, Emily would need to make an overnight stay at Mary Jane's home – presented to her as a prestigious address which, of course, Emily had never visited.

Joseph Barnett was informed of the appointment with death on Monday, 29 October 1888. It was time for him to leave Millers Court.

Parting is Such Sweet Sorrow

Joseph Barnett and Mary Jane Kelly had lived comfortably and happily in room number 13, Millers Court, for approximately six months.

During that time they had been quiet and considerate neighbours and though Mary Jane had expressed an interest in another man; a man named Joe Flemming, her relationship with Joseph Barnett seemed amicable enough.

It came as something of a surprise then, when on the afternoon of Tuesday, 30 October 1888, sounds of domestic disharmony filtered through the environs of Millers Court.

Domestic disharmony quickly developed into domestic violence and, surprisingly, it was Joseph Barnett, the quiet man, who seemed most irate. Curses and blows were exchanged, objects were thrown; a bottle crashed through a windowpane leaving jagged shards of broken glass strewn across the court.

Joseph Barnett stormed from room number 13, his face a thundercloud.

Everyone testified to the violence of the tirade.

Later, Joseph would give two reasons for his uncharacteristic behaviour. He first stated that the primary cause was money, or rather the lack of money.

Later on, he would say that the problem occurred after Mary had taken a bad woman into their home, a German woman named Julia and, if he didn't actually say that Mary Jane had lesbian tendencies, there were plenty of people who said it for him.

Doubtless both matters rankled. The rent was heavily in arrears and, with Joseph out of work, that was not a problem likely to be soon resolved.

As for Mary Jane taking a woman into her bed. It was likely true.

She was drinking heavily and had probably returned to a life of prostitution: an intolerable situation for a decent man like Joseph

Barnett, a man who had often stated his objection to such a lifestyle.

And what of Mary Jane herself? (Remarkably unmarked, given the violence of the tirade.) Well, she didn't care what Joseph Barnett did.

She fancied another man, she confided; a man named Joe Flemming who visited her clandestinely, though surprisingly, nobody had ever met or even seen Joe Flemming.

The argument in room number 13, Millers Court, had been a stage-managed, fully orchestrated row, given for the benefit of the credulous.

Joseph Barnett had left Millers Court and, not only had he left, he had been seen to have left.

The stage was set for bloody murder!

Mary and Joseph had a plan and, in order to execute that plan, Joseph Barnett could no longer live in room number 13, Millers Court.

How else could Mary Jane Kelly be murdered by Jack the Ripper?

The Plan

Joseph Barnett and Mary Jane Kelly had a plan. It was of course a plan devised many months prior to Joseph Barnett's departure from Millers Court, which was itself merely an indication that the plan had come to fruition.

The plan was the basis for the anagram which, when constructed, signed the death warrant of six vile whores.

The first five whores were not selected on the basis that they were any more or any less objectionable than any of the other whores. They had simply collided with the anagram. Their deaths were virtually accidental.

Number six was different. She was specifically selected and had been from the very beginning. It is probable that if number six had not existed, then the series of crimes attributed to Jack the Ripper would not have occurred for, without Mary Jane Kelly's expertise and above all her obsessive hatred and desire for revenge, the plan was unviable.

Number six bore a superficial physical resemblance to Mary Jane Kelly, which was of course a necessity. This physical resemblance was not too surprising, for number six was Mary Jane Kelly's hated first cousin, the same cousin who, Joseph Barnett said, had been the cause of Mary Jane's downfall. It was the fact that Mary Jane Kelly hated her first cousin coupled with the fact that their age and physical appearance were similar, that had made the plan viable. In order that the *differences* in their physical appearance be obliterated Mary Jane Kelly would need to make a few alterations, not to herself, but to her cousin...posthumously of course.

The argument of 30 October 1888, signalled the fact that number six had been invited to, and had accepted, an invitation to Millers Court. It was time for Joseph Barnett to vacate, and to be seen to vacate, room number 13, Millers Court.

It is worth recording that number six had never been to Millers Court nor even to the East End. She had accepted the invitation to Mary Jane Kelly's home in the belief that Mary Jane lived in comparative comfort.

Getting number six to the East End would be relatively easy.

Getting her into room number 13, Millers Court, might require a little persuasion.

The Cast of Players

Before examining the murder in room number 13, Millers Court, Friday, 9 November 1888, it is necessary to meet the people who contributed to the events of that night, however slight their contribution.

Nobody has been omitted and no witness has been contradicted, except where stated, (one instance).

Following the introduction of The Players, it will become necessary to meet the real Mary Jane Kelly, and the real victim.

Joseph Barnett's account is as near as possible, verbatim, and is written in the first person singular.

The Cast are introduced in no particular order.

Joseph Barnett

My name is Joseph Barnett and I resided, until Tuesday, 30 October 1888, with Marie Jeanette Kelly at room number 13 Millers Court.

On 30 October following an argument with Marie, I moved to Bullers Lodging House, 24/25 New Street, Bishopsgate, but, because of the murder and the attendant publicity, I was requested to leave that establishment and I presently reside with my sister at number 21, Portpool Lane, Gray's Inn Road.

I had lived with Marie for approximately one year and six months, the last eight months in room number 13, Millers Court. I would not have left her, save for her violent habits.

Or I left her because:

a) I wasn't earning sufficient money as a result of which she had resorted to prostitution. (Statement to Police) or,
b) She had taken in a prostitute named Julia, a German woman, and I objected to her doing so. That was the only reason I left. (Inquest statement and newspaper interview)

I am a labourer/fish porter but I have been unemployed for the past 3 or 4 months.

Marie was known as Mary Jane Kelly which I understand was her maiden name but her real name was Marie Jeanette.

Marie was born in Limerick but she was taken to Wales when she was very young. I do not know how long she stayed in Wales. Her parents were fairly well off. Her father's name was John and he was a ganger/gaffer/foreman in some iron works in Carmarthenshire or Caernarvonshire. She married when she was very young, about sixteen. She lived with her husband for two or three years but he was killed through some explosion. She married a collier named Davis or Davies – Davies I think. Marie went to Cardiff where she spent eight or nine months in an infirmary and lived a bad life with her cousin. This cousin was, as I often told her, the cause of her downfall.

Then she came to London, about four years ago, where she lived in a fashionable house in the West End.

Marie had one sister, a respectable woman, who followed her aunt's occupation travelling from market place to market place with materials. This sister was very fond of her.

She told me she had six or seven brothers all at home save one who was in the army but I never spoke to any of them. The one in the army was named Henry but he was known, amongst his comrades, as Johnto. I believe he is serving with the Second Battalion Scots Guards, and I understand they are currently on duty in Ireland. He came to see her once but, beyond that, she neither saw nor corresponded with any of her family.

On her arrival in London she made the acquaintance of a French lady residing in the neighbourhood of Knightsbridge who, she informed her friends, led her into the degraded life which has brought about her untimely end. She made no secret of the fact that, whilst she was with this lady she drove about in a carriage and made several journeys to the French capital and, in fact, led the life of a lady. When she first came to London, staying in the West End of town, a gentleman there asked her to go to France with him, so she described to me.

She said she went to France but she did not like the part and returned after two weeks and went to the East End where she found accommodation on the Ratcliffe Highway, but she did not say for how long she was there.

Marie first stayed with a Mrs Buki who resided in one of the thoroughfares off the Ratcliffe Highway, now known as St George's Street. Both women went to the French lady's residence and demanded Kelly's box which contained numerous costly dresses. Her father came from Wales looking for her but, hearing from her friends that he was enquiring about her, she stayed out of the way.

Then she was living near Stepney gas works (or Pennington Street) with a man named Morganstone – I never saw that man in my life – but she did not say for how long.

Marie also lived with a man named Joseph Flemming and he passed as her husband. She was very fond of him. He was a mason's plasterer and lived in Bethnal Green Road. Flemming used to visit her.

I picked up with her in Commercial Street, Spitalfields, last Easter twelve month (Good Friday). We had a drink together and I arranged to see her again the next day. On that day, Saturday, we agreed to remain together and I took lodgings in George Street, not far from where the George Yard murder was committed, and where I was known, and we lived comfortably together. From George Street we moved to Paternoster Row, Dorset Street, but were evicted from there for getting drunk and not paying the rent. We then lived in Brick Lane until finally making the move to Millers Court. Marie occasionally went to the Elephant and Castle district to visit a friend who was in the same position of life as herself.

She was anxious because of the murders and used to ask me to get her the evening newspapers. I would read the accounts of the murders to her. She had a little boy aged six or seven years living with her.

Although we had parted we remained on the best of terms and I continued to visit her.

I last saw her Thursday evening, 8 November 1888, for about one hour, between six thirty and seven thirty, or seven forty five, and told her that I regretted being unable to give her any money. We did not have a drink together. I believe her to have been a woman of sober habits but I have, on occasion, seen her the worse for drink. I understand my brother met her later that evening and spoke with her (See Maurice Lewis).

I went with the police to Millers Court and I saw the body of the deceased by peering through the window. I am positive it was her. I recognised her by her hair and her eyes.

I first heard about the murder from my sister's brother-in-law and I went directly to the police station.

I was questioned for two and a half hours and was able to give a satisfactory account of myself.

My clothing was examined for bloodstains. The police were satisfied and I was allowed to leave.

George Hutchinson

George Hutchinson has been dealt with in a previous chapter. It is, however, worth recording the scant description we have of George. Taken from news reports:

> A man who knew Mary Jane Kelly. Apparently of the labouring class but of a military appearance.

And,

> A "down on his luck" groom.

Thomas Bowyer

Thomas Bowyer (otherwise known as Harry) said to be an Army pensioner: employee of John McCarthy. Resided at number 37, Dorset Street.

At approximately 10.45 on the morning of Friday, 9 November 1888, Thomas Bowyer was instructed to go to room number 13 Millers Court for the purpose of collecting rent arrears of twenty-nine shillings.

Bowyer knocked at the door of the room and, receiving no reply, he endeavoured to look through the keyhole but could see nothing.

Recalling that a window of the room had been broken during a recent memorable row between Joseph and Mary, he ventured around to the side of the building, went to the broken window and pulled back the material which obscured his view.

"I saw two lumps of flesh lying on the table. Then I saw a body on the bed and blood on the floor. I went and got Mr McCarthy.

I knew the deceased. I never saw her drunk but one time. I knew Joseph Barnett as well but I never saw him the worse for drink."

John McCarthy

John McCarthy was, in the year 1888, thirty-seven years of age.

He was a lodging housekeeper (McCarthy's Rents) and a chandler. He lived and worked at his premises at 27, Dorset Street, Spitalfields and was effectively Joseph and Mary's landlord.

At about 10.45 on the morning of Friday, 9 November 1888, John McCarthy was disconcerted to discover that the rent arrears in respect of room number 13, were twenty-nine shillings (six weeks) overdue.

Deciding that immediate action was necessary, he despatched his employee, John Bowyer, with the instruction to collect the outstanding sum, or else...

Bowyer returned after an elapsed time of approximately five minutes and informed Mr McCarthy that he should be aware that a serious incident appeared to have taken place in the court.

McCarthy accompanied Bowyer to Millers Court and, acting on Bowyer's agitated urging, went to the broken window of room number 13 and parted the overhanging material.

For a moment McCarthy was so shocked he was unable to speak. Then he turned to Bowyer and said: "Harry, don't tell anyone about this. Go and get the police."

As Bowyer hastened away, McCarthy recovered his composure and followed.

Both men hastened to the police station in Commercial Street (400 yards) returning fifteen minutes later with the Duty Inspector (Inspector Beck).

At the inquest John McCarthy said:

I very often saw the deceased worse for drink.
    She was an exceptionally quiet woman when sober but when she was drunk she had more to say. But I never saw her helpless through drink.
    It was more the work of a devil than that of a man.
    I have no doubt it was the woman I knew as Mary Jane Kelly.

Mary Ann Cox

Mary Ann Cox is described in contemporary newspaper reports as:

> A wretched looking specimen of East End womanhood.

And is probably the same person described anonymously, in a different news report, as:

> A doleful-looking body with negress-type features.

Surprisingly, her age is estimated, in *The Jack the Ripper A–Z*, by Paul Begg, Martin Fido and Keith Skinner, as just thirty-one years.

Mary Ann was a widow and described herself as, "an unfortunate".

She resided in room number 5, Millers Court and had known Mary Jane for about eight months.

Mary Ann Cox testified that at approximately 11.45 p.m. on Thursday, 8 November 1888, she walked into Dorset Street from Commercial Street, with the intention of returning to her room to warm her hands at the fire.

In front of her, walking toward the entry to Millers Court, was Mary Jane Kelly in the company of a man. Both Mary Jane and the man, she judged to be extremely intoxicated. Mary Ann caught up with the couple as they were entering room number 13.

> I said: "Goodnight, Mary Jane."
> She could scarcely answer me but said: "Goodnight."
> The man turned round and banged the door (closed?).
> I shortly afterwards heard her singing: "A violet I plucked for my mother's grave."
> I went out shortly after midnight and Mary Jane was still singing.

In the statement taken by the police and again at the inquest, Mary Ann Cox returns to her room at one o'clock and Mary Jane is still singing. She (Mrs Cox) goes out again, shortly afterwards and returns at three o'clock. All is quiet.

A news report makes no mention of this one o'clock return and it seems unlikely for, if Mary Ann arrived home at 1 a.m. and went out again say fifteen minutes later, it seems likely she would have seen and been seen by Elizabeth Prater who had stood at the Millers Court entry from 1 to 1.30 a.m., and Elizabeth stated that nobody had entered or left the court during that time. Furthermore, Elizabeth Prater had not heard Mary Jane singing during that half hour, if at all; indeed Elizabeth Prater stated that all was quiet during that time.

It is submitted here that Mary Ann Cox was incorrect in her estimate of time in so far as this related to her return visit assuming always that there was a return visit. She is the only witness in this book who has been contradicted and if she is not contradicted, then Elizabeth Prater must be incorrect in her estimate of time.

When Mary Ann Cox returned to her room for the last time that night, at approximately three o'clock, there was no light showing in room number 13 and all was quiet. She went to bed and slept. She heard nothing unusual.

The man she saw in the company of Mary Jane Kelly she described thus:

36 years of age.

5'5" tall (A little taller than Mary Jane).

Carried a quart pot (presumed to contain ale).

Complexion fresh but possibly, blotches on face.

Small side whiskers and a thick carroty moustache.

Shabby dark clothes. Long dark overcoat and black felt hat/billycock hat. His boots were worn for he made no sound as he walked.

Mary Jane Kelly was wearing a red top and a dark shabby skirt. Her hair was down. (Ordinarily Mary Jane wore her hair pinned up.)

Elizabeth Prater

Elizabeth Prater, described in a newspaper report as a garrulous young woman, was married to a boot machinist by the name of William Prater.

Perhaps Elizabeth was a shade too garrulous for William's liking for he had deserted her some five years earlier, leaving her to fend for herself. It is not recorded how Elizabeth obtained her living.

She lived alone in room number 20, Millers Court, which was the room immediately above room number 13, and she had done so since July 1888, at which time she had become acquainted with Mary Jane Kelly. Elizabeth obviously liked Mary Jane:

> She was tall and pretty and fair as a lily.

Elizabeth had last seen Mary Jane alive at approximately nine o'clock on the evening of Thursday, 8 November 1888.

> We stood talking at the entry to Millers Court and she had said: "I hope it will be a fine day tomorrow as I want to go to the Lord Mayor's Show."
> Then she went one way and I went the other.
> I said: "Goodnight, old dear," and she said: "Goodnight my pretty."
> She always called me that.
> That was the last I saw of her. She wore neither hat nor jacket but then neither did I, as I have neither. [Sobs violently] I'm a woman myself and I've got to sleep in (over) that place tonight where it happened.

Elizabeth Prater had stayed out that night until one o'clock on the morning of Friday, 9 November 1888. When she returned she took up station at the entry to Millers Court until 1.30, waiting for a young man who never appeared. Apart from a brief conversation with John McCarthy she spoke to nobody. During that half an hour, Elizabeth had seen no one enter or leave the court.

At 1.35 she retired to her room, barricaded the door with two tables, climbed fully clothed into bed, "as was my custom," and fell asleep. There was no sound from room number 13.

(This last comment assumes some importance when considered against the evidence of Mary Ann Cox.)

Sometime between 3.30 and four o'clock Elizabeth was awakened by her pet kitten rubbing its nose into her face.

Almost at the same instant she heard a cry:

"*Oh murder!*"

She thought she heard the cry repeated, though much fainter.

Elizabeth turned over and went back to sleep.

At 5.30 she arose, went across the road to the Ten Bells public house, consumed some rum, returned to bed and slept until eleven o'clock.

Sarah Lewis

Sarah Lewis was, by profession, a laundress and lived with her husband, at number 24, Great Pearl Street, Spitalfields. (In 1871 Joseph Barnett lived at number 24½ Great Pearl Street.)

It was not a relationship without problems and, in the early hours of Friday, 9 November 1888, she had deemed it advisable to vacate her abode and seek shelter in a friendlier environment.

Sarah Lewis was friendly with a woman named Keyler (or Keiller) and this woman resided, with her husband, in room number 2, Millers Court, on the first floor, which was situated directly opposite to room number 13 but on the next level.

Presumably the Keylers were used to late and unannounced arrivals, for Sarah Lewis seems to have entertained no doubt that she would be made welcome, notwithstanding the lateness of the hour.

At the inquest into the death of Mary Jane Kelly, Sarah Lewis deposed that she entered Dorset Street heading for Millers Court at some time between the hours of two and three o'clock. (In a newspaper interview she was more specific, giving the time as 2.30, as indicated by the church clock).

As Sarah approached the entrance to Millers Court she noticed a man standing against the wall of Crossinghams Lodging House, immediately opposite to the court.

Sarah Lewis stated, at the inquest, that she could not describe the man but in a newspaper interview she described him thus:

> He was not tall and he was stout. He wore a wideawake hat (a hat with a low crown and a wide brim). He appeared to be looking up the Court as though he were waiting for someone.

To her knowledge Sarah Lewis had never seen and certainly did not know Mary Jane Kelly.

Sarah also saw a man and a woman pass up Millers Court. Both appeared to be intoxicated. The phrase "pass up Millers Court" suggests that the couple went beyond room number 13 which was the first door on the right and Sarah could scarcely have failed to notice had the couple entered that particular room.

Sarah appears to have gained admittance to room number 2 without preamble and, gratefully, she was allowed to rest in a chair. She slept until she was awoken by the church clock chiming the half hour. The time was 3.30.

Fifteen to twenty minutes later, at approximately 3.50, Sarah heard the voice of a young woman scream: "*Murder!*"

It was a loud scream and it was not repeated. She did not investigate the cause, not even looking out of the window for, as she would testify, such sounds were unremarkable.

In a newspaper interview Sarah Lewis adds:

> I did not take any notice especially as a short time before there had been a row in the Court.

Astonishingly, this information does not appear to have been thought worthy of further consideration and Sarah was not asked to elucidate.

Mrs Kennedy

Most writers consider Sarah Lewis and Mrs Kennedy to be one and the same person and it may well be so, for there are many similarities between the stories they tell. There are also essential differences, therefore it will be assumed here that Mrs Kennedy is an entity in her own right.

Mrs Kennedy gave this interview to a newspaper:

> On the night of the murder, I was staying with my parents at a house in Millers Court immediately opposite to room number 13.

(Sarah Lewis was visiting Mrs Keyler at a room opposite number 13 but on the first floor.)

> I turned the corner into Dorset Street at about three o'clock (Sarah Lewis arrived on Dorset Street at 2.30) and I saw three people standing outside the Britannia public house at the corner of Dorset Street.

(Sarah Lewis did not report seeing these three people.)

> One was a man, a young man, respectably dressed, with a dark moustache, talking to a woman. Both the man and the woman appeared to be intoxicated. There was another woman standing by. This woman was poorly clad and had no hat.

(From this description it can be assumed that the first woman, the drunken woman, wore a hat or bonnet. It seems likely that, to Mrs Kennedy, a woman with no hat [and with her hair down] would be considered poorly clad.)

> The man said to the drunken woman:
> "Are you coming?"
> The drunken woman, who appeared to be obstinate, turned in the opposite direction to which the man wished her to go.

(It is assumed here that the man wished the woman to proceed toward Millers Court.)

> I took no further notice. I did not retire to rest immediately but sat up.
> At some time between 3.30 and four o'clock I heard a woman scream: "*Murder!*"
> The cry was not repeated and I took no further notice.
> I was detained in the Court, by the police, and gave a statement to this effect.

(Mrs Kennedy did not report seeing a man standing outside Crossinghams Lodging House, as did Sarah Lewis.)

Maria Harvey

Maria Harvey is described as a young woman. She has married status but there is never mention of her husband.

Her last address (Maria was temporarily homeless) is given as 3, New Court, Dorset Street and her occupation that of laundress.

Mrs Harvey and Mary Jane Kelly seem to have enjoyed an extremely close affinity, indeed Maria had slept with Mary Jane the Monday and Tuesday immediately preceding the murder, since Maria was temporarily homeless.

A reporter who attended the inquest into the death of Mary Jane Kelly wrote:

> Maria Harvey was the "Mrs Gamp" of the day; an amusing witness who provoked general laughter by her decisive dogmatism of manner. She and the coroner were at loggerheads regarding the question of whether certain articles of apparel were two shirts belonging to one man or one man's two shirts [sic].

Maria and Mary Jane spent the afternoon of Thursday, 8 November 1888, in each other's company. Maria claimed to have been in room number 13, Millers Court, when Joseph Barnett arrived. She stated that the time was five minutes to seven and that Mary and Joseph appeared to be on the best of terms. (See Lizzie Allbrook.)

Maria considered it discreet to depart but not before she left some items of clothing with Mary Jane. These items she had taken in for laundering and/or cleaning and she had nowhere else to keep them.

This is a list of items Maria Harvey claimed to have left with Mary Jane Kelly on the evening of Thursday, 8 November 1888:

A bonnet (her own).
A man's black overcoat.
Two men's shirts.
One boy's shirt.
A black bonnet with black strings.
A pawn ticket for a shawl – for two shillings
One little child's white petticoat.

At the inquest, Maria Harvey stated:

> I have seen nothing of them since except the overcoat.

Whether any of these items were subsequently returned to Maria Harvey is not known. It has been assumed that they were destroyed in the fire lit by Jack the Ripper.

Lizzie Allbrook

Lizzie Allbrook was a young woman, just twenty years of age.

Lizzie had a room in Millers Court (number not stated) and worked at a lodging house in Dorset Street.

> I knew Mary Jane Kelly very well as we were near neighbours. The last time I saw her was on Thursday night, about 8 o'clock. I left her in the room with Joe Barnett. (See Maria Harvey.)
>
> About the last thing she said to me was: "Whatever you do, don't you do wrong and turn out as I have."
>
> She had often spoken to me in this way, and warned me against going on the streets as she had done.
>
> She told me she was heartily sick of the life she was leading and wished she had money enough to go back to Ireland where her people lived. I don't believe she would have gone out as she did if she had not been obliged to do so in order to keep herself from starvation.
>
> She had talked to me about her friends several times and, on one occasion, she told me she had a female relative who was an actress on the London stage.

Maria Harvey and Lizzie Allbrook

There is no essential incompatibility between the statements of Maria Harvey, Lizzie Allbrook and Joseph Barnett, as they relate to the evening of Thursday, 8 November 1888.

Joseph Barnett stated that he was with Mary Jane Kelly for approximately one hour between seven and eight o'clock.

Joseph Barnett said:

> There was a woman in the room when I arrived.

Maria Harvey said:

> I left when Joseph Barnett arrived, about five minutes to seven. Joseph and Mary appeared to be on the best of terms.

So the woman in the room when Joseph Barnett arrived was Maria Harvey.

Joseph Barnett further stated (but at a different time and place):

> There was a female with us in the room whilst we were together.

Lizzie Allbrook said:

> The last I saw of Mary was about eight o'clock when with Joseph Barnett. I left her in the room.

So what happened was this:

Joseph Barnett arrived at room number 13, Millers Court at just before seven o'clock when Maria Harvey was with Mary Jane.

Maria Harvey stayed just long enough to determine that Joseph and Mary appeared to be getting on well together: then she left them alone. Some time after, say just before 7.30, Lizzie Allbrook arrived and was invited in. Lizzie stayed in the room for say twenty minutes, conversing, then she left.

Joseph Barnett left shortly afterwards, just after eight o'clock.

The time difference clearly indicates that Joseph Barnett was talking about two different events.

Confusion has resulted in assuming that the "woman in the room, when I arrived" and "the female with us when we were together" are one and the same person when, quite evidently, they are not.

Caroline Maxwell

Caroline Maxwell was the wife of Henry Maxwell and they resided at number 14 Dorset Street.

(In the year 1891, number 14 provided accommodation for forty people. The names, Henry Maxwell and Caroline Maxwell, are not in evidence.)

Henry was employed at Crossinghams (35, Dorset Street) in the capacity of lodging house deputy and Caroline assisted her husband at this establishment which stood directly opposite to Millers Court.

Caroline Maxwell made this statement to the police:

I have known the deceased woman during the last four months and she was known to me as Mary Jane.

She lived with a man named Joe Barnett but he had recently left her. Since that time I understand she had become an unfortunate.

I was on speaking terms with her although I had not seen her for three weeks until last Friday morning, about half past eight.

She was standing at the corner of Millers Court in Dorset Street.

I said to her: "Why, Mary Jane, what brings you out so early?"

She said: "Oh Carrie, I feel so ill. I have the horrors of drink upon me as I have been drinking for some days past."

I said: "Why don't you go to Ringers and have half a pint of beer? That'll make you feel better."

She said: "I've just had a drink and brought it all up again." And she pointed at some vomit, in the gutter.

I said: "Well you have my sympathy. I know how you feel."

We then parted. She back to her room I suppose, and I went to Bishopsgate on an errand.

I returned to Dorset Street around nine o'clock and I then noticed the deceased standing outside The Britannia public house talking to a man. I was some distance away but I'm sure it was her.

(Caroline had been to Bishopsgate. She would therefore have returned from the west via Artillery Passage, Ravens Row, Crispin Street then walked east along Dorset Street until she reached her house. The distance from number 14 to the Britannia: fifty to sixty yards.)

The man looked to be about thirty years old, around 5'5" tall and stout. He was dressed like a market porter (or dark clothes and a sort of plaid coat). I didn't notice his hat and I'm doubtful that I could identify him.

Mary Jane wore a dark dress, black velvet body and coloured wrapper around her neck (or maroon shawl) and no hat.

Caroline told this same story at the inquest into the death of Mary Jane Kelly and, despite a severe caution, she would not be bullied into changing her mind.

Joseph Barnett sat there, listening to every word. He must have been wondering when the penny would drop.

It is Caroline Maxwell who has provided the only meaningful word portrait of Mary Jane Kelly.

From the *Daily News*, 10 November 1888:

> A pleasant little woman, rather stout, with a fair complexion. Rather pale. She spoke with a kind of impediment.

(On 24 May 1889, Caroline's husband, Henry Maxwell, aged fifty-two years, died at the Bakers Row infirmary. The cause of his death is given as pneumonia – exhaustion. At the time of his demise Henry was still residing at number 14, Dorset Street, and his occupation is shown as lodging housekeeper.

The census for the year 1891 fails to register Caroline Maxwell living in Dorset Street.)

Maurice Lewis

This extract from *The Jack the Ripper A–Z*:[2]

> Lewis, Maurice
> Informant. Acquaintance of Mary Jane Kelly. Tailor living in Dorset Street, who told the press he had known Kelly for about five years. He claimed to have seen her in The Britannia, about 10 a.m., 9 November 1888 (i.e. several hours after her death). He also said he saw her drinking with "Danny" and "Julia" in The Horn of Plenty on the night of the murder. Since "Danny" was said to be Joe Barnett's nickname, and he had left Mary Kelly rather than have "Julia" to live with them, the group poses the questions whether Lewis correctly identified Barnett and Kelly or whether Danny was really Barnett's nickname.

Also an extract from *The Jack the Ripper A–Z*:

> Caroline Maxwell, Maurice Lewis and an unnamed woman mentioned in The Times all reported seeing Kelly out of doors at times between 8 and 10 a.m. (i.e. several hours after medical and other evidence indicated she was dead).

---

[2] Paul Begg, Martin Fido and Keith Skinner, *The Jack the Ripper A–Z*, Headline Book Publishing Ltd, 1992.

In the first account, Maurice Lewis doesn't state whether Mary Kelly was alone or with company when he allegedly saw her in The Britannia on the morning of the 9 November but, whilst his account has not been incorporated into the murder at Millers Court, it is not disputed. Regarding his sighting of Mary Jane, "Danny" and "Julia" in The Horn of Plenty on the night of the murder: a neutral position is taken since "Danny" and "Julia" are not clearly identified characters. (See Joseph Barnett, who stated that his brother (Daniel?) met Marie and spoke with her on the evening of the murder.) This sighting too is not incorporated into the murder at Millers Court.

I have assumed that Maurice Lewis' alleged statement, that he had known Mary Kelly for about five years, should have been translated as five months.

With this exception, none of the above is disputed, but I have preferred the unsubstantiated accounts that Maurice Lewis saw Mary Kelly at roughly the same time that she met and spoke with Caroline Maxwell.

Neither Maurice Lewis nor the unnamed woman mentioned in *The Times*, were called to give evidence at the inquest into the death of Mary Jane Kelly.

Julia Venturney

Julia Venturney was a widow who lived with a man named Harry Owen in room number 1, Millers Court. By profession, Julia was a charwoman.

> I knew the woman Kelly, knew her for about four months. She lived with Joe Barnett. They seemed to live quite happily together. He wouldn't let her go on the streets, wouldn't live with her if she did he said, and he was very generous and kind to her.
>
> She told me she was married and, though she lived with Joe Barnett, she said she was very fond of another man named Joe. This other Joe, she said, ill-treated her on account of the fact that she lived with Joe Barnett. I never saw this other Joe.
>
> She used to get tipsy occasionally and one time she broke a window when she was drunk.
>
> I last saw her on the morning of the 8 November about ten o'clock. She was in her room having breakfast with another woman. (Presumed to be Maria Harvey.)

My room is opposite hers and on the night of the murder I couldn't sleep: only dozed, but I heard nothing unusual. I certainly didn't hear any singing and I didn't hear a scream.

Julia

Julia is not to be confused with Julia Venturney.

Joseph Barnett stated that Julia was German, and that he had left Millers Court because Mary Jane Kelly had allowed this "bad woman" into room number 13.

Joseph Barnett was telling the truth.

How else could Jack the Ripper kill this bad German woman?

The Leading Lady

The Cast would scarcely be complete without the leading lady. It is now time to meet the girl from Limerick.

Mary Kelly, the Girl from Llymaryke

> Marie Kelly was born in Limerick, but she was taken to Wales when she was very young. Her father, John, was a foreman in some iron works in Wales. Marie married when she was very young, about sixteen, but after two or three years her husband was killed through some explosion. She married a collier named Davis or Davies – Davies I think.
>
> Joseph Barnett, 1888

Mary Kelly did come from Limerick but it is unlikely that she was ever in Ireland.

To understand this statement it is necessary to look at Limerick and Mary Kelly not as identities but simply as words.

MARY KELLY has a phonetic consonant structure of MRKL. LIMERICK has a phonetic consonant structure of LMRK.

The same phonetic consonant structure – in a different order.

Whether Joseph Barnett did shorthand cannot be known but he certainly understood the principle: that only the consonant sounds are written; the vowels added later – luxury of time permitting.

Look at LIMERICK like this. LI meri CK. The centre section is Meri.

Now reverse the order of LI with CK like this. CKLI. Now write the two sections like this. Meri Ckli and add a vowel: Meri Ckeli.

Joseph Barnett would fine-tune this later; deciding that Meri sounded more like Marie than Mary. Or, at least, that is what I originally supposed.

To emphasise the point, write Mary Kelly like this:
LLYMARYKE.

And so... MERI CKeLI came from LLYMARYKE.

We can now discover Mary Jane Kelly's real name.

In order to arrive at the name "Mary Kelly", Joseph Barnett had to have a starting point and that starting point was Mary

Kelly's real name; which means that Mary Kelly's real name has a phonetic consonant structure of LMRK. Working on the basis that he would not change her first name, Mary, the order of the consonants must be MR then LK or KL. Her real name then is Mary KL: Mary Cole, Mary Keel, Mary Eccle maybe. Or, Mary LK: Mary Lock, Mary Leekey, Mary Ollick perhaps.

To discover Mary Kelly's real name, read the words of Joseph Barnett, written at the top of this chapter.

Remember, you are looking for a name with a phonetic consonant structure of MRLK or MRKL.

So…would the real Mary Kelly please stand up.

Mary Collier

So Mary Kelly's real name was Mary Collier but it appeared that Joseph Barnett had "cheated". Mary Collier does not have a phonetic consonant structure of MRKL. Mary Collier has a phonetic consonant structure of MRKLR. It was disappointing until I remembered. Joseph Barnett had developed a stutter.

He hadn't said, MARY KELLY came from LIMERICK.

He'd said, MAR-RY KELLY came from LIMER-RICK.

Now:

MAR-RY KELLY has a phonetic consonant structure of MRRKL.

LIMER-RICK has a phonetic consonant structure of LMRRK.

MARY COLLIER has a phonetic consonant structure of MRKLR.

To emphasise the point. They all have the same phonetic consonant structure.

Which now brings us to Millers Court.

MILLERS COURT has a phonetic consonant structure of MLRSKRT.

The S and URT are reserved for Yours Truly.

The remainder spells:

M COLLIER.

Which brings us to the staggering conclusion that Joseph Barnett selected Murder Headquarters, not just for the location but because Millers Court contained an anagrammatic construction of Mary Kelly's real name. And, even more staggering, he had been constructing the anagram and planning the murders for at least six months before Martha Tabram was killed at George Yard buildings and, probably, a great deal longer.

The Anagram

These are the "pure" letters carried forward after the Mitre Square murder of Catherine Eddowes but not including the Berner Street murder of Liz Stride.

> UYSR
> BNER STREET
> ILLERS COURT

Now that the real name of Mary Jane Kelly is known, the name Collier can be subtracted from the anagram.

These then are the last of the "pure" letters.

> UYSR
> BNER STREET
> SURT

It will be assumed that both YOURS TRULY and MASON are required to complete the anagram and therefore additional information is added as hereunder.

> UYSR
> DUTFIELDS YARD BNER STREET
> ROOM NUMBER THIRTEEN SURT

YOURS TRULY and MASON will be deducted from the new balance leaving this situation.

> DUTFIEDS RD BER STREET
> R NUMBER THIRTEEN

This then is the message to date.

> Required, Whores.
> Yours Truly,
> Barnett (Master Mason)
> Mary Collier
> George Buck

In order to complete the anagram you will require the inclusion of a few more letters (from where?) and a little imagination.

It is worth remembering that Joseph Barnett tried to keep the anagram as *tight* as possible.

The Police

Before proceeding to the murder at Millers Court it is worth introducing the three senior policemen who opposed Jack the Ripper.

Sir Charles Warren

Sir Charles Warren was born in the year 1840. He joined the Royal Engineers in 1857 and pursued a distinguished and valiant career.

He succeeded Sir Edmund Henderson as Commissioner of the Metropolitan Police in the year 1886, resigning 9 November 1888, (the day of Mary Jane Kelly's murder) following two stormy years in office. He returned to the Army.

The appointment of Sir Charles as Commissioner was, initially, popular with the general public but at the Lord Mayor's Show in 1886 a section of the crowd became unruly and were summarily dealt with by the enthusiastic application of police batons.

On 13 November 1887, there was a mass demonstration by the unemployed in Trafalgar Square: a demonstration that would go down in history as Bloody Sunday. Warren, reverting to his military background, summoned in the troops.

The unemployed, numbering an estimated 20,000, faced 4,000 police constables plus detachments of the Life Guards and the Grenadier Guards. The National Gallery accommodated 300 Grenadier Guards, brandishing fixed bayonets, with orders to fire if necessary. It wasn't necessary. The police smashed into the demonstrators, striking them down until Trafalgar Square resembled a bloody battleground.

At least 200 men required hospital treatment, with many more limping home untended. It is recorded that at least two men died of their injuries.

The Times applauded Sir Charles who received a Knighthood for his "outstanding work".

One wonders if Joseph Barnett and George Buck were there that bloody day and, if so, how they fared. And had Joseph planned to *discover* the body of Mary Jane Kelly on the first anniversary of that day? We shall never know.

It is worth recording that Sir Charles Warren was a Freemason, a fact acknowledged by The Grand Lodge Library staff (See Martin Short's excellent book, *Inside the Brotherhood*) and it is worth recording that it was Sir Charles Warren who ordered the "The Juwes" message in Goulston Street to be immediately erased.

That is not to say that there were not sensible reasons for that decision (though why the word "Juwes" could not be erased and an innocuous word such as "poor" substituted is not understood); it is just to record the fact that, whilst another officer made the recommendation, it was Sir Charles who gave the order, acting against the advice of other senior policemen.

It is also worth reiterating that Sir Charles Warren, Commissioner of the Metropolitan Police, resigned within hours of being informed of the Millers Court murder!

Dr (later Sir) Robert Anderson

Robert Anderson was born in the year 1841. He was the Assistant Commissioner, Metropolitan Police, CID, in charge of the Whitechapel murder investigation from 6 October 1888, until the closure of the file in the year 1892.

Robert Anderson claimed, many times and in writing, that the identity of Jack the Ripper was known. It is a claim marred by the fact that his suspect is said to have been a poor Polish Jew who lived in the vicinity of where the murders took place and who was later incarcerated in an asylum. Further proof of this man's guilt, if further proof was needed, is the fact that an unnamed witness identified this man as the murderer.

Researchers have pondered over the question: who can this man possibly be? For those of you who can't wait to find out, the answer is: either Aaron Kosminski or David Cohen. Well, there you have the opinion of the Assistant Commissioner, Metropolitan Police. CID.

Sir Robert made many valuable contributions of this nature and it was something of a surprise to find these less than flattering observations in *The Jack the Ripper A–Z*:

> No doubt an irritating and opinionated man, inclined, as pious people are, to claim that an action was morally justified because his principles debarred him from committing an immoral one. He clearly loved being taken for a man of mystery and power: one who knew more of vital importance than it was possible for him, in the national interest to divulge.

Bernard Porter
(Origins of the Vigilant State)

and

> His tenure of Office was considered to be characterised by the comfortable placidity for which the majority of our public functionaries are remarkable. Moreover, his temperament, so admirably adapted to his social and religious proclivities, was not such as best fits one for the work of the CID.

Police Review
(On the occasion of Anderson's retirement!)

A merciful veil is drawn across the unpleasant reviews.

Inspector Frederick George Abberline

Frederick George Abberline was born in the year 1843. He joined the Metropolitan Police in 1863 and, two years later, he was promoted to the rank of sergeant. During the year 1867 he was a plain-clothes officer investigating Fenian activities.

In the year 1873 he was promoted to the rank of Inspector and transferred to H Division, Whitechapel, where he remained until 1887, having been promoted in the year 1878 to Local Inspector (Head of H Division CID.)

In 1887 he was transferred to Scotland Yard at the special request of James Monro and Frederick Williamson. He was promoted to Inspector First Class in 1888 during which year he assumed the role of Metropolitan Police Inspector in charge of detectives investigating the Whitechapel murders.

He was promoted to Chief Inspector in the year 1890 and retired, on full pension, two years later, just short of his fiftieth birthday.

Although Abberline was not the officer in overall charge of the Jack the Ripper murders, he was the officer with the most intimate knowledge of the East End, and its people, and he was the man at the coal face.

Frederick George Abberline was undoubtedly a brave and resourceful policeman, and he had many commendations to prove it but, since we are concerned here only with Jack the Ripper, the question must be asked: what was Inspector Abberline's most significant contribution to the investigation?

In order to answer this question let us take a trip to Bramshill Police Staff College. On a wall there, preserved for posterity, hangs a walking stick. The head of the walking stick is carved in the shape of a human face. There is an inscription. It reads:

THE WHITECHAPEL MURDERS

The Whitechapel murders in 1888, commonly known as the Jack the Ripper murders, took place in London between 31 August and 9 November. The Officer in charge of the investigation was Inspector (later Chief Inspector) Frederick G. Abberline and this stick appears to have been presented to him by his team of seven detectives at the conclusion of the enquiry.

Whilst the murderer was never identified, it is known that Inspector Abberline favoured the theory that The Ripper was a Dr. Alexander Pedachenko, or Ostrog, an alleged Russian anarchist living in the London area at the time, and the head of the stick may well be based on his features.

The stick was found amongst the possessions of Ex-Chief Inspector Hugh Pirnie (Dorset and Bournemouth) by his son, Commander Ian Pirnie, R.M. and presented, by him, to the college.

Chief Inspector Pirnie served on the Directing Staff from March 1950 to December 1953.

Finally, perhaps the most important person in this story... the victim.

Please allow me to introduce Julia.

A German Cousin – Julia

> She lived a bad life with her cousin who was, as I often told her, the cause of her downfall.
>
> Joseph Barnett, 1888

Joseph Barnett felt compelled, by his "code of honour", to inform the world who really died in room number 13, Millers Court, on the night of 8–9 November 1888.

So what had Joseph Barnett said?

"I left Marie because she had allowed a prostitute named Julia, to share our bed."

Some writers have confused Julia with Julia Venturney, notwithstanding the fact that Julia was not a prostitute, was not a German and ignoring the fact that Julia Venturney had a room of her own.

Almost certainly Julia was not a prostitute, though she was probably a woman of easy virtue (certainly in the opinion of Joseph and Mary Jane) and a woman Mary Jane detested. Otherwise Joseph Barnett was telling the truth. Joseph had to leave Millers Court so that Julia could be murdered in room number 13.

So what else had Joseph Barnett said?

"Julia was a German." And indeed, Julia was German.

Julia was Mary Jane's Cousin-German, which is the more concise way of saying Cousin (*Collins English Dictionary*) – German from the French word Germain/English *Germane* (related to), Latin: *Germanus*. Cousin is also an archaic word for a prostitute. So, Julia was Mary Jane's first cousin – *viz.* that they shared the same grandparents on the spear or on the distaff side of the family.

I have assumed that Mary Jane's cousin Julia, and her female relative on the London stage, are one and the same person.

So, the woman who died in Millers Court on the night of 8–9 November 1888, was Mary Collier's Cousin-German – stage actress/dancer – woman of easy virtue – the woman responsible for Mary Jane Kelly's downfall. Once Mary Jane had loved her first cousin Julia, but that love had turned to hate.

So who was cousin Julia?

That question will be considered after the real Mary Collier has been introduced.

In the following story, the part of Julia is played by Emily.

The Murder at Millers Court

Two little whores, shivering with fright,
Seek a cosy doorway in the middle of the night,
Jack's knife flashes, then there's but one,
And the last one's the ripest for Jack's idea of fun

Joseph Barnett, 1888

A Perfect Night For Murder

It was fifteen minutes to midnight when Mary Jane and George turned into Dorset Street. They were unaware that they were being trailed by Mary Ann Cox. The couple turned into Millers Court and walked to the door of room number 13. Mary Jane unlocked the door and she entered. George followed her inside.

"Goodnight, Mary Jane." The raddled Mary Ann Cox peered into the room. George turned and glared at her.

Mary Jane rejoined, "Goodnight."

George savagely slammed the door closed.

As Mary Ann Cox wended her way to room number 5, she heard Mary Jane singing plaintively, "A violet I plucked from my Mother's grave..."

At 12.25 on the morning of Friday, 9 November 1888, Mary Jane Kelly made preparation to leave room number 13.

George quietly opened the door and peered out. His face looked blotchy under the flickering yellow gas light. All was quiet. George turned and whispered to Mary Jane; "All clear."

She pulled the shawl over her head and moved to his side. She clutched his arm. "I'll be back as near to three o'clock as I can. I won't be earlier than half two."

"I'll be there at a quarter past, just in case."

She shivered as she left the warm room. George closed the door behind her.

Mary Jane glided silently through the dark tunnel that gave access to Murder Headquarters. She turned right out of Millers

Court onto Dorset Street and headed for the cab rank at Liverpool Street station. There she hired a four-wheeled growler.

She settled back as the cab proceeded on the four-mile journey – the journey that would end in the graveyard for her hated cousin.

George drank some beer and considered the plan.

Leave Millers Court about ten past two. Stand outside The Britannia and await the arrival of the cab.

Let Marie take Emily as far as she can before moving forward. Then… be respectful. You're there to escort the ladies home. But, if push comes to shove… George looked thoughtfully at his big left fist.

Joseph Barnett had left room number 13, Millers Court, at just after eight o'clock on the evening of Thursday, 8 November 1888. He went directly to New Street where he was a resident of Bullers Lodging House which was itself situated near to Bishopsgate police station and just half a mile from Millers Court.

Joseph was well aware that, when the murder was discovered, he would be the prime suspect and it was therefore essential that his presence was acknowledged to be elsewhere than Millers Court and by as many people as possible.

There is no surviving transcript of Joseph Barnett's alibi but there is no doubt that it was genuine.

Emily was in the company of her friends from the theatre. The performance had finished at 10.30 and the players had freshened up and changed in the dressing rooms. It was nearly 11.30 when everyone was ready and many of them headed for the late night bars and cafes scattered round and about theatreland.

Where this theatre was cannot be ascertained but many of the principal London theatres, in the year 1888, were in the vicinity of the Strand in the area now covered by Aldwych. This location is preferred notwithstanding the fact that, in the year 1888, there were many provincial theatres situated much closer to the East End. Undernoted is a selection of West End theatres (some of which have disappeared) and the entertainment on offer 8–9 November 1888:

Olympic Theatre	*The Two Orphans* (Set in Paris)
Opera Comique	*Carina*
Globe Theatre	*The Monks' Room*
Gaiety Theatre	*Faust Up To Date*
Royalty Theatre	*French Plays*
Savoy Theatre	*The Yeomen of the Guard*
Lyceum Theatre	*Prince Karl*

In the company of her friends, by pre-arrangement, Emily went to a restaurant or public house in the vicinity of the theatre.

The arrangement was that Mary Jane would join them at about one o'clock. (It seems likely that, in the days preceding the murder, when it is reported that Mary Kelly was absent from her usual haunts, she had insinuated herself into this company.) This would give Emily time to have a meal with her friends.

At midnight Emily enjoyed a plate of fish and chips which she washed down with cheap wine. It was her last supper.[3]

George finished the beer. He stood up and stretched. He felt sleepy and there still remained an hour and a half to go before zero hour. He stoked the fire and he added some wood.

From upstairs he heard the sound of someone dragging a heavy object across the floor. He remembered that Mary Jane had said that a woman named Elizabeth Prater lived up there. Well, there was no law against Elizabeth rearranging her furniture. Perhaps Elizabeth was barricading herself in. Very sensible – it's dangerous out there. He'd take a stroll to clear his head. It was 1.28 a.m. when George left room number 13. He locked the door behind him and he put the key in his pocket.

The hands of the clock shifted to a quarter past two.

Mary Jane stood up. "Time for us to leave. It's probably still raining. I'll get a carriage and bring it to the door. No sense in both of us getting wet."

Emily looked up. "All right. I'll wait near the door."

---

[3] Forensic evidence indicated that the victim of the Millers Court murder had eaten a meal consisting of fish and potatoes some three to four hours before she was killed.

Homeward Bound

A small group of inebriated well-wishers helped push Emily into the cab. They waved as the cab moved away and they continued to wave foolishly until the vehicle turned onto the Strand and disappeared from view.

The cab jolted its way past the church of St Mary Le Strand and, bearing into view on the left hand side of the street, the entrance to the Opera Comique. A torn poster proclaimed, under a wavering yellow light, "Carina".

The street was devoid of the garish illumination of a few hours earlier. Mary Jane leaned across Emily and pulled down the blind. She did the same on her own side.

"I hate this time of night – everything seems so dirty."

Emily didn't respond. She'd had a wonderful evening. She'd told everybody precisely what she thought of them. But she'd had far too much to drink and she wished now that she hadn't stuffed herself with fish and chips. Emily was feeling a little sick.

The time, 2.45 a.m. The appointed hour was drawing near. George pushed himself away from the grimy wall of Crossinghams Lodging House. He walked slowly, counting off the thirty-five paces to the corner where stood The Britannia public house.

Only the distant sound of thunder somewhere far off in the darkness disturbed the tranquillity of the night. It was the ominous quiet that preceded a storm. It was a perfect night: a perfect night for murder.

Past the Law Courts now and into Fleet Street where stood the grand edifices of the newspaper industry – giant printing machines, even now, rolling off tomorrow's news. Emily, who was destined to play a prominent, if anonymous, role in tomorrow's news, shifted irritably.

"These things are so uncomfortable. I feel sick."

"We'll be there soon. Just ten more minutes."

"I hope you've got a comfortable bed. I could sleep forever."

"I'm sure you will."

They fell silent, each with their so different thoughts. One of life. The other – death.

Past the great cathedral of St Pauls. Its clock showed the hour eleven minutes to three.

Joseph Barnett had left The Magpie in the company of his drinking companions and they had returned together to Bullers Lodging House. His suggestion that they retire to the communal room for a game of cards had not been greeted, initially, with enthusiasm, but his purchase of a bottle of whisky tipped the balance of goodwill in his favour. He must be careful not to play too well. Better to be a good loser this evening. He looked at the clock – ten minutes to three.

Mary Jane took a sideways look at Emily and noted that her head was down as though she were asleep – unlikely she knew, given the bone-shaking motion of the cab. Best not to talk to her though.

Past the Aldgate Pump and now, on the left, Mitre Square where Catherine Eddowes had been murdered just six weeks earlier – murdered by a fiend known as Jack the Ripper. And the City of London is behind them now. A sudden and dramatic change in the quality of the area. No longer the fine imposing buildings of the commercial district – only old, dilapidated houses and shops. It is for this reason that Mary Jane had pulled down the blinds.

Mary Jane took another look at Emily. No change. Good – she won't need to be distracted. Only three more minutes.

George looked up at the Christchurch clock – five minutes to three. He shivered. It was raining again.

Joseph Barnett noted the time – five minutes to three. He played the ten of diamonds to the Jack of diamonds. He looked out of the window – it was raining again.

It was five minutes to three when the four-wheeler clattered into Whitechapel High Street. Mary Jane peered out through a gap in the blind. It was raining again.

The carriage turned left onto Commercial Street. Just sixty seconds now. Sixty seconds from Dorset Street – and Home Sweet Home.

Home Sweet Home

George heard the approach of the cab as it clattered its way along Commercial Street, towards the point where he stood: the doorway of The Britannia public house.

The cabbie reined over to the right-hand side of the road and the vehicle came to a halt in front of Christ Church.

"We're here." Mary Jane shook Emily.

"All right." Sleepily, Emily fumbled to open the left hand door.

"No. Not that side." Mary Jane restrained her. "That's the road. It's safer this side." And Mary Jane opened the right hand door and stepped out onto the pavement. Emily followed and Mary Jane helped her negotiate the step, keeping her close, not allowing her to take in the view. Not that the view was immediately unpleasant.

Hawksmoor's Christ Church still overlooks the spot today as it has done since the year it was built, 1720. The church stands in its own grounds and trees overhang the pavement. The park is surrounded by a low wall atop which are high railings.

Set into the wall, a drinking fountain, inscribed:

Erected by the Metropolitan Free Drinking Fountains Association, 1860.

Just beyond the church, on the corner of Church Street (now Fournier Street) stands, as it stood in 1888, The Ten Bells public house – a handsome enough building – and a glimpse of once proud Georgian houses on Church Street. This was the centrepiece of a once prosperous area and darkness helped conceal the fact that its grandeur was long past its prime. Mary Jane had chosen well – the place and the time.

Mary Jane paid the cabdriver. He flicked the reins and the carriage moved away, up Commercial Street in the direction of The Royal Cambridge Music Hall.

Emily had just lost her last best chance.

Now that the cab was gone the panorama opened up. Across the street, Spitalfields Market; the present building erected in the year 1887. On the corner, just up from the market, almost opposite to where stood Mary Jane and Emily, The Britannia public house. Part of Dorset Street was also visible. The area had taken on a dingy, derelict appearance. And there was a smell – a smell of decay.

"Come on or we'll get wet."

Mary Jane seized Emily's arm and urged her across Commercial Street toward The Britannia.

Emily allowed herself to be pulled across the street but, drunk as she was, she was now filled with a sense of apprehension bordering on foreboding.

There was a man standing outside the pub. He was looking at them. Suddenly, Emily was frightened. She was sobering up fast now and she hesitated.

George saw the hesitation.

He walked towards them. It was time for him to take over.

"Good morning, Marie. And good morning to you, madam." George doffed his hat and gave a slight bow. He handed the key to room number 13 to Mary Jane.

Mary Jane turned to Emily:

"This is George, Emily. George is here to see us safely home."

George moved to Emily's side, taking her arm.

Emily was breathing hard now and her heart was pounding. George wasn't her idea of an escort. Her legs were trembling and she felt weak from a sense of fear. And then she saw Dorset Street. She stopped and pulled away.

"I don't want to." Emily's voice quavered.

The moment had been anticipated. George would have to hit her. Mary Jane moved back to give George room.

Mrs Kennedy turned into Dorset Street. She heard the drunken man speak. "Are you coming?" But the well-dressed woman backed away. Mrs Kennedy noted that the other woman, the poorly dressed woman, stood back from the other two.

Mrs Kennedy walked on and entered through the entranceway to Millers Court.

Emily thought of shouting to the woman, but what use would she be? Emily wanted to scream but her throat had dried and she could scarcely swallow. She looked around in desperation.

Perhaps a policeman? But there was no policeman.

The punch hit Emily in the stomach. Her mouth exploded open – her legs collapsed under her. George grabbed Emily before she fell.

The three "drunken" people staggered toward the Millers Court archway.

One woman was so drunk she couldn't stand. Just three late-night revellers.

Forty staggering steps and they would be there. Mary Jane took the lead. Half dragged, half carried into the black tunnel, Emily made a desperate attempt to break free.

Sarah Lewis frowned. *Somebody having a row in the court. Nothing unusual.*

Mary Jane opened the door to Murder Headquarters. She moved across the room and she lit a candle.

George bundled Emily into the room, his hand clamped tightly over her mouth. He kicked the door shut.

Mary Jane moved back to the door and she locked it.

The trap was sprung.

This Woman is Armed and Dangerous

George forced Emily into a chair. The candle illuminated the tiny room with a flickering, dirty yellow light. The room was hot and it smelled of smoke. The fire glowed red and angry in the tiny grate.

The "Fisherman's Widow" watched the drama unfold.

Mary Jane placed her face close to Emily's face – looking, searching, probing into her bulging, frightened eyes. She kept her voice low – a whisper:

"Listen to me, Emily."

Emily struggled vainly in George's grip.

"Are you listening?"

Emily stopped struggling and nodded dumbly.

"George doesn't want to hurt you. You don't – do you, George?"

George put his mouth close to Emily's ear. "No, I don't *want* to hurt anybody."

"There... there you see." Mary Jane patted Emily's knee. "George is only doing me a favour... because I wanted to punish you. I wanted you to know how I live now. I wanted you to know to what depths you have brought me. And so your punishment is to stay with me. Here, here in this room with me. For this one night. In the morning you may go. Do you understand?"

Emily nodded. Maybe she wouldn't be raped and murdered after all.

"Now Emily, there are people upstairs. Not nice people like George, but people who are sensitive to noise. So, if you scream, those people could come down here to see what the noise is about and those people could do unpleasant things to a girl like you. Isn't that right George?"

George whispered into Emily's terrified ear. "I've heard it said... I've heard it said, they've done terrible... *'orrible* things. I've heard it said... they keeps rats... *rats* as pets. And... and I've heard it said they eats... *eats*... hooooman flesh."

155

Emily's frightened eyes; giant orbs of terror; looked up at the ceiling. She nearly stopped breathing when she thought of what might be up there.

"Now... Emily. George will let you go. He'll let you go if you promise not to scream. Do you understand?" Emily nodded. "If you do scream – I'll open the cupboard. And you won't like what's in the cupboard." Emily's terror stricken eyes swivelled towards the cupboard. *What horror was in the cupboard?*

"Let her go, George. But...if she screams..."

George pleaded. "Please don't open the cupboard while I'm here!"

An explosion of fear erupted in Emily's brain. Even George was afraid of the thing in the cupboard!

George slowly released his grip on Emily. The sound of her frightened breathing filled the tiny room. The pounding of her heart threatened to break her ribs. She looked beseechingly at her arch tormenter, her eyes imploring mercy.

Mary Jane examined Emily's frightened face for a sign that she might panic and scream, but noted that she was frozen with dread. Mary Jane looked at George. "I don't believe we'll need you any longer, George."

"Do you want me to wait outside – just in case?"

Mary Jane pretended to think for a long moment. "Yes – just in case."

George moved toward the door. "I'll wish you both goodnight then. Sweet dreams."

George opened the door and quietly he closed it behind him. He left Millers Court for the last time. He would return to Dorset Street, to meet with Mary Jane at nine o'clock, as arranged.

Mary Jane moved to the door and locked it. The time was 3.30. Emily felt an enormous sense of relief. George was gone. Marie had locked the door. That must mean he wasn't coming back. She wasn't to be raped after all. She could endure this awful place until daylight came, then she could leave. Marie had said so. Emily was overwhelmed by a sense of salvation. Some awful thing ran across the floor, a huge disgusting bug thing, but it didn't matter. She was saved.

But Emily was locked in a tiny room alone... alone with Jack the Ripper.

Emily turned and looked at Mary Jane. "Marie, I'm truly sorry, I..."

Mary Jane's soft voice interrupted. "Keep your voice down," and she pointed at the ceiling. "We'll talk in a minute – in bed. I'll put the kettle on. We'll have some tea." She balanced the already filled kettle on the fire.

Emily looked doubtfully at the bed. Nothing in this room looked clean. And now Emily was aware of the smell. She felt light headed. She thought of bottling the smell and purveying it as perfume. She would call it A Thousand Years of Slime and Vomit. She could bottle it and sell it. People would queue for days to get some.

Emily was on the verge of hysteria.

"Did you mean what you said – I can go in the morning?" Emily remembered to whisper.

Mary Jane absently poked the fire. "Yes, I meant what I said. Take your dress off and get into bed. There's not much of the night left and there are things I want to say."

Emily looked around, with distaste. *Where does she expect me to put my clothes? The cupboard? No! Definitely not the cupboard.* Emily shuddered. She looked enquiringly at Mary Jane but Mary Jane was preoccupied poking the fire. *The table will have to do. It's filthy but I'll lay them across the table. No sense in upsetting her.* And Emily proceeded to undress.

She took off her bonnet. She noted how battered it was. She didn't feel drunk anymore, just a little weak. And she wasn't as frightened as she had been. She didn't believe there was anything in the cupboard, not any longer. Marie had said that just to frighten her. But she wasn't about to open the door to find out. She knew she'd been a fool to trust Marie. *Just humour her. Do nothing to upset her. Agree with everything she says.*

Emily found a convenient nail in the wall and she hung her bonnet on it. She sat on the chair and unbuttoned her boots. She pulled them off. She undid the fastenings on her dress and shrugged out of the garment. The floor was bare board and it was filthy. Her dress dragged in the dirt as she gathered it up and laid it on the table. She unlaced her stays and removed them. She looked again at the bed. It had to be done. She sat on the edge of the bed and turned back the grey sheets. They felt damp, and her flesh cringed.

Taking a deep breath she placed her feet between the sheets and wriggled into bed. She badly wanted the toilet. *I don't suppose there's a bathroom.* She almost laughed at the absurdity of the idea. Her eyes chanced on the bucket. She shuddered.

Emily moved to the far side of the bed, nearest to the grimy wall. She pulled up the covers and lay her head on the dirty pillow. She was suddenly overwhelmed with exhaustion and she closed her eyes. Filled with a sense of loneliness and self pity, she longed for sleep. Oblivion. Death? The word screamed in her brain. She sat up, suddenly terrified again. No! No, not death! Just a new tomorrow. A new beginning. Just the chance to live again… to love again… to hope again… to dream again. She fell back, drenched with perspiration. She was exhausted by fear. But she'd learned her lesson.

There was no forgiveness. There never would be.

Mary Jane removed the kettle from the fire, the tea seemingly forgotten. She stood up.

"Do you know where you are, Emily?"

The voice brought Emily back to full awareness. *Was this a trick question? Treat it lightly.*

"Well… I'm here. Here in this room."

The voice. It had a life of its own. It was smooth… like silk. "I mean the locality. Do you know what part of the world this is?"

No… no, Emily wasn't sure. Not far from the West End obviously. The journey had only taken about fifteen minutes, Emily didn't know London very well. "I don't know. I'm not sure." But suddenly, Emily knew that she wasn't going to like the answer.

"You're in Whitechapel."

Whitechapel? Emily knew the name, knew it well, It had been in the papers a lot recently, and now Emily was once again filled with dread. Whitechapel was the home of Jack the Ripper! *Keep calm! Keep calm!* But her voice quavered.

"I think I've heard of it."

The voice spoke again.

"Of course you have. Jack the Ripper lives here." And Mary Jane moved slowly to the cupboard. "Here... here in this very room." And she pulled open the cupboard drawer.

Emily was breathing hard again. She was frightened. She was very, very frightened, and Marie's voice. It sounded so sinister, like a voice, a voice from the grave. *Keep calm!*

Emily's mouth trembled. Her voice, scarcely audible, shook violently, "I'm sure he won't bother us."

Mary Jane heard the nail biting fear. It was the moment she'd waited for for so long. She closed the cupboard drawer and she moved slowly and deliberately to the side of the bed. She kept her left hand behind her back.

"Well Emily. He won't bother me."

Emily stared at her. Eyes like saucers now. Her whole body was shaking uncontrollably.

And Marie! Marie had become someone else. But, no! *Something* else! Her face was white and terrible. Her features were a mask of hatred. And her eyes! Her eyes were yellow pools of venom and wickedness. The flickering candlelight moved across the contours of Marie's face illuminating a monster Emily had never seen before. But she knew who it was. It was Satan! Emily knew at that moment, that she was about to die.

"You see... I am Jack the Ripper." And Mary Jane slowly brought her left hand from behind her back and showed Emily the glittering blade.

Emily stared, appalled, transfixed, as Mary Jane held the knife, moving it to and fro before her face, hypnotising her with terror.

Warm liquid spilled from Emily's loins.

The time was eleven minutes to four o'clock.

Elizabeth Prater stirred, as the gentle kitten nuzzled her face with its nose. Sarah Lewis and Mrs Kennedy rested and waited for the dawn of a new day. A better day perhaps until, finally, death would transport them to a kinder place.

"*Murder!*"

For one person in Millers Court, death was an immediate consideration.

Emily didn't know she'd screamed. Didn't know she'd pulled the sheet over her face with her left hand whilst trying to ward off the knife with her right. But she felt the knife slice into her thumb. She felt Marie's right hand gripping her face, pushing her head back into the pillow. She felt her neck being sawed apart. She felt her brain explode with terror.

Mary Jane was breathing hard. She'd judged the moment well. She was pleased that she'd used the blunt knife and sawed across the throat. She was satisfied that Emily's death had been as unpleasant as she so richly deserved.

She looked into Emily's dead eyes and whispered, "I told you you could go in the morning."

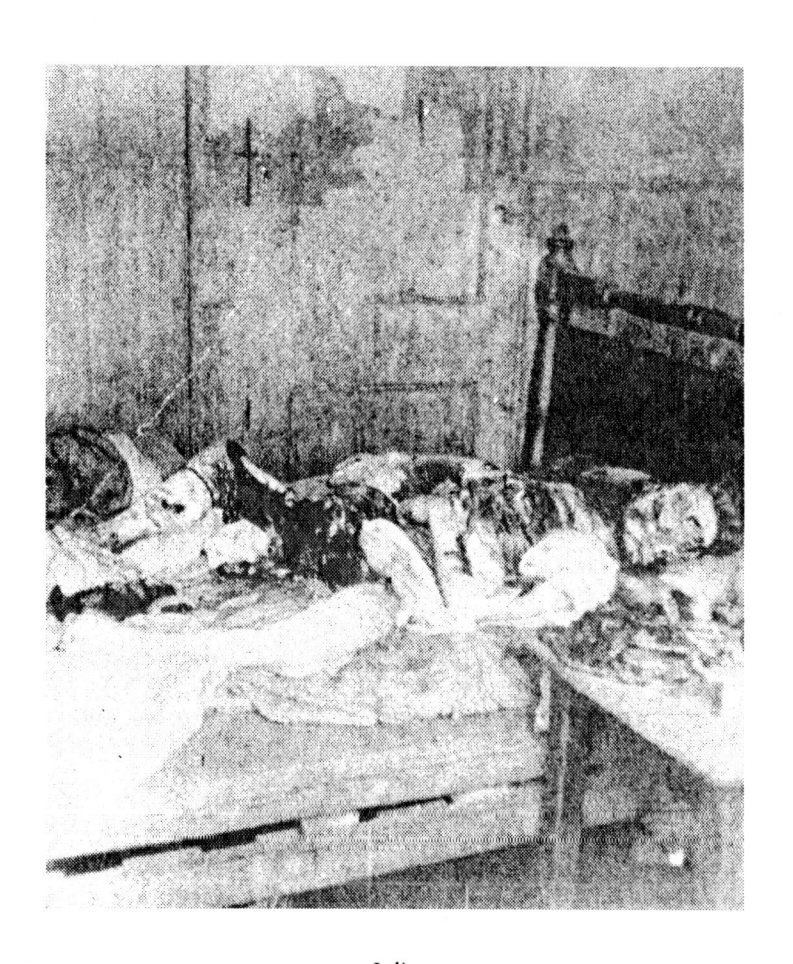

Julia

A Cousin – Once Removed

For a long time she sat in the chair, just staring at the corpse of her recently departed cousin. She experienced an unfamiliar feeling of unease and suddenly her mind seemed to slide towards a precipice. A sharp intake of breath. She wondered if she had destroyed her own soul – she was afraid of Hell. For a long time she listened to the sound of the wind, and the pattering of the rain on the window panes and she remembered better times.

But there was work to be done – she couldn't rest. Mutilate Emily's body and disfigure her face. Burn Emily's clothes and burn her own bloody garments. And then four years of torment would be over – she would die avenged. She looked at her watch – quarter to five.

She poked the fire into life and she fed wood to the tired flames. Mary Jane took Emily's bonnet and she slashed it into strips with the knife. The pieces of the once elegant hat were consigned to the fire.

She picked up Emily's dress and she ripped it to rag, the easier to burn.

She ate two slices of bread and butter and drank deeply from a bottle of ginger beer.[4]

She moved to the cupboard and she selected a scalpel. Holding the instrument between her teeth she moved to the bed. She grasped Emily's dead body with both hands and she dragged it across to the near side of the bed. She took the scalpel from between her teeth and she commenced the grisly work of mutilation.

After ten minutes the candle guttered as it began to expire and she lit a new, and the last, candle. It would be enough. Occasionally she stopped and fed torn strips of Emily's clothing into the fire.

Three hours and ten minutes later her gory task was done.

---

[4] Four empty ginger beer bottles and a plate with pieces of bread thereon were found in room number 13 after the murder.

(Emily's throat had been cut from ear to ear, back to the spinal column, which itself was deeply notched. Her breasts, nose and ears had been hacked off.

The stomach and abdomen had been ripped open and the liver, heart, kidneys and uterus removed. Chunks of flesh had been cut from the victim's arms legs and torso. The face had been slashed into bloody ribbons until the features were totally unrecognisable, though the eyes (so much like Mary Jane's own eyes) remained carefully untouched.

And afterwards Mary Jane arranged the torn, mangled pieces of dismembered flesh in a crazy bloody jigsaw about the room. On the bed, on the table and even hanging from picture hooks – like grisly Christmas decorations.)

It was nearly eight o'clock. Critically she surveyed her handiwork, then she unpinned Emily's long hair (so much like her own hair) and she coaxed it out so that it cascaded across the bloody sheets. The effect was strangely beautiful.

She had seen horrific sights during the war – men with mangled arms and legs, their bodies torn asunder. When she closed her eyes she could still hear them screaming in their agony as she sawed off their mutilated limbs.

But this was somehow different. This bloody gargoyle, was her once dearly beloved cousin. But it didn't look like Emily. It didn't look like anybody – except perhaps a woman who had never existed – a woman named Marie Jeanette Kelly.

Satan could scarcely have done better.

The room was uncomfortably hot now, and the smoke made her eyes smart.

She stripped off her own bloodstained dress and tore it into strips and some of the material she fed into the fire. She went to the bucket, half filled with water, and she washed the blood from her hands and arms and she rinsed her face. Then she selected the dark red dress from the cupboard and she put it on. She combed her hair.

It was twenty-five minutes after eight o'clock.

She added wood to the fire and threw on the last remaining torn remnants of her bloody dress.

Smoke came back into the room and made her cough. She drank the last of the ginger beer, but it only succeeded in making her feel nauseous. She needed fresh air.

She moved to the window and looked out. The rain had all but ceased. The court was empty. She unlocked the door and pulled it ajar. She sucked greedily at the cold air. Then she pulled the door open, just wide enough to pass through, and stepped outside. She shut the door behind her and she locked it.

Mary Jane passed through the narrow archway and walked onto Dorset Street. The time was half past eight.

Maurice Lewis, the tailor who resided on Dorset Street, glanced through his window. He saw Mary Jane as she came out of Millers Court but he took no further notice of her.

Mary Jane spewed into the gutter and she wiped her mouth with the back of her hand. She felt a little better and she walked a few steps, breathing deeply of the cold, damp air.

"Why, Mary Jane, what brings you out so early?"

Mary Jane quite liked the large, good-hearted, Caroline Maxwell, but she would have preferred not to have encountered her at that precise moment.

"Oh Carrie, I do feel so ill. I have the horrors of drink on me for I have been drinking for several days past."

"Have half a pint at Ringers, that'll soon make you feel better."

Mary Jane indicated the pool of vomit. "I've already had one and I've brought it straight up."

"Well, you have my sympathy – I know how you feel." Caroline Maxwell gave Mary Jane a reassuring smile. "I must go. I have to get my husband some breakfast. I hope you soon feel better." And Caroline proceeded on her way.

Maurice Lewis noticed Mary Jane Kelly as she walked back through the arched entranceway that led to Millers Court.

Mary Jane opened the door and quickly she stepped inside. She locked the door behind her.

She surveyed the room of death, through the haze of smoke.

Hell must look like this.

The fire was still burning but little, if any, of the material was recognisable. It was good enough. There was nothing incriminating in the ashes.

(Mary Jane didn't know it, but small fragments of Emily's dress and bonnet had survived; fragments that Maria Harvey, when called in by the police, to do an inventory, would not be able to recognise as having belonged to the deceased.)

It was time to leave Murder Headquarters for the last time.

Mary Jane wiped off the knife and the scalpel, and she rinsed them in the bucket of bloody water; then she dried them. These items she placed in a bag together with Emily's heart, which she first wrapped in a sheet of newspaper.

She put on the black velvet bodice and the lavender coloured scarf, then she surveyed the room. Was there something she'd forgotten? The water, what to do with the bucket of water?

She sluiced the water across the grimy floorboards where it immediately soaked away, leaving the boards with an unfamiliar wet sheen.

Just before leaving, she piled some underclothes, and the shirts that had been entrusted to her by Maria Harvey, onto the fire and she balanced the kettle on top of the smouldering pile. It was over. This had been her home for nearly nine months. She felt a feeling of emptiness. She knew that things were going to get worse, knew she was travelling downhill, knew her life was nearly over. She shrugged. *What did it matter – what did anything matter? But the evil one who'd caused it all was dead,* and she smiled at the ghastly, bloody mess that had once been a beautiful woman.

Her voice was soft – a caress. "Goodbye, Emily. Have a nice funeral."

She picked up the bag, moved to the door and unlocked it. She looked back. One last, long look.

Mary Kelly left the smoking hell that was room number 13, Millers Court, never to return. It was five minutes to nine o'clock, Friday, 9 November 1888.

She locked the door and she placed the key in the bag. Then she walked out onto Dorset Street, turned left, and headed towards The Britannia. George was waiting for her. *Good old reliable George. George would never let you down.*

He gave a broad smile. "You look terrible."

She smiled back. "I had a bloody awful night."

George laughed. "Drink?"

"Yes – but not here."

"No, not here."

George Buck and Mary Collier walked away, past The Ten Bells which would, 100 years later, briefly bear the name, The Jack the Ripper. And from there, they walked on... on into history. But George would return – for the greatest curtain call in the history of crime.

Bad News

On the morning of Friday, 9 November 1888, Joseph Barnett left Bullers lodging house, crossed over New Street and entered the bar of The Magpie public house.

(The Magpie is still there today, as is the edifice of Bullers.)

Joseph took a window seat and sipped his pint. He looked at the clock. The hands showed the time at 10.42.

By now it was all over, he mused. The German woman was dead. Marie was on her way home.

Nothing to do. Nothing to do but wait until the discovery of the latest horrible murder.

He reflected that this discovery would probably take place about Monday or Tuesday. By that time, decomposition would have reduced the corpse to a state where it would be impossible to ascertain, with any degree of accuracy, when the murder had taken place.

Nothing to do but build an alibi. Joseph was going nowhere near Millers Court and he would ensure that he had witnesses galore to prove it. It was a situation not without its advantages. Bullers was comfortable, the pub was pleasant, the landlord friendly. Nothing could mar the tranquillity of the weekend.

The hands on the clock showed 10.45.

Thomas Bowyer attempted to gain admittance to room number 13, Millers Court, but found the door locked against him.

He moved around to the side of the building where he remembered a window had been broken. He put his hand through the aperture and he pulled back the material obscuring his view of the interior.

Joseph Barnett didn't yet know it but Jack the Ripper was in trouble.

It was 12.45 when Catherine Beer's brother-in-law, John Beer, entered the pub and pulled up a chair.

"I've been looking for you. I've got bad news."

And so John Beer told Joseph Barnett that the police were in Millers Court, in force, and appraised him of the rumour that Mary Jane had been murdered by Jack the Ripper.

Joseph Barnett didn't have to pretend to be incredulous.

"Who told you that?"

"Everybody and anybody. It's common talk."

"I'd better get down there. You can finish my beer," and Joseph rose to leave.

"It's like a police barracks down there. Be careful."

"I'm always careful." But he knew he hadn't been careful enough.

He walked in the direction of Millers Court, his mind racing with unanswered questions. *How had the murder been discovered so quickly? Had the building caught fire? Had Marie got away? If she had got away, had she been seen? If she had been seen, then it was all over.*

Joseph rubbed his neck. The hangman's noose was beginning to chafe.

At approximately 3.30, Joseph Barnett presented himself at Commercial Street police station where he was interviewed by Inspector Abberline. He was escorted to room number 13, Millers Court, where he identified the mutilated body as being that of Marie Jeanette Kelly.

"I know her," he said, "by her hair and her eyes."

Jack the Ripper noted that the door had been smashed in. *So Marie had locked the door and she'd got away.*

His alibi was checked and he was released at six o'clock.

As he walked away, along Commercial Street, towards Dorset Street, he passed a stout woman proceeding in the opposite direction, headed towards the police station.

Her name was Caroline Maxwell and Caroline was about to smash a massive hole in Jack the Ripper's armour.

No News is Good News

The evening of Friday, 9 November 1888. George sat at the bar in The Town of Ramsgate. After a late night he'd retired to his bed and he hadn't got up until six o'clock. George was drinking his first pint when Joseph Barnett walked through the door. George ordered another beer. They moved to a quiet corner and sat down.

"How did it go? " Joseph sipped his beer.

"Perfect."

"No problems?"

"Nothing we didn't anticipate."

"And Marie?"

"On her way home."

Joseph took a long drink.

"They've found her."

"Already?"

"You hadn't heard?"

"It was a long night, I've only just got up. This is my first."

Joseph gave a wry smile: "Let's hope it won't be your last."

"As bad as that?"

"Maybe not. Tell me everything. From the beginning."

They talked and they drank, and they both agreed. If nobody came forward to say they had seen or spoken to Mary Jane Kelly after she had been "killed", then there really was no problem.

Caroline Maxwell had been in Commercial Street police station for an hour. She was becoming irate. Caroline didn't like being called a liar. Did they think she was stupid?

The Inquest

The inquest into the death of Marie Jeanette Kelly was opened Monday, 12 November 1888, at 11 o'clock. The venue was Shoreditch Town Hall, an impressive building which today has the look of a beleaguered fortress.

Joseph Barnett would be the first witness and he had only a rough idea of the forces that might be arraigned against him.

He had learned, from George, that he (George) had been seen entering room number 13 with Marie on the night of the murder. That witness might be at the inquest (Mary Ann Cox was in attendance) which meant that George was disqualified from attending for fear he might be recognised. A rescue then could not be effected until all the facts were known.

The evidence given by all the witnesses at the inquest, have already been given in The Cast list though, where witnesses also gave newspaper statements, the information has been amalgamated. Nothing has been added, omitted or altered, and no witness has been "conveniently" ignored.

One witness is, however, worthy of special consideration. That witness is a man named Joseph Barnett.

Consider the newspaper reports regarding Joseph Barnett, related specifically to the way in which he gave his evidence at the inquest into the death of Marie Jeanette Kelly:

> The witness stuttered occasionally.
>
> He spoke with a stutter and evidently laboured under great emotion.
>
> He had a curious habit of beginning his answer with the last word of each question asked.

One person who had arcane knowledge understood Joseph Barnett very well. That person was, of course, coroner Roderick Macdonald. After Barnett had concluded his testimony, Dr Macdonald uttered these immortal words:

"You have given your evidence very well."

He surpassed himself when he abruptly concluded the proceedings with this less than reassuring statement:

"There is other evidence which I do not propose to call: for, if we at once, make public every fact brought forward, in connection with this terrible murder, the ends of justice might be retarded."

(Though whose justice, Dr Macdonald neglected to say.)

This comment is taken directly from Tom Cullen's excellent book, *Autumn of Terror*:

> What did he (Dr Macdonald) mean by this extraordinary statement? Was he being guided by Scotland Yard, which had been so anxious to get the inquest out of Coroner Wynne Baxter's hands? What were the police trying to hide?[5]

The inquest was over but Jack the Ripper was not totally happy. He had seen Caroline Maxwell take the stand and he had heard her give evidence. She was his worst nightmare. He knew her for what she was, an honest woman who would not submit to the bullying tactics employed by Macdonald. She was a formidable adversary and she would need to be neutralised.

Joseph Barnett left the inquest and headed south to Wapping and an appointment with George Buck.

---

[5]Tom Cullen, *Autumn of Terror: Jack the Ripper, his crimes and times*, The Bodley Head, London, 1965

Thou Shalt Not Bear False Witness

Joseph Barnett left the inquest, bade his farewells and headed in the direction of St George's-in-the-East.

It was nearly two o'clock when he turned into Cinnamon Street and walked into the taproom of The Pear Tree.

George was sat at the far corner of the bar and Joseph strolled over and sat down.

"You're late." George pushed across a full pint. "It's flat."

Joseph Barnett took a long drink.

"Took longer than I thought."

"How bad?"

"Well…"

And so Joseph Barnett told George everything that had happened at the inquest and they both agreed. It wouldn't be long before someone put two and two together.

Caroline Maxwell represented a menace that needed to be defused.

George Buck was about to walk into the lion's den.

Attack is the Best Form of Defence

George "Hutchinson" walked into Commercial Street police station at six o'clock on the evening of Monday, 12 November 1888; more than three days after the discovery of the Millers Court murder, and several hours after the inquest into the death of Mary Jane Kelly had closed.

The police investigation staggered under the weight of "Hutchinson's" "new evidence", fell back and finally collapsed. It would never rise again.

But Inspector Abberline did not release the body of the victim for burial until several more days had elapsed. Perhaps he was waiting for a missing person's report; a missing persons report that never came.

Success had been achieved.

Mary Jane Kelly had been seen with Jack the Ripper just one hour before she was murdered. Caroline Maxwell had been relegated to the status of "mistaken witness".

So why didn't George come forward earlier?

Neither George nor Joseph knew the full extent of the problem. They couldn't formulate a plan until all the evidence had been taken and a verdict given.

And, had George been required to attend the inquest as a witness, there might have been those present who knew him: knew his name wasn't Hutchinson.

As it was, George was taking an enormous risk: a risk that was never originally envisaged: a risk made necessary by the too early discovery of the Millers Court murder.

The Anagram – the Final Solution

The seven missing letters are NO FORTY.
The anagram is:

GEORGE YARD
BUCKS ROW
HANBURY STREET
DUTFIELDS YARD – NO FORTY, BERNER STREET
MITRE SQUARE
ROOM NUMBER THIRTEEN, MILLERS COURT

The solution to the anagram is:

The required number of dirty whores
died for better run streets.

Yours Truly,

Barnett (Master Mason)
Mary Collier
George Buck

But something is wrong. There is an R and an N unaccounted for.

The Anagram – Trials and Tribulations

When Joseph Barnett originally envisaged the anagram he knew he had to keep the number of murders within manageable limits: include his own name; include the names of Mary Collier and George Buck, and have sufficient letters left over for a meaningful message, without leaving a letter debt. If these strictures were not onerous enough, he could only operate within a very small area and the last murder would need to be committed at his (or, more specifically, Mary's) own residence. In order to achieve these objectives he would need to conduct a feasibility study of the chosen murder sites and it seems most likely that Hanbury Street and Berner Street gave him the biggest headache.

He knew the Whitechapel streets well but, undoubtedly, a map was an essential requirement, and he pored over this as he devised and pondered the content of the anagram; alternately selecting a site; discarding a site; amending the wording of the anagram.

First, he had to make provision for the names (his own name and the names of his two accomplices). The last murder would be the easiest to commit, for it would take place indoors. He needed a secluded address for his Murder Headquarters but also an address that provided essential letters for the anagram.

Millers Court was near perfect and, probably, he bribed the tenant of room number 13 to vacate the premises so that he and Mary could take up residence.

Having conceived the last murder (Millers Court) first, he then conceived the first murder (George Yard), the second (Bucks Row) and the third murder (Hanbury Street). But although George Yard, Bucks Row and Hanbury Street were the final choices, it is most probable that Hanbury Street was a decision taken with some reluctance, and Joseph Barnett must have pondered the problem, and the possible alternatives, for a long time before finally deciding to take the considerable risk of killing at number 29.

The structure of the message must have been adjusted many times, though the meaning remained essentially the same.

Joseph Barnett would have been quite happy to commit more murders than the actual six; maybe as many as ten, but he couldn't control the letter debt and the more killings there were, the more letters, and the more letters the more indecipherable the message would become.

It was Berner Street: Berner Street in conjunction with Dutfields Yard that the dictates of the anagram finally decreed would be the "sweeper".

Joseph Barnett couldn't do the anagram without leaving a letter debt: an R and an N, though it wasn't for want of trying.

So... how did he overcome the problem?

Jack the Ripper would have to stutter!

The Man Who St-St-Stuttered

> The witness, Barnett, had the curious habit of repeating the last word of every question put to him. He appeared to be labouring under great emotion and his concentration was apparent. He gave a very odd impression and occasionally, he stuttered.
>
> (From press reports of Joseph Barnett giving evidence at the inquest into the death of Mary Jane Kelly, November 1888)

Joseph Barnett needs every ounce of concentration, for he has come to this inquest with the intention of imparting information and, in addition or perhaps more particularly, he must ensure that the anagram is correctly presented. His biggest danger is a loss of concentration.

He repeats the last word of every question. This buys him thinking time.

First he must give his name – Joseph Barn-nett. He's accounted for the extraneous letter N by adding this letter to the solution but without increasing the value of the original letters.

He has already accounted for the extraneous letter R. Indeed, the letter R shouldn't be considered as extraneous at all, since Mary is always referred to as Mar-ry.

So, the final solution to the anagram is:

The required number of dirty whores
died for better run streets.

Yours truly,

Barn – nett. (Master Mason)
Mar – ry Collier.
George Buck.

The phonetic consonant link between Mar-ry Kelly, Limer-rick and Mary Collier is now broken, by reason of the fact that this link was never compatible with the completed anagram. Because of this fact Mary Collier is now, incorrectly titled, Mar-ry Collier.

The Anagram – the Murder That Never Was

The manner in which the anagram developed prescribed that the message be constructed in the format of a letter. The letter required an initial salutation, e.g. *Dear Sir,* but, of course, any salutation would suffice, always provided it was plausible, e.g. *My Friends,* etc. However, the salutation was limited by the available street names, the suitability of the venue for bloody murder and last but, by no means least, the accumulation of letter debt. It would also be necessary to take into consideration that a letter N remained outstanding.

Whilst he endeavoured to compose a salutation, Joseph Barnett knew he had some flexibility inasmuch as he could introduce a new word into the message or he could amend an existing word, but the room for manoeuvre was small.

Joseph searched through a map of the Whitechapel streets, experimenting with various alternatives; looking for a street name that would provide him with an acceptable salutation and, at the same time, eliminate the letter debt. But it was to no avail. Finally, and with great reluctance, he selected Baroness Road. This road was a commercial/residential thoroughfare, nearly 300 yards in length, providing good cover for nefarious activity and, Baroness Road, abbreviated to Baroness Rd, gave Joseph Barnett the inspiration for "Dear Boss". Resigned to a letter debt; better to repeat the same letters; another letter N and another letter R. He would need to stutter twice on each letter.

But the "Dear Boss" murder (the proposed sixth in a projected sequence of seven) was the murder that never happened.

It was a murder scheduled to take place around 18 October 1888, but it was aborted and could not be re-scheduled. Why?

Presumably because the police cordon was too tight and it is possible that Joseph and/or George and/or Mary were apprehended and questioned regarding their suspicious behaviour, as they trawled the area around Baroness Road in an endeavour to procure a victim. The proposed murder on Baroness Road had therefore to be abandoned. There is no other logical explanation.

Having said that, it is interesting to note that Joseph Barnett did not write the first of his "Dear Boss" communications until 25 September 1888 – well into the murderous series. Possibly, the reason he delayed his correspondence for so long, was due to his reluctance to resign himself to the fact that he could not resolve the problem of the letter debt. Also that he was never fully committed to, or prepared for, the Baroness Road murder.

(Baroness Road (named in honour of Baroness Angela Burdett-Coutts) exists today. It is sited just 200 yards from where Joseph Barnett resided in the year 1881; number 1, Horatio Street.

The impressive Gothic structure known as Columbia market, exists now only in photographs. The Market Inn, St Thomas's church and rectory, the shops and the houses are all gone.

Today's abbreviated Baroness Road is little more than a pathway that snakes through a housing estate – not even a faint echo of 1888.)

The Anagram – the Intended Solution

This was the construction of the anagram at 25 September 1888, when Joseph Barnett compiled his famous "Dear Boss" letter, which was dated just five days before the night of the double murders.

> GEORGE YARD
> BUCKS ROW
> HANBURY STREET
> DUTFIELDS YARD, NO 40, BERNER STREET
> MITRE SQUARE
> BARONESS RD
> ROOM NUMBER THIRTEEN, MILLERS COURT

The intended solution to the anagram, as it was envisaged at 25 September 1888 was:

Dear Boss,

The required number of dirty whores
died for better run streets.

Yours Truly,

Master Mason – Bar-rn-n-nett
Mar-ry Collier
George Buck

Joseph Barnett, assuming he had successfully committed the Baroness Road murder, was nonetheless restricted to stuttering only once on the R of Mary. In order to obtain the additional letters (another letter R and another letter N) he would had to have stuttered once on the R of Barnett and twice on the N of Barnett.

Homicide at Horsleydown

It was 10.30 on the morning of 4 June 1889. John Regan, a waterside labourer – having nothing better to do – idled on the Thames foreshore at St George's Stairs, Horsleydown, opposite St Katherine's Dock. He watched whilst two boys threw stones at a bundle floating on the water.

After a short while, the two boys grew bored, and they went away in search of a more interesting pursuit. But John Regan was not a man to be bored so easily and he decided to investigate the mysterious bundle. With some difficulty he managed to coax it to shore, noting as he did so that the outer wrapping appeared to be an apron.

John, his curiosity getting the better of him, untied the rope that bound the bundle together and, having appreciated that the contents were not entirely to his liking, rushed away in the direction of the nearest police station. The police confirmed John's worst fears. The bundle contained bloody human flesh. The bundle and its contents were quickly conveyed to the mortuary for further examination, where it was established that the bloody human flesh was a female torso.

Later that same day, a youth named Isaac Brett, a woodchopper of Lawrence Street, Chelsea, whilst bathing under Albert Bridge, found a parcel. It was wrapped around with a piece of lady's ulster, marked with the name L E Fisher and tied with a boot lace. The parcel contained a human leg.

Two days later, on 6 June 1889, a Battersea Park gardener, named Joseph Davis, came across a bundle wrapped around in a soiled linen garment, which proved to be a further piece of the "L E Fisher" ulster. The bundle contained part of a human body, though what part cannot now be ascertained. Joseph Davis took it along to the police station.

Two days passed. It was on 8 June 1889 when a newspaper reporter named Claude Mellor chanced to walk past the house of Sir Percy Shelley; a house which was situated on the Chelsea

Embankment. There he noted, just inside the railings of that establishment, reposed part of a human being's anatomy (what part is not stated). Claude Mellor reported the matter to the police.

Similar discoveries were made at roughly the same time, off Copington Wharf; at Bankside; Southwark; West India Docks and at other sundry locations. Some of these parts had been wrapped, others had not. An inventory established that most of the cadaver had been recovered: the most notable exception being the head.

The remains were examined by Drs Bond, Hibberd and Kempster, and they concluded that the parts were all of the same woman. They considered that, in life, she had been twenty-four to twenty-five years of age, 5'4" to 5'6" in height, fair of skin with well-shaped hands, though the nails had been thoroughly bitten. She had been pregnant and the fact that her right hand was tightly clenched indicated that she had died a painful death. Rudimentary skill such as that possessed by a butcher had been shown in the dismemberment of the body.

It was finally established, with reasonable certainty, that the victim's name was Elizabeth Jackson, aged twenty-four years. She had been employed in service but had, of late, encountered hard times.

She was not a known prostitute.

Verdict: Murder by person or persons unknown.

Killing on Castle Alley

Alice McKenzie was a 45-year-old prostitute, originally from Peterborough, but Alice had lived in the East End of London for some years. In the year 1889 she was consorting with a man named John McCormack, and John and Alice lived together in a common lodging house situated at number 52, Gun Street, Spitalfields.

Alice was an enthusiastic drinker and an inveterate pipe smoker and, on the afternoon of 16 July 1889, she and John had quarrelled – possibly over her bad breath – though this is only surmise.

Somewhat chagrined, Alice, in a fit of pique, embarked upon another heavy drinking bout.

Around ten past seven she took George Dixon, a blind lad who also resided at number 52, Gun Street, into a pub, not far from The Royal Cambridge Music Hall. George Dixon heard Alice McKenzie say: "Stand a lady a drink?" and a man respond: "All right."

It is doubtful that any connection can be inferred from this incident and the subsequent demise of poor Alice, but the possibility exists and cannot be ignored.

Alice McKenzie returned George Dixon to the lodging house at number 52, Gun Street, and fortified with a few drinks sallied forth alone to the late night delights of the Spitalfields streets. She was adjudged, by her landlady, to be "more or less drunk."

The last positive sighting of Alice placed her on Brick Lane at approximately 11.40. Alice was staggering south along Brick Lane and was seen by her friend, Margaret Franklin, who was sitting talking with acquaintances at the Brick Lane end of Flower and Dean Street.

Invited to stop and chat, Alice demurred: "I can't stop now," she confided, and continued on her way.

But Alice was about to be stopped... permanently.

At fifteen minutes after midnight, 17 July 1889, PC Joseph Allen, number 423H, ate a sandwich under a street light in Castle Alley (then an extension of Old Castle Street – now amalgamated with Old Castle Street) just south of the communal wash house. Having enjoyed his brief repast, Constable Allen proceeded on his way. It was approximately 12.20.

Another constable, Walter Andrews, number 272H, entered Castle Alley only moments later. A perusal of the area assured him that all was well, and he too departed the scene. The time was 12.25.

PC Andrews returned to Castle Alley at approximately 12.50. The decor had changed. A dead body now reposed under the very street light where PC Allen had enjoyed his light supper.

The dead body was that of Alice McKenzie. Blood oozed from wounds to her neck. Her skirts had been pulled up and her abdomen had been crudely mutilated.

Joseph Barnett had returned.

But now he was working alone.

It was a sad travesty of the glory days of 1888. An attempt to emulate the handiwork of the ferocious Mary Jane Kelly had failed.

But... Jack was back!

The Package on Pinchin Street

Pinchin Street was, and is, in Jack the Ripper's heartland, just two streets away from Berner Street, where Joseph and George had murdered Liz Stride, in Dutfields Yard, almost a year earlier. And it was Pinchin Street where Arthur Dutfield had transferred his business just prior to the Berner Street murder and, it was Pinchin Street where police whistles signalled the discovery of another gruesome killing.

It was 5.30 a.m., 10 September 1889, when PC Bennett, number 239H, turned into Pinchin Street, St George's-in-the-East. He had patrolled the same area just thirty minutes previously and had seen nothing untoward. This time he noted a bundle under one of the railway arches and he decided to investigate.

The bundle contained a female torso complete with arms. He noted that the lower part of the torso had been severely gashed. PC Bennett called for assistance, and the torso was conveyed to the mortuary.

A number of vagrants, residents of the arches, were questioned but they all claimed to have seen nothing.

The torso, and arms were examined by Doctor Clarke and Doctor Sergeant who concluded that the deceased had been approximately thirty-three years of age, slim, 5'3" in height with shapely, well-kept hands; neither of which was clenched. Some anatomical skill had been exhibited.

The head and the legs were never recovered and the identity of the victim could not be ascertained.

Inquest verdict: Murder by person or persons unknown.

Slaughter in Swallow Gardens

Swallow Gardens is a misnomer, for there are no gardens and there are no swallows, and one would need to travel back to the early days of the nineteenth century if one wished to encounter either.

This fact is tacitly acknowledged by the local council who have removed the name altogether. Swallow Gardens is now an alleyway with no name, and it deserves none.

A short narrow passageway, it survives today, still connecting Chamber Street with Royal Mint Street. It is straddled by an enormous, double-track railway arch which blots out the sun, and, to compensate, the railway company have generously provided three huge lights which are attached to the underside of the railway arch. They provide a ghostly yellow illumination for the traveller brave enough to venture into this forsaken place.

Exiting from Swallow Gardens onto Royal Mint Street, across the road, just eighty yards away, is a pleasant early Victorian public house named The Crown and Seven Stars (but presently masquerading as The Artful Dodger). It was just 100 yards to the rear of this building in the year 1858, that Jack the Ripper was born – at number 4, Hairbrain Court.

Possibly Joseph Barnett had enjoyed a drink in The Crown and Seven Stars on the night of Thursday and Friday, 12–13 February 1891, and had then gone for a nocturnal stroll. Later he would meet a woman: a woman named Frances Coles.

Frances Coles was the daughter of a boot maker. She was just 5' tall with brown hair and brown eyes and, in the year 1891, just twenty-six years of age.

Frances was considered an attractive woman though a dissipated life of alcohol and prostitution was rapidly taking its inexorable toll and, if truth be told, Frances had begun to smell. She had spent the night of Wednesday and Thursday, 11–12 February with James Thomas Sadler, a ship's fireman, and together they had spent most of Thursday drinking at various pubs in the Spitalfields area.

By eight o'clock, both Sadler and Frances Coles were extremely drunk and they parted after a quarrel. Frances staggered back to the common lodging house on White's Row, where she had spent the previous evening. She sat at a table in the kitchen and fell into a drunken stupor.

Some time later, Sadler arrived at the lodging house, his face bleeding, his clothes begrimed and torn. "I've been robbed," he announced, "and I'd do for them what done it, if I could get me hands on them." This was dire news indeed, and augured badly for a restitution of connubial bliss.

The lodging housekeeper, after some considerable difficulty, persuaded Sadler to leave the premises. Later, when Frances was sufficiently revived to walk unaided, she too left the lodging house. The exact time of her departure is disputed but a mean average puts the hour at approximately one o'clock.

Shuttleworth's eating house in Wentworth Street obviously enjoyed a brisk late night trade for, at 1.30, Frances Coles was tucking into a plate of mutton and bread in that worthy establishment. She stayed on the premises for about fifteen minutes and, during that time, was asked to leave the premises three times; from which fact we can deduce that her charm and possibly her fragrance had failed to impress the management. Whatever the reason, Frances Coles was persuaded to take her custom elsewhere, which she did at approximately 1.45. Last seen, Frances was staggering in the direction of Brick Lane.

It was 2.30 when PC Ernest Thompson, number 240H, marched resolutely westward on Chamber Street. PC Thompson was new to the force and this was his first night on the beat by himself. Ahead of him, in the darkness, he could hear footsteps.

Thompson deduced they were the footsteps of a man: a man also walking westward, towards Mansell Street.

Whoever it was, Thompson considered the individual was in no particular hurry and, in any event, it was of no importance.

The footsteps were all but inaudible as PC Thompson turned left, into Swallow Gardens.

There was a bundle lying in the centre of the narrow passageway and, as Thompson approached, he shone the beam of his lantern onto the offending obstruction.

The "obstruction" was Frances Coles. Blood was pouring from savage wounds to her throat and, as the horrified PC took in the scene, he saw Frances Coles open and then slowly close her right eye!

If Frances was not already dead she had certainly expired before the arrival of a doctor. This doctor was of the opinion that Frances had been violently thrown to the ground, after which act of violence her attacker had slashed her throat three times – from left to right, from right to left. And from left to right again.

So far as can be ascertained, Joseph Barnett never killed again, but when he killed Frances Coles in Swallow Gardens he was just 150 yards from his birthplace: number 4, Hairbrain Court.

Swallow Gardens

Crown and Seven Stars today, renamed the Artful Dodger
(A bas-relief of the Crown and Stars surmounts the building still)

Savagery in Salamanca Place

Salamanca Place, a side road of Salamanca Street, which itself leads onto the Albert Embankment near to Lambeth Bridge, and runs parallel with Broad Street.

In the year 1902 it was an area that enjoyed an unsavoury reputation.

At 4 a.m. on a June Sunday in the year 1902, Charles Whiting, an employee in the works of Messrs Doulton, had just completed a job after working all night in the Broad Street depot. There was still a kiln needing to be changed at the Salamanca Works and he, together with a fellow workman named Muntzer, set off on the short journey to Salamanca Place.

Dawn had already broken and the light was good as the two men neared the gates of Messrs Doulton.

As they approached they noted, in front of the gates, what appeared to be a pile of rubbish.

Closer examination revealed the "rubbish" to be a pile of human remains and atop the heap was a human head, the eyes of which stared vacantly at the two appalled men.

Skirting around the grisly sight, they entered through the gateway and alerted the nightwatchman, John Cox.

As the three men stared, transfixed by the ghastly sight, two young men presumed without any justification to be medical students, passed by, and one casually remarked to the other, "Oh, it's just a woman's head."

John Cox ran to fetch a policeman and returned with PC Birton who immediately called for reinforcements.

The reinforcements duly arrived and the remains were transported to the mortuary where they were examined by a police surgeon.

The remains were female. In life the woman had been aged twenty-five to thirty years, 5'0" tall, slim and muscular and the cause of death was given as possible suffocation.

She had been dismembered with little or no skill, her backbone sawn in two and her limbs wrenched off. The head had been partially boiled and/or roasted, resulting in considerable disfigurement of the features. One ear was shrunken and several teeth were missing. She had been scalped. Such hair that remained was colour, black

The woman was never identified.

Verdict: Murder by person or persons unknown.

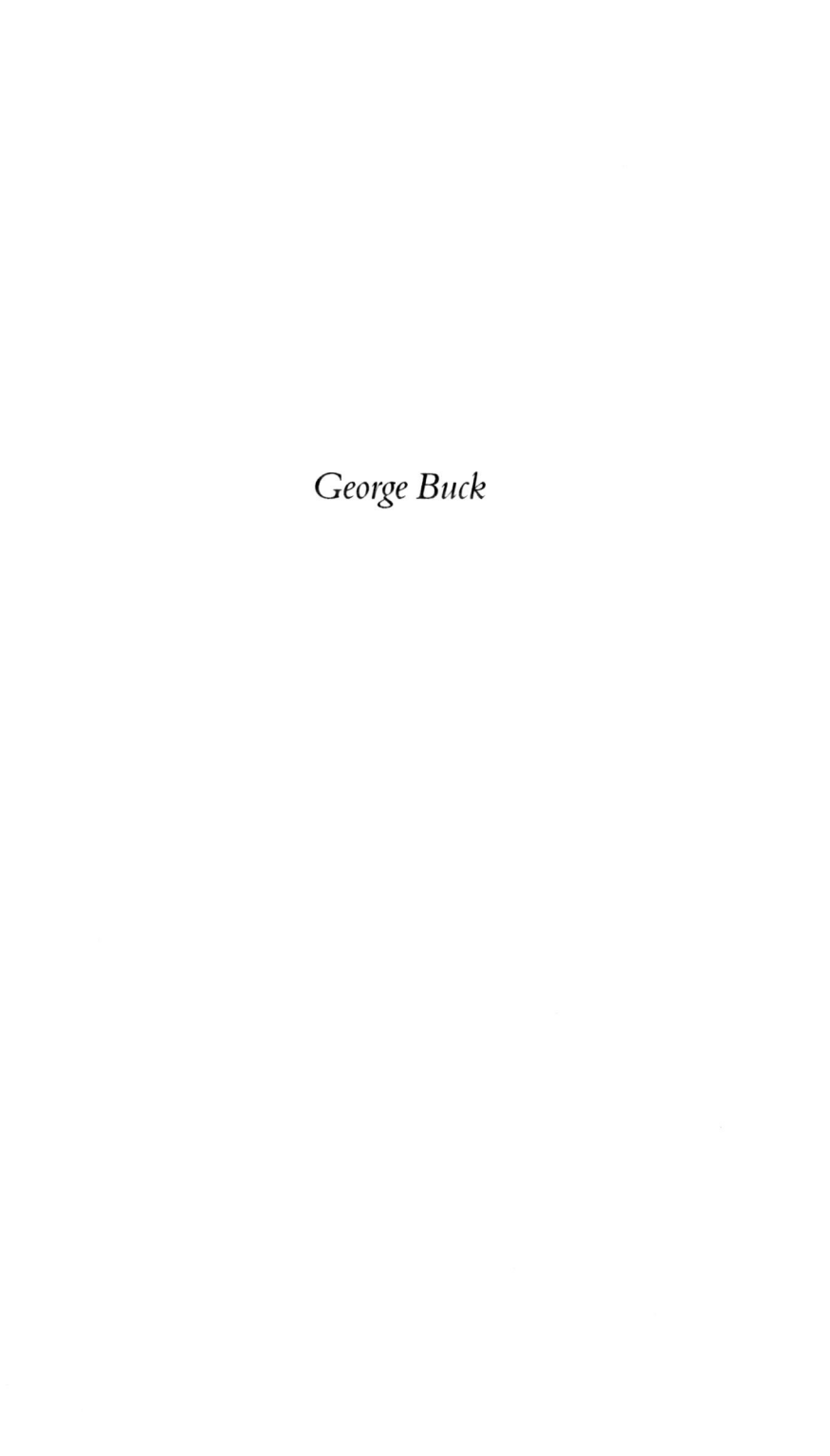

George Buck

George Buck

It seemed possible that George Buck worked with Joseph Barnett at Billingsgate but there was no licensed fish porter by that name. There was, however, a Henry Buck. Perhaps George was a relative.

Henry Buck

Henry Buck was born circa 1847 in Bethnal Green (from the censuses).

His father was named Thomas and Thomas was, by trade, a hawker (from Henry's marriage certificate).

There is no birth certificate on file for a Henry Buck born in Bethnal Green, in respect of the five-year period 1845 to 1849 so that we do not know the name of Henry's mother, neither do we have any details of Henry's early life. (There are six Henry Buck births recorded during this period though none are in respect of Bethnal Green.)

On Guy Fawkes' day, 5 November 1866, at St Philip's church, Bethnal Green, Henry married a girl named Caroline Smith, the daughter of John Smith, a horse dealer.

Both Henry and Caroline gave their age as nineteen years and both signed the register with their mark, an "X", as did their two witnesses.

Henry and Caroline gave their address as Tyssen Street (no number), Bethnal Green, and Henry gave his occupation as "hawker".

In the year 1871, Henry and Caroline are living at number 25, Nelson Street, Bethnal Green.

Henry, at the age of twenty-four years, has given up hawking and is now a porter.

Caroline, who was the same age as Henry when they married is now three years younger, at just twenty-one years. The couple have two children: Caroline aged three years and Emma – who was born on Christmas Day, 1870 – just three months old. (On the birth certificate for Emma, Henry gives his occupation as fish porter.)

In the year 1878 Henry was issued with a Billingsgate Porter's Licence, number 286. There are two addresses on the licence. The first is shown as 9, Turin Street, Bethnal Green, the second as 3, Valley Place, Orange Street, Bethnal Green.

Henry is shown as being thirty years old, 5'6" tall and fair.

The census of 1881 records that the Buck family are residing at number 9, Turin Street, Bethnal Green. In a ten-year period Henry has aged an extra year and is now thirty-five whilst Caroline has aged an additional two years. She is now only two years younger than Henry at thirty-three years.

Daughter Caroline is not recorded on the 1881 census and is presumed dead. Emma is now ten years old and she has two sisters, Clara, seven and Sarah, two, and a brother, Henry, aged four.

(The absence of a birth certificate for Henry Buck, senior, is a handicap in establishing whether he had a brother and particularly a brother named George. If there is a link it has not been established. In seeking a common denominator we do know that Henry's father is named Thomas. There are no other family details.)

It seems probable that Henry Buck and Joseph Barnett were acquainted given that they resided in the same area and worked at Billingsgate at the same time.

There was another Billingsgate porter with the surname Buck – John Buck.

John Buck

John Frederic Buck was born 3 November 1870, at Hill Street, St Albans, Hertfordshire. His father was a brewer's collector named John Buck and his mother was named Ellen Buck née Frisby. Ellen had been born in Whitechapel.

In October 1889, John Buck was granted a Billingsgate porters licence, number 1857.

John's age is shown as twenty years (in actuality he was nearly nineteen).

Eyes: Grey

Hair: Fair

Complexion: Fresh

His address is given as number 9, Suffolk Street, Field Road, Forest Gate.

Forest Gate is sited on the Romford Road not far from Romford itself. (George Hutchinson, in his statement, said that he had told Mary Kelly that he had spent all his money going to Romford, which may or may not be significant.)

The censuses for the years 1881 and 1891 record that the Buck family reside at number 9, Suffolk Street, Field Road, Forest Gate.

This was the situation in 1881:

Ellen Buck	Widow	Aged	Forty-one years.
Emily	Daughter		Twenty years.
Herbert	Son		Sixteen years.
Arthur	Son		Fourteen years.
John	Son		Eleven years.
Mabel	Daughter		Six years.
Ernest	Son		Seven months.

I have not found any evidence that John had an older relative, named George but the possibility exists.

Henry Buck and John Buck are the only individuals with the surname Buck to be issued with a Billingsgate porter's licence.

The Search for George Buck

If George Hutchinson was in reality George Buck, it could be proven, by default, provided the anagram could be solved, but was there anything else in support of the theory?

Searching through the newspapers for statements made by Joseph Barnett, there was the strangely named Mrs Buki. But why Mrs Buki? Why not Booki, Boucki, Boucky or any other spellings with the same phonetic consonant structure? Probably the news reporter wrote down what he had heard and guessed at the spelling from the sound.

So what had Joseph Barnett said?

"She [Mary] had first stayed with Mrs Buki in St George's Street."

There it was again – BUK in close proximity to GEORGE. There might be another explanation but it looked interesting.

After George Hutchinson had made his appearance at Commercial Street police station he was interviewed by newspaper reporters, but sadly they gave very little information relating to George himself.

Of the working class.
Of military appearance.
A down-on-his-luck groom.

No age is even approximated, though we can assume George is mature but not aged.

So what of the sightings of Jack the Ripper? Descriptions here don't help for there is no real point of comparison. But assessments of age assist in narrowing the field.

Witness sightings of a stout man, 5'5" to 5'6" indicate an age range between twenty-eight years to thirty-seven years.

The number of births for George Buck circa 1845 to 1860 were too numerous to consider each one individually. But if the vicinity of Ratcliffe Highway is assumed to be the correct location for George Buck's birth, and it is a big assumption, then there is only one candidate.

He was born George Buck, 8 October 1853, at number 5, Mary Ann Street, St George's-in-the-East. His father, Francis Buck was, by occupation, a carman. His mother was named Elizabeth Buck, née Allen. Elizabeth was the informant and she signed her name with her mark: an "X".

In the year 1851, two and a half years before George was born, the census records that the undernoted people resided at number 5, Mary Ann Street.

		AGE	BORN
Francis Buck	Head and carman	26	Aldgate
Elizabeth	Wife	28	Poplar
Francis	Son	5	St Geo.

But after careful consideration it was obvious that, at this stage, birth details were not relevant, since this birth and many of the other George Buck births could have ended in a death prior to the year 1888, and our interest is confined to a George Buck who was alive and well, in November of that year.

The search for George Buck then would be confined to all George Bucks who died after November 1888.

George Buck Died after November 1888

Please note: the initial G after a first name could indicate the name George but it is not necessarily so.

Date	Name	Age	Place died
Dec 1888	Nil		
Mar 1889	George	42	Lancaster
	George	30	Middlesboro
	George Harrison	39	Dover
Mar 1890	Henry George	31	Poplar
Jun 1891	George	31	Sculcoates
Dec 1891	George Frederick	40	Whitechapel
Dec 1892	George William	31	Swaffham
Mar 1893	George	30	Lambeth
Mar 1895	George Henry	35	Wakefield
Dec 1895	George	34	Alverstoke
	George Frederick	34	Greenwich
Mar 1897	George	40	Abergavenny
Jun 1899	George	44	Depwade
Dec 1899	George Edward	50	Pancras
Mar 1902	George	54	Shoreditch
Dec	George	47	Han. Sq.
Sep 1904	Herbert J G	45	Kings Lynn
Dec	George	48	Norwich
Mar 1906	George Isaac	50	Hambledon
Jun 1907	Arthur G	50	Kingston
Dec	George	60	Warwick
	George	50	Mutford
	George	61	Knaseboro
Sep 1908	Arthur G	57	Croydon
Jun 1909	George	58	Pancras
Sep	George	50	Farnham

DATE	NAME	AGE	PLACE DIED
Jun 1910	Reginald G	56	Whitechapel
Mar 1911	George	61	Ripon
Sep	George	63	Bedwelty
Mar 1912	George H	60	West Derby
Mar 1915	George R	70	Tynemouth
Jun 1916	George	66	Haslingden
Mar 1918	George Henry	57	London City
Sep	George	56	Carlisle
Sep 1922	George	69	Leeds
Dec	George	73	Henstead
Mar 1923	George J P	75	Flegg
Jun	George H	63	Aston
Sep	George W J	64	East Preston
Mar 1924	Walter G	64	Norwich
Jun	George	73	Sculcoates
	William G	70	Exeter
Mar 1925	Alfred G	70	Haslingden
Dec	George	62	Wellingbro
Jun 1926	George	78	Wayland
Sep	George M	77	Bournemouth
Jun 1921	George	76	Bedford
	George	80	Smallburgh
	George R	62	Linton
Dec 1928	George	76	Blofield
Mar 1929	George	66	Camberwell
	George	67	Wakefield
	George Levi Thomas	75	Uckfield
Jun	George	74	Preston
Dec	Henry G	68	Reigate
	Isaac G	68	Yarmouth
Mar 1930	George	81	Aylsham
	William G	75	Wandsworth
Jun	Reuben G	69	Cambridge
Mar 1931	George	68	Stepney
	George	76	Devonport

Date	Name	Age	Place died
Jun	George J	72	Rochford
Sep	George	86	Poplar
Dec	George W G	71	Reigate
	Edward G	78	Wandsworth
Dec 1932	George	77	Dudley
	George	78	Burton
	George S	72	W. Ward
Mar 1933	Richard G	74	West Ham
Jun		69	Knaseboro
Jun 1934	George J	78	Newport M
Dec	George	77	Islington
Sep 1935	George	76	Alnwick
	Alfred G	73	Islington
Mar 1937	Alfred G	83	Northampton
Sep	George	73	Wolverhampton
Dec	George	84	Erpingham
	George H	80	Dartford
	Henry G	76	Essex S W
Dec 1938	George G	79	Cambridge
	George M	77	Aylsham
Mar 1939	George H	81	Chelmsford
Mar 1940	George Thomas	81	Essex S W
Sep 1941	George H	85	Worthing
	Harry G	90	Stoke
Dec 1942	Frederick George	85	Battersea
Jun 1943	William G H	83	Poole

And checked to 1955.

The Death of George Buck

A Shortlist.
Death recorded after December 1888. Born/died London area.

		AGE	DIED
1890			
Mar	Henry George	31	Died Poplar, born Bethnal Green 1858
1891			
Dec	George Frederick	40	Died Whitechapel, born Whitechapel 1851.
1902			
Mar	George	54	Died Shoreditch, born Whitechapel
1918			
Mar	George Henry	57	Died London City, born Bow
1940			
Mar	George Thomas	81	Died Essex SW, born Bethnal Green

Census 1881

This is a list of London based George Bucks taken from the surname indexed census for the year 1881 – seven years before the Whitechapel murders. (The 1891 Census is not surname indexed).

At 21, Kenilworth Road, Bethnal Green lived: George Buck, aged thirty. Unmarried. Wine cooper. Born Whitechapel. Aged thirty-eight years in 1888.

At 8, St Pauls Road off Rhodeswell Road, Limehouse, Mile End lived: George Buck, aged twenty-two. Unmarried. Paper maker. Born Germany. Aged thirty years in 1888.

At 13, Stafford Road, Bow, off Roman Road, lived: George D. Buck, aged thirty-five. Married to Sarah M Buck with four children. Printers lithographer. Born Sussex. Aged forty-three years in 1888.

At 9, King John Street, Mile End Old Town, Stepney Green lived: George Rd Buck. Aged twenty-two. Unmarried. Cigar sorter. Born Ratcliffe. Aged thirty years in 1888.

At 10, Hayfield Cottages, east Ferry Road, Poplar, lived: George Buck, aged thirty-eight. Widower. Four children, eldest twelve years. Bricklayer and Plater in Iron works. Born Alderton, Suffolk. Aged forty-six years in 1888.

At 7, Castle Square, Old Castle Street, Bethnal Green lived: George Buck, aged forty. Born Bethnal Green. Married to Mary. Porter. Seven children. Aged forty-six years in 1888.

At 31, Denbigh Place, Pimlico, St George, Hanover Square, lived: George Buck, aged twenty-one. Unmarried. Porter. Born Bath. Aged twenty-nine years in 1888.

At 13, Newby Place, Poplar, lived: George Buck, aged thirty-three. Born Flettenham, Norfolk. General Labourer. Aged forty-one years in 1888.

(1888 ages based on assumption of survival.)

The Real George Buck

In endeavouring to find the man who called himself George Hutchinson, the only criteria was the establishment of an age range, and this was arbitrarily set at between twenty-five years and forty years, an estimate based on witness sightings and allowing a latitude of three years plus or minus.

The number of men named George Buck who fell roughly within this age range and whose deaths were recorded within the period October/December 1888, to October/December 1955, totalled eighty-seven.

With no other guidelines, this number was dramatically reduced to just five, by the process of eliminating all George Bucks who died outside the London area, and with particular preference being given to those who were born, and whose death was recorded, within the area of the East End. However, regarding deaths, I accept that the boundaries have been stretched a little. I accept too that the age range has been stretched (once) by reason of the fact that the ages recorded in the various censuses is, more often than not, inaccurate.

There is one enduring, additional piece of information. George Buck was literate, as indicated by the fact that George Hutchinson signed his *nom de guerre*, on his statement to the police. It must be emphasised that there is a very distinct possibility that George was not a local man, as evidenced by the fact that he was able to masquerade as George Hutchinson without fear of being denounced.

The following five profiles represent the prime London suspects. They are not listed in any particular order – and no conclusion has been reached.

George Henry Buck

George Henry Buck was born 3 May in the year 1860, and was therefore twenty-eight years old (two years younger than Joseph Barnett) at the time of the Whitechapel murders.

George Henry was the son of George Buck, a commercial traveller who was originally from Saffron Walden, and Elizabeth Buck née Barnard, who was originally from Essex.

The birth of George Henry Buck took place at number 21, Three Colts Street, Limehouse, a street which runs southward from the Commercial Road.

The census of 1861 records that George Buck, then aged twenty-seven and his wife Elizabeth, then aged twenty-five, lived at this address with daughter Frances, then aged five, and newly born George Henry, then aged just ten months.

George Henry Buck married a woman named Minnie (or Annie) Mary circa 1857 but, at this time, I have not been able to positively trace a marriage certificate.

At 10.30 on the morning of Saturday, 2 March in the year 1918, George Henry Buck left his home at number 13, Langton Street, St Luke's, Islington.

(Langton Street ran in an east–west line from the east side of Central Street. No part of Langton Street survives today. Only the derelict Langton Arms public house on the corner of Paton Street and Norman Street testifies to the fact that near here, once, was Langton Street. Tennis courts, part of Finsbury Leisure Centre, now cover the area where once stood the home of George and Minnie.)

Kissing Minnie Mary goodbye, George Henry walked to his place of work, up Langton Street, and on into Norman Street, then turned right, through Helmet Row, past St Luke's Church (still standing but gutted by incendiaries) across Old Street and into upper Whitecross Street. The Whitecross market was busy at this hour and the journey took him a little longer than usual, but he had plenty of time; for God had decreed that, after today, George Henry Buck would never need to work again. On past The Green Man and Still public house, past the King's Arms at the crossroads with Chiswell Street, until he reached Silk Street.

(Today, George Henry could go no further along Whitecross Street. This area, close to St Paul's Cathedral, was so badly bombed in 1941 that scarcely a building survived. The Barbican Centre straddles the place where once George Henry worked at the Midland Railway Goods Depot then situated on Whitecross Street.)

George Henry Buck was a railway barrowman and this Saturday was just another working day.

At approximately 2 p.m. George Henry had just finished loading goods onto a horse drawn road wagon which was second in line in a queue of such wagons, but only the lead wagon had a horse ready in the shafts. George Henry climbed onto the "dicky" (the footwell where the carman placed his feet) and proceeded to place a tarpaulin cover over the wagon.

In order to better accomplish this operation, George Henry braced his back against the loaded wagon immediately in front of the one he was working on: leaning back at an angle across a four- to five-foot drop.

Carman William Leamer, unaware that George Henry was dependent on the front wagon for support, took the bridle of the horse standing ready in the shafts and led the animal and the lead wagon forward. Suddenly deprived of his support, George Henry went over backwards falling the four or five feet onto the hard road surface. His body crashed onto the ground and George Henry sustained a fractured skull and two fractured ribs.

City police constable, 74A, Joseph Bates, attached to Moor Lane police station, was instrumental in removing the injured man to St Bartholomew's Hospital where he was duly admitted at 2.30 p.m.

George Henry was attended by house surgeon W Jolliffe but, despite his ministrations, the injured man never regained consciousness. George Henry Buck was pronounced dead at 6.15 a.m., 4 March 1918.

His widow, Minnie Mary, in her deposition at the post mortem, stated that George Henry was a sober man who had never been ill a day in his life. It is doubtful that she derived any comfort from the fact that George Henry's life was insured with The Forester's Society, in the sum of £12.

(The voters register for the year 1919 records Minnie Mary Buck as Annie Buck.)

George Thomas Buck

George Thomas Buck was born Monday, 8 March in the year 1858. He was therefore, at the time of the Whitechapel murders, thirty years of age, just seventy-eight days older than Joseph Barnett, and it must be possible that they schooled together.

George Thomas was the son of John Buck, bricklayer, and Mary Buck née Godier, and he was born at 55, Lessada Street, Bethnal Green.

(Lessada Street is gone now. It ran in a north/south line from Roman Road, just a few yards east of The Grand Union Canal.)

The census for the year 1851 does not record Lessada Street, whilst the census for the year 1861 does not record anyone by the name of Buck living on Lessada Street.

On 11 November in the year 1893, George Thomas Buck, then aged thirty-four, married Florence Louise Booth, then aged twenty-two, at St Thomas's Church, Westham. He gave his occupation as zinc worker and his address as 35, Latt Road. Florence gave her address as 54, William Street.

On 23 April 1905, Florence Louise Buck gave birth to a son. The birth took place at 23, Burleigh Road, Enfield. George Thomas and Florence Louise named their son George Samuel John.

George Thomas Buck, a retired zinc worker, died 12 February 1940. He was aged eighty-one years and his address was given as 63, Harris Street, Leyton. The cause of death was given as senile decay. His son George Samuel John Buck was the informant.

Henry George Buck

Henry George Buck was born Thursday, 11 March in the year 1858. He was therefore thirty years of age at the time of the Whitechapel murders, just seventy-five days older than Joseph Barnett which means that Joseph and Henry George, in common with George Thomas, could have schooled together.

Henry George Jnr was the son of Henry George Buck Snr, a chair maker, specialising in children's chairs, and his wife Mary Buck née Jolliffe. Henry George Buck Jnr was born at number 10, Simpsons Place, west, off Birdcage Walk, Hackney Road, Bethnal Green (Birdcage Walk is now named Columbia Road. Simpsons

Place which lay alongside Ion Square is gone). Neither the census of 1851 nor the census of 1861 records anyone by the name of Buck living at number 10.

Sometime before 1881, the family moved to number 9, Blanchard Street, Hackney. The census of 1881 records this situation:

Henry George Buck aged sixty-four, chair maker, born St George's-in-the-East, his wife, Mary, aged forty-seven, born London City, their children, Henry George, aged twenty-three, chair maker, born Bethnal Green, Samuel, aged sixteen, halter maker, Mary A, aged seven, (blind in one eye) and Charlotte, aged three. By the time of the 1891 census the family are still living at the same address. Samuel and Henry George have left the family home and there has been one new addition, Eliza, then aged four.

Henry George Buck married Eliza Burden, daughter of Samuel Burden, a cellar man, on Christmas Day, December 25, 1884, in Old Ford parish church, Bow. The bridegroom was aged twenty-five years. The bride was aged just eighteen years.

On 15 March 1888 (as Joseph Barnett and Mary Jane Kelly were settling into number 13, Millers Court) Henry George and Eliza were blessed with a son. The child was born at 46, Ford Road, Poplar. The happy couple named their only child Henry Samuel.

Henry George Buck, cabinet-maker and journeyman, living at number 32, Ranwell Street, Bow, with his in-laws, celebrated his thirty-second birthday March 11 1890, in the Poplar Sick Asylum (now St Andrew's Hospital). He died there 16 March just sixteen months after the Millers Court murder.

The cause of his demise was given as "morbus cordis mitral" which, translated, means "death from a morbid heart/mitral valve disease", a heart condition which may be congenital or may be caused by an earlier bout of rheumatic fever or by syphilis. It is doubtful that any inference can be drawn by the oblique reference to syphilis.

The registrar duly recorded the death. Henry George's mother, Mary, was the informant and she gave her address as 9, Blanchard Street, Hackney. The young widow was left weeping at 32, Ranwell Street, with her family and her young son. The future must have looked very bleak indeed.

George Frederick Buck

George Frederick Buck was born 27 September in the year 1851. He was therefore thirty-six or thirty-seven years old at the time of the Whitechapel murders: six years and eight months older than Joseph Barnett.

George Frederick was born at number 11, Hobsons Court, Whitechapel, the son of Nicholas Buck, a labourer, and Harriet Buck née Lee.

The census of 1851 records that Nicholas Buck, a labourer, then aged forty-two years and originally from Germany lived at this address with his wife Harriet, then aged just thirty-one, herself originally from Mile End.

Nicholas and Harriet had, at that time, three sons, John aged fourteen, James aged ten, and Nicholas aged six. At the time of the census, Harriet was three months pregnant with George Frederick.

The census of 1861 does not record the names of either John Buck or James Buck but it does record the name of Frederick, then aged nine years, so it is assumed that the family knew George Frederick as "Fred".

Harriet Buck, who has aged rather badly, is now forty-four years old and is a laundress whilst her husband, Nicholas, is aged fifty-three years. The younger Nicholas, then aged seventeen, is now a carman. Number 11, Hobsons Court, now houses a 23-year-old lodger; a chair maker named John.

The census of 1871 does not record the name of Harriet Buck and her death is therefore presumed. Nicholas Buck is no longer a labourer but is now a tobacconist. The younger Nicholas, now twenty-seven, is still a carman whilst his brother (still known only as Frederick) aged nineteen, is a warehouseman.

John, the lodger, has gone (perhaps he ran off with Harriet) but number 11, Hobsons Court now houses two new lodgers, Fred Callard, aged twenty-one, and Albert Burton, also aged twenty-one.

On Christmas Eve, 24 December 1871, George Frederick Buck married Amelia Frances Moore Burr, the daughter of James Burr, a horse keeper. The bridegroom was aged twenty-three years. The bride was aged twenty-one years.

The ceremony took place in the parish church of St Philip's, Stepney. The bride and groom gave their address as 22, New Street, Stepney, and they were both sufficiently literate to sign their own names.

(New Street has been renamed Newark Street. Number 22 is no longer in existence. St Philip's, Stepney, became derelict and was torn down in the year 1883 and a new church was constructed. The new St Philip's (so vast it was known as the Cathedral of the East End) was consecrated in the year 1892, by the Bishop of Wakefield. The church was declared redundant in the year 1979. It is now the library of The Royal London School of Medicine and Dentistry.)

The census of 1881 records that Nicholas Buck then aged seventy-two years, is a retired tobacconist from Germany and he has ceded his role as head of the family to his son, George Frederick Buck, then aged twenty-nine, and now a brewer's servant (a drayman).

George Frederick has had a busy ten years. He married Amelia in 1871 and fathered five children, Frederick, then aged seven, Amelia, then aged six, Florence, then aged five, Rebecca, then aged three and little Henry, then aged just one year.

The younger Nicholas, aged thirty-seven and unmarried, is no longer a carman but, like George Frederick, a brewer's servant.

There are no lodgers at number 11, Hobsons Court.

The census of 1891 (two and a half years after the Whitechapel murders) records that the Buck family now live at number 14, Hobsons Cottages but the move is, almost certainly, more apparent than real, for the undernoted reasons:

(In 1889, the dwellings which were located in two short streets, Hobsons Place and Hobsons Court, suffered a reduction in their number (presumed demolished) and the name Hobsons Court was changed to Hobsons Cottages. The houses were, almost certainly, renumbered so it is assumed here that number 11, Hobsons Court and number 14, Hobsons Cottages are one and the same house.)

This census fails to record the names of both Nicholas Buck Snr and Nicholas Buck Jnr.

The family of George Frederick has prospered and increased by two, Esther E, then aged seven, and Lilian Charlotte, then aged four.

(Lilian Charlotte Buck was born 13 April in the year 1886, (two years prior to Joseph and Marie taking up residence at number 13, Millers Court) at number 11, Hobsons Court.)

Number 14, Hobsons Cottages now houses a lodger; William Toomey, aged thirty-five, a numerical printer.

(Hobsons Place and Hobsons Cottages have gone now. They were situated adjacently and ran in a north-south line from the south side of Pelham Street, now named Woodseer Street, which itself is just thirty yards north of Hanbury Street where Annie Chapman was murdered at number 29. It is worth recording that Hobsons Court/Cottages was situated just 500 yards from Millers Court. The streets are buried now under a block of flats rejoicing in the name Hobsons Place. Fifty yards from Hobsons Place, on Albert Street (now Deal Street) are some pleasant Victorian cottages named respectively Albert Cottages and Victoria Cottages. They give an excellent indication of what Hobsons Cottages/Place must have looked like in the year 1888.)

On 10 November 1891, at number 14, Hobsons Cottages, and exactly three years and one day after the murder at Millers Court, George Frederick Buck died. The cause of death was given as pulmonary tuberculosis otherwise known as consumption.

George Buck

George Buck was born 4 February 1846, at number 32, Underwood Street, Whitechapel, Mile End New Town.

George's father was a man named William Buck and William was employed as a slop cutter. George's mother was named Amelia Buck née Wrench.

The census for the year 1851 at number 42, Devonshire Street, Stepney, records this situation:

William Buck, aged thirty-one years, a slop cutter, born Brentwood, Essex. Amelia Buck, aged thirty years, born Shoreditch. Sons William aged seven years and George aged five years. Also at number 42, lived Isabella Wrench, sister of Amelia, aged eighteen years, unmarried, and her son James Wrench, aged two years.

On 5 April 1854, at number 42, Devonshire Street, Stepney, George and William acquired a sister. She was named after her mother, Amelia. In 1854 William was still employed as a slop cutter.

Circa 1875, sister Amelia married a man named Ernest Walker and the union produced at least six children.

In the year 1888 George was aged forty-two years.

The census for the year 1901, at number 25, Regents Row, Haggerston records this situation:

Amelia Walker, aged forty-five years, a widow. Sons Albert, aged eighteen years, Thomas aged fifteen years, James aged twelve years, George aged ten years, Samuel aged nine years and Alfred aged six years.

Whether brother George married or not cannot be ascertained by reason of the fact that the number of George Bucks who married during the relevant period are too numerous to consider individually, and because I have been unable to locate George in any census after 1851.

On 10 January 1902, George Buck, aged fifty-four years, a picture frame maker (journeyman) died at number 25, Regents Row, Haggerston. Cause of death given as "Phillusis Pulmonalis" and exhaustion. Amelia Walker, sister of the deceased, was the informant.

George Buck – the Invisible Killer

This is where, reluctantly, I decided to end the search for George Buck.

There is only the signature of George Hutchinson as a point of comparison (as far as I can ascertain) and that isn't enough.

It is also possible that George died on foreign shores, so that there would be no record of a death in this country. But, even if he did die in this country, there is a major obstacle in working backwards from a known death when investigating a relatively common name. It is this:

Taking a given year of death and subtracting the age of the deceased from that year gives the year of birth – except that is not necessarily true. Certainly there are always two years to consider because the month of birth is unknown (did he die before his birthday or after his birthday?) Add to this, that the age of the deceased might be incorrectly shown and that the place of birth indicated on the birth certificate may conflict with the place of birth shown on the census and throw into the mix the possibility that the birth may not have been registered at all, and one is in danger of reaching an unsatisfactory conclusion.

It is only necessary to say that Joseph, Mary and George freely roamed the streets of Whitechapel and on those streets they murdered six women, seemingly without fear of being discovered or denounced – but Joseph and Mary (who always stayed in character – Mary as Mary Jane Kelly) didn't suddenly have to masquerade as somebody else. This suggests that George was, like Mary, a stranger to the district and that during the time he resided in the East End, was always known as George Hutchinson.

It is for this reason that I have reached the conclusion that George was from out of town, with this cautionary comment:

George only broke cover to save Joseph Barnett (Mary was, almost certainly, undetectable) following the too early discovery of the Millers Court murder, so that a desperate situation dictated a desperate remedy.

The risk was justified on that basis and, if that risk had never been taken, George Buck would have remained forever – the invisible killer.

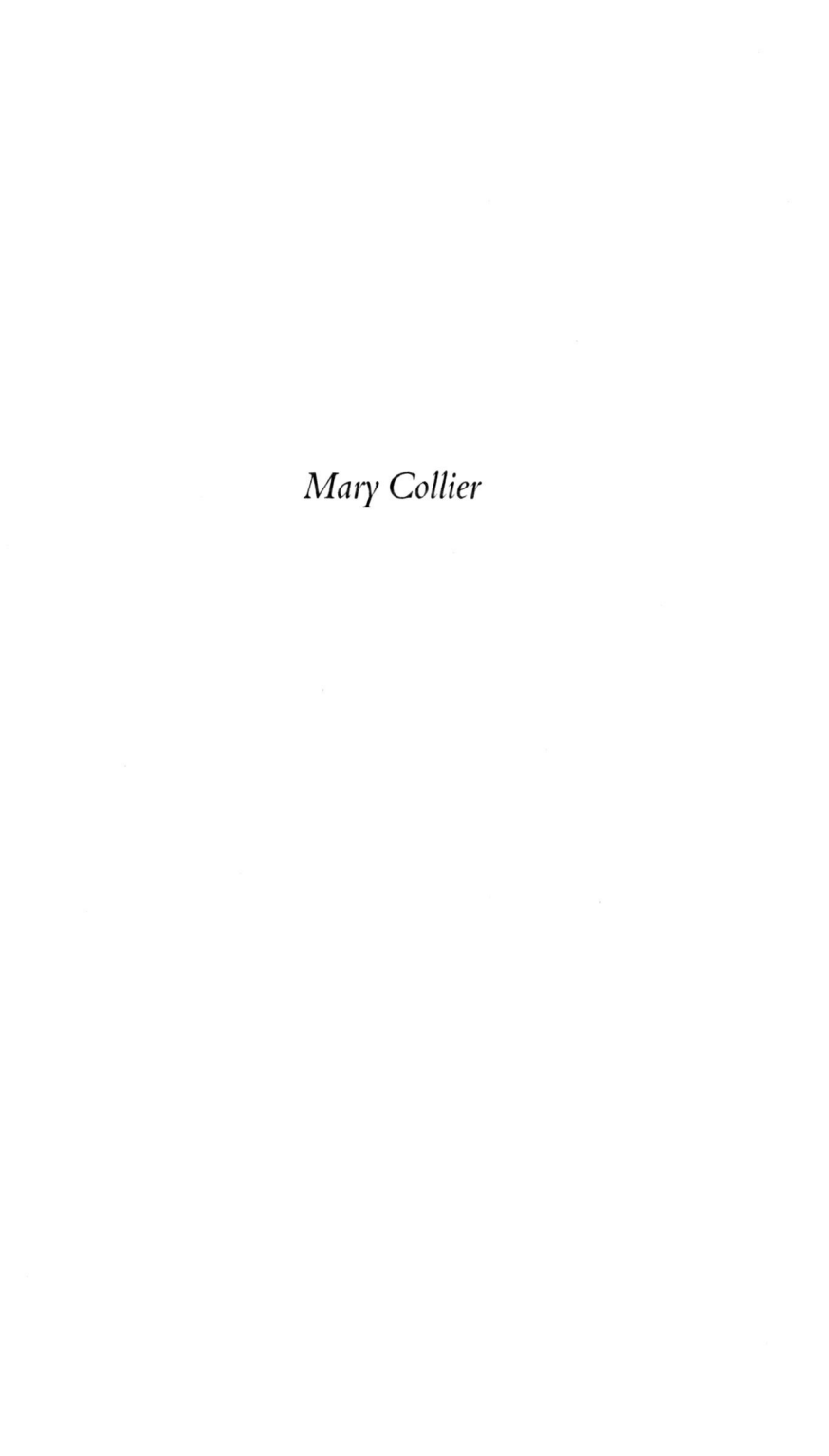

Mary Collier

The Search for Mary Collier

In order to find Mary Collier it was essential to know the answer to two questions.

1. Did Mary have a second name and, if so, was it Jane or Jeanette?
2. Was Collier a maiden name or a married name?

Joseph Barnett had said:

> She was known as Mary but her real name was Marie: Marie Jeanette Kelly: Kelly being her maiden name.

He had also said:

> She married a collier named Davis or Davies.

But what did he mean by this? The obvious, and intended interpretation is: she married a miner surnamed Davis or Davies.

But nothing with Joseph Barnett is that straightforward.

Since Mary's real name was Collier: was this her married name? Or is the interpretation: she (a woman named Collier) married a man named Davis or Davies?

It seemed a good idea to look for the death of a man named Collier, a fairly young man; a man who had died sometime between 1878 and 1885 preferably in Wales.

Collier is a name found principally in Manchester or in the immediate surrounding area, otherwise there are scatterings of Colliers throughout the country – the largest enclave being in London; but there are very few people with the name Collier to be found in Wales. This was something of a blessing, for it considerably reduced the number of candidates.

Even though the net was cast in a wide arc, there were only two men who could have been Mary Jane's husband and, after viewing their respective death certificates, they were eliminated.

It was time to look for the birth of a Mary Collier; all second Christian names considered; Jane being preferred.

Joseph Barnett's estimate of her age (twenty-five) could not be relied on and it seemed probable that Mary Jane was older. An upper age limit of thirty-two seemed reasonable and so the search began from the year 1856. Originally, it seemed likely that Mary Jane was born in Wales: Limerick having been disposed of otherwise London was the most probable venue.

There were several possibilities but only one probable. She was born Mary Jane Collier, 25 October 1862, at 29, King Street, Haggerston west, Shoreditch, just over one mile north from the murder epicentre. Mary Jane attained her twenty-sixth year in October, 1888.

(Anyone searching for King Street, Haggerston West, on a modern map will be disappointed. King Street underwent a name change to Loanda Street in the year 1879, and Loanda Street disappeared in the 1960s when the whole area was re-developed.)

Mary Jane's father was named James (Barnett had said "John") and he was a plasterer (Barnett had said, "A foreman in an iron works"). A foreman in an iron works could be some sort of masonic rank, not an occupation, but there was no obvious reason to change James to John. Mary Jane did have a sister named Mary (after her mother) and a brother named Henry. There was no sign of the other five or six brothers and given the fact that James and Mary were a mature couple in their thirties such a large increase in the family seemed unlikely, for the future.

The acid test would be Mary Jane's marriage. If this Mary Jane was Mary Jane Kelly she should have married circa 1878 and, preferably, she should have married a man named Davis or Davies.

But Mary Jane hadn't married in 1878, or between 1874 and 1888. Mary Jane Collier, if she married at all, married after 1888. This Mary Jane was not Mary Jane Kelly.

It was now time to concentrate on marriage transactions involving all females named Mary Collier (all additional Christian names considered) anywhere in the country during the period 1872 to 1884.

There were seventy-one possibilities. Most of these had married in, or in the area around, Manchester and these were checked against Davis or Davies with negative result. There were three in London that were deemed worthy of further investigation and three in Wales, but as the marriage certificates came in and each was considered, it became obvious that none of the brides could possibly have been Mary Jane Kelly.

There was the gradual realisation that Mary Collier was not a maiden name; it was a married name, and, irrespective of the fact that there had been no success in tracing the death of "Mr" Collier it was decided to return to that arena and start again from a different tack.

Barnett had said:

She married a collier named Davis or Davies.

And that is how it has always been construed, but did he mean:

She married a Collier named Davis or Davies.

In other words, was there a man named Davis or Davies Collier, and was he married circa 1878 to a woman named Mary: a woman who had become Mary Collier?

William and Mary

William Lindsey Collier was born in Witney, Oxfordshire, in the year 1825. His father, James, was a butcher. Ten years later, in the year 1835, William Lindsey was presented with a brother; a brother named Edward. (It is probable that there were other children in addition to these two.)

The next time we hear of William and Edward it is 30 March in the year 1851. They are sharing an address in Reading, the capital town of the county of Berkshire, situated just forty miles west of London; with a population, in the year 1851, of just 21,456 souls.

The address which the brothers shared was number 20, Broad Street, which comprised of a shop and living accommodation. (The building survives today – currently trading as O2).

In addition to themselves, this abode provided accommodation for a 37-year-old woman – a servant named Elizabeth Lovegrove, born in the City of London.

William Lindsey Collier was, by profession, a chemist and druggist (in the year 1859 he became a member of The Pharmaceutical Society of Great Britain) and he conducted his business from the ground floor shop. In addition, William manufactured soda water, lemonade, ginger beer and, sometimes, British wine. He was also an oil and colourman. His brother Edward acted as his assistant.

But life was not all toil and, when William was not busy working he was busy courting a local girl… a girl named Mary.

Mary Rusher Davies was born in the year 1830 in Reading; the first child of Philip Davies who had also been born in Reading; and Mary Davies née Rusher, who had been born in Banbury, a small town in Oxfordshire situated seventy miles north-west of London, and with a population, in the year 1851, of less than 3,000 souls.

Philip Davies was, by profession, a grocer and tallow chandler, though he liked to describe himself simply as, "a gentleman". In addition to Mary Rusher, Philip and Mary produced three other children; all girls. There was Susan, born circa 1833, and Martha and Elizabeth, born circa 1836. Their home at 24, Russell Street, Reading, (the house is still there today) also provided accommodation for a servant girl named Mary Crisp, a 21-year-old who had been born in Pangbourne.

It cannot be ascertained when or how William Lindsey Collier and Mary Rusher Davies first met but Russell Street and Broad Street are situated in close proximity to each other. And, in Broad Street, located in Reading's town centre, both William Lindsey Collier and Philip Davies ran their respective businesses.

On 6 May in the year 1851, at the congregational chapel, Broad Street, Reading, and according to the rites and ceremonies of the independent denomination: William Lindsey Collier and Mary Rusher Davies were joined together in holy matrimony. (The site is currently Waterstones bookstore).

The witnesses gave their names as Samuel Davies, Philip Davies, Susan Davies and James Collier. The registrar gave his name as Frederick West.

It had been a spring day full of joy and promise and, it is to be hoped, the happy couple enjoyed a blissful honeymoon.

When they returned, they returned to number 20, Broad Street and it is assumed that William's brother Edward and the servant, Elizabeth Lovegrove continued in residence.

It was at number 20, Broad Street, Reading, on 9 April 1852, that Mary Rusher Collier gave birth to a son. And it was at number 20, Broad Street, Reading, on 21 December 1853, that Mary Rusher Collier gave birth to a second son. This second son William and Mary named William James.

On 15 February 1856, again at number 20, Broad Street, Reading, Mary Rusher Collier gave birth to her third and last child, a son. This third son William and Mary named, John Osborne.

They had named their first-born son, Philip Davies... Philip Davies Collier.

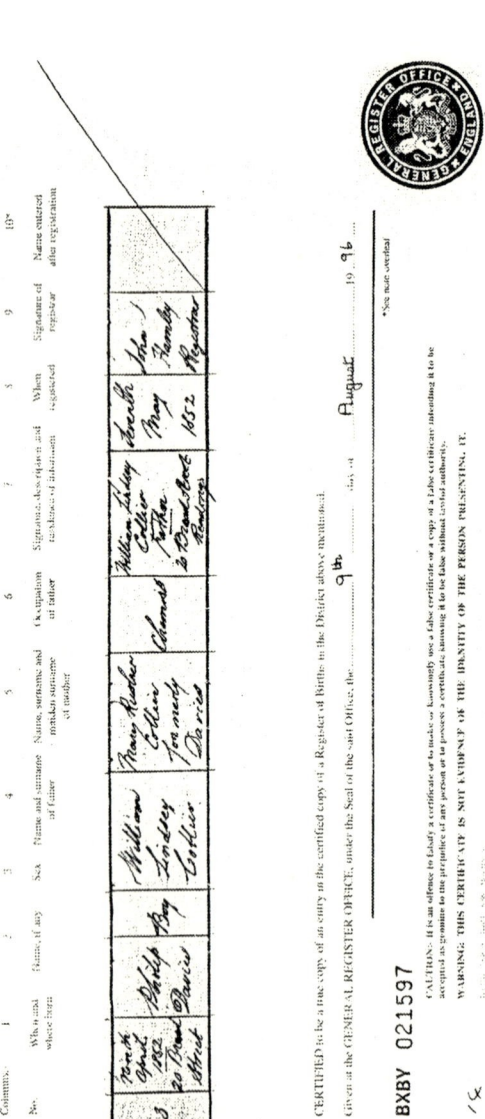

CERTIFIED COPY OF AN ENTRY OF BIRTH

GIVEN AT THE GENERAL REGISTER OFFICE

Application Number: B007478

REGISTRATION DISTRICT: Reading

1852. BIRTH in the Sub-district of St Lawrence Reading in the County of Berks

No.	When and where born	Name, if any	Sex	Name and surname of father	Name, surname and maiden surname of mother	Occupation of father	Signature, description and residence of informant	When registered	Signature of registrar	Name entered after registration
1	Ninth April 1852 20 Broad Street	Philip Davies	Boy	William Lindsey Collier	Mary Hester Collier formerly Davies	Chemist	William Lindsey Collier Father 20 Broad Street Reading	Seventh May 1852	John Family Registrar	

CERTIFIED to be a true copy of an entry in the certified copy of a Register of Births in the District above mentioned.

Given at the GENERAL REGISTER OFFICE, under the Seal of the said Office, the 9th day of August 19 96

BXBY 021597

CAUTION: It is an offence to falsify a certificate or to make or knowingly use a false certificate or a copy of a false certificate intending it to be accepted as genuine to the prejudice of any person or to possess a certificate knowing it to be false without lawful authority.

WARNING: THIS CERTIFICATE IS NOT EVIDENCE OF THE IDENTITY OF THE PERSON PRESENTING IT.

*See note overleaf

Philip Davies Collier, birth certificate, 9 April 1852

Philip Davies Collier

Philip Davies Collier was born at number 20, Broad Street, Reading, on Good Friday, 9 April 1852. It is presumed here that he and his two brothers were brought up and schooled in Reading. Philip Davies decided that, when he grew up, he wished to follow in his father's footsteps and become a chemist.

William James was similarly inclined. If John Osborne ever nurtured the same ambition, he changed his mind for he would choose a career as a bookseller.

In 1859 or 1860 the family had need of larger premises and they removed to number 149, Friar Street, Reading, (the building no longer exists) next door to the Great Western coal offices, whilst 20, Broad Street was taken over by Martin Abijah – tailor, woollen draper and undertaker. (He would continue in this business until at least 1890.)

Operating from number 149, Friar Street, William Lindsey Collier continued his business but on a larger scale, and he increased his range to include the sale of photographic equipment. It was an endeavour sufficiently ambitious to justify the employment of a man, a boy and a seventeen-year-old apprentice; the latter named Henry Gillman, who resided with the family.

Mary Rusher was kept busy in the shop and accordingly it was considered necessary to employ a young woman; Mary Ann Bunce, as a nursery governess to look after the children; together with a servant girl named Mary Ann Crook.

The family were still living at number 149, Friar Street, when William Lindsey Collier had a presentiment of death and on 28 January in the year 1870, he prepared his last will and testament.

On 2 August of that year he died. Charles Cook of Child Street, Reading was in attendance. At the age of just forty-five years, William Lindsey Collier had allowed his health to deteriorate to a considerable degree. The cause of his death was given as heart disease, dropsy and exhaustion.

In his will, William Lindsey Collier left a sum, stated as being less than £1,500, to his well beloved wife Mary Rusher. In her care he left three sons, Philip Davies, aged eighteen years, William James, aged sixteen years and John Osborne, aged fourteen years.

The 1871 census records that the reduced family were still residing at number 149, Friar Street, with four additional persons (presumed to be Mary's relatives) all named Davies. There is no mention of the business and Mary Rusher's income is stated to be derived from interest and rent. (It seems likely that George Davies, aged twenty-nine years, and described as a chemist, was running the business until the sale of 149, Friar Street could be effected.)

Some short time after this sad period Mary Rusher Collier removed to a house which was situated just 200 yards from the Davies family home in Russell Street. Kelly's Directory for the year 1874 records that Mary Rusher Collier was living at number 153, Oxford Road, Reading, whilst the property at 149, Friar Street, was being managed by J R Knowles (chemist & dentist – he was still there in 1890).

Assuming that the move was made in 1871 (there is no extant copy of Kelly's Directory for 1871, 1872 or 1873) it is likely that her three sons joined her at this address. (The house is still there today.) But the 1881 census records that all the sons have departed and Mary is living at 153, Oxford Road with servant and companion Eliza Anderson then aged thirty years.

It seems probable that, following their father's death, Philip Davies and his brother, William James, had an immediate need of employment and possibly they continued working at 149, Friar Street, employed by J. R. Knowles. It is likely that, following the death of William Lindsey, the three sons stayed with their mother for a year or two, at 153, Oxford Road, before Philip Davies and William James decided to seek their fortune in London. It seems probable that they decamped circa 1872–1873 leaving John Osborne at home.

When we next encounter Philip Davies Collier he has achieved his ambition to become a chemist or, more correctly, he styles himself as such, for there is no record of his having achieved a qualification in any branch of chemistry (this applies equally to William James Collier).

(The Pharmacy Act of 1868 required that all pharmaceutical chemists, and chemists and druggists, must be registered in order to practise, though this would not have precluded Philip Davies, or William James, from practising as assistant to a druggist/chemist.)

He is living in the old French Quarter of central London, on the north side of Oxford Street (presumed) and he has found employment with a chemist or in a hospital (presumed).

Philip is about to embark upon a venture that will change his life.

It is October in the year 1876, and Philip Davies Collier stands not only on the threshold of matrimony but on the threshold of embracing a new religion.

Assuming that Philip met his beloved sometime between 1874 and 1876 it is to 153, Oxford Road, Reading, that he took her to meet his mother, Mary Rusher Collier.

The betrothed of Philip Davies Collier will marry a Collier named Davies.

And should the name of Philip's betrothed chance to be Mary, she will then become a woman named Mary Collier.

So... who *did* marry Philip Davies Collier?

Number 153, Oxford Road, Reading

The French Connection

> She made several trips to Paris and rode about in a carriage.
> She was known as Mary but her real name was Marie.
>
> Joseph Barnett 1888

At the outbreak of the French Revolution in the year 1791, a considerable number of the French aristocracy crossed the Channel and sought refuge in England.

Most came to London and specifically to the area north of Oxford Street. So great was the initial influx that part of the Middlesex Hospital on Mortimer Street was requisitioned for their accommodation; though how the patients fared is not recorded.

Large numbers of the French aristocracy settled in the area and soon the streets of St Marylebone echoed with the great names of the *ancien régime*: de Polignac, de Montalembert, de Castries, de la Tour du Pin, and many other great families.

There was an immediate need to cater for the refugees' spiritual requirements and, initially, divine offices were celebrated variously in a house in Paddington Street; at St Patrick's, Soho Square; and in the various embassy chapels.

This was however only a temporary solution and, accordingly, a site was purchased in Little King Street to facilitate the construction of a chapel. Building commenced almost immediately and, it is said, many of the clergy and even members of the French court aided the workmen with their own hands; the sooner that the chapel might be completed.

The chapel was blessed and dedicated to Notre Dame de l'Annonciation, on 15 March 1799, and there, most if not all of the Bourbon monarchs who came to England as exiles or as visitors – Louis XVIII, Charles X, Louis Philippe and Queen Amélie, the Duchess d'Angoulème – heard Mass at the chapel. The Duc d'Orléans took his first communion there, and the

Prince Imperial, his last before he left England for the Zulu war (1879) in which he was killed.

With the restoration of the monarchy in the year 1814, many of the *émigré* returned to France and the congregation dwindled.

Soon afterwards the little chapel was raised to the status of Chapel Royal of France by letters patent of Louis XVIII, and endowed with an income from the royal treasury which was subsequently withdrawn in the year 1848. Thereafter, the chapel began to experience serious economic difficulties and was dependent for its survival on private donations. The situation was further exacerbated by the fact that a large number of the *émigré* who had chosen to stay in England, removed to the area of Leicester Square. The chapel's status was reduced to that of a private chapel, open for public worship under the patronage of the Toursel family.

A new French church, dedicated to Notre Dame de France, was opened in Leicester Place, off Leicester Square, in the year 1865 and the chapel's return to its former glory was now impossible.

A subscription list was raised, which attracted the great names of old France and the Empire, and so the little chapel survived to celebrate its centenary in 1899. Abbé Toursel had rededicated the chapel to St Louis of France.

The last service was held on the morning of Sunday, 12 February 1911. The closing ceremony was preached by the Abbé Henri Vatan. The building, which had had its glorious day was reduced to ignominy. It served, at various times, as a furniture warehouse, a day nursery, an undertaker's mortuary chapel, a Protestant prayer room and a synagogue.

John Yeowell, whose article in *The Royalist* (reprinted in *The Author*) has been used extensively for this information, had this to say in 1958:

> The old Chapel Royal of St Louis of France is the second oldest post-Reformation Catholic place of worship in London. If action is not taken very soon we shall witness its further desecration and eventual destruction.

Little King Street underwent a name change and, certainly within the year 1876, was known as Little George Street. Later still it was named Carton Street and today it is a cul-de-sac without a name (almost directly opposite to the Worcester Arms public house on George Street) reduced in status to a service road and car park.

The French Chapel Royal is no more. The site where once it stood is now covered by an office block.

It was in the little chapel, in the year 1876, that a beautiful French woman married a Collier named Davies. Her name was... Marie.

French Chapel, Little George Street

Wedding Bells

> She married a Collier named Davis or Davies – Davies I think.
>
> Joseph Barnett, 1888

On Friday, 6 October 1876, Philip and Marie travelled to the French Catholic chapel, Little George Street, and there Philip Davies Collier was baptised into the Holy Roman Catholic faith.

Abbé Louis Toursel made the entry in the register and signed his name. Canon, Joseph Toursel, countersigned. Philip Davies Collier appended his signature in full and the entry was witnessed by Marie, giving her first name and her surname only.

The following day, Saturday, 7 October 1876, dawned overcast and wet but, undaunted, Philip and Marie returned to the little chapel and there they were married – to love honour and cherish until death should part them.

Canon Joseph Toursel made the entry in the register and signed his name. D S A Ballard and W J Collier witnessed the entry. Philip Davies Collier signed his name in full and, this time, so did Marie... Marie Thérèse Julien.

So... who was Marie Thérèse Julien?

Entry of baptism – Philip Davies Collier

Jill the Ripper

The question should not be, is it possible that Marie Thérèse Julien was Mary Jane Kelly? But rather, is it possible that Marie Thérèse Julien was *not* Mary Jane Kelly?

Joseph Barnett styled himself Jack the Ripper and he was certainly a killer and he was the leader of the Murder Squad, but it was Marie Thérèse Julien, in the guise of her alter ego, Mary Jane Kelly, who was the Ripper in deed. And it was Marie Thérèse Julien who single-handedly killed, and then tore into bloody pieces, her hated cousin, on that long ago, cold, wet night of 8–9 November 1888, in room number 13, Millers Court.

In a later chapter, Marie Thérèse Julien will be considered in more detail and reviewed against a checklist.

Entry of marriage, P D Collier and M T Julien

CERTIFIED COPY OF AN ENTRY OF MARRIAGE — GIVEN AT THE GENERAL REGISTER OFFICE

Application Number R 001842

1918-70. Marriage solemnized at the Church of Marylebone in the County of Middlesex

When Married	Name and Surname	Age	Condition	Rank or Profession	Residence at the time of Marriage	Father's Name and Surname	Rank or Profession of Father
1918 23 October	Philip David Collier	24	Bachelor	Chemist	3 Gospel Place	William Sidney Collier (dec'd)	Chemist
	Marie Thérèse Julien	25	Spinster	—	3 Gospel Place	Joseph Jean Etienne Julien	Coach-maker

Married in the Parish Catholic Church according to the Rites and Ceremonies of the Catholic Church by Licence, by me, J. Fauvell

This Marriage was solemnized between us: Philip David Collier / Marie Thérèse Julien
In the Presence of us: G.L.A. Pollard / M.J. Collier

Thomas Louis Nickols, Registrar

CERTIFIED to be a true copy of an entry ... Given at the General Register Office ... 18th day of July 96

Marriage certificate, P D Collier and M T Julien

A Man Named Morganstone

> At one time Marie lived with a man named Morganstone. I never saw that man in my life.
>
> Joseph Barnett 1888

According to which version you read, Joseph Barnett stated that Marie lived with a man named Morganstone either near Stepney gas works or in Pennington Street. The actual location is, almost certainly, irrelevant since Morganstone never existed.

This is an abridged extract from John J Robinson's book, *Born in Blood, The Lost Secrets of Freemasonry*:

> On March 13 1826, Captain William Morgan of Batavia, New York, signed a contract for the printing of a book that he said would reveal the secret grips, signs and rituals of Freemasonry. In the consternation that broke out among the local members of the order, the printer's shop was set on fire and, in what he termed an act of harassment, Morgan was arrested and jailed for non-payment of debt. An anonymous benefactor paid the debt for him, but as Morgan left the jail he was seized by men waiting out front and forced into a coach that immediately dashed off on the road north. He was taken to the abandoned Fort Niagara and held there as a prisoner. That much was confirmed later when five Masons confessed to the abduction and confinement. The Masonic version was that he was released, or escaped, and fled to Canada, whilst the anti-Masonic story was that his captors had taken Morgan on the river in a boat, where he was tied to heavy stones and then rolled overboard. No body was ever recovered, but the public, and many Masons, were convinced that Morgan had been murdered to protect Masonic secrets.
>
> As arrests were made and a trial set, the public learned that the local sheriff, the judge, and some of the jurors were Masons. The sheriffs of the towns through which the kidnappers had passed were Masons. So was the secretary of state of the United States, and it came out that New York Governor DeWitt Clinton was a past Grand Master. It appeared that Freemasonry might be

functioning as an underground government.

Impromptu Masonic conventions were called at which the murder of Morgan was condemned, and thousands of practicing Freemasons resigned from the order. An Anti-Masonic party was organized as a third political party in the United States, with formal fund raising, its own newspapers, and the first national convention at which a nominee for president was selected. The most vocal champion of the Anti-Masonic party was Congressman John Quincy Adams, who had served as the sixth president of the United States. Masons claimed that the alleged murder of Morgan was just an excuse for Adams to attack Freemasonry, that he was bitter that he had been denied a second term as president because of the popularity and political machinations of Freemason Andrew Jackson.

Whatever the reason, Adams passed up no opportunity to condemn Freemasonry, alleging that the murder of Morgan had been in line with the murderous oaths of the Masonic order. He appealed to all Freemasons to abandon the order and to help abolish it once and for all since it was totally incompatible with a Christian democracy...

...For a while it appeared that Adams would have his wish, as the Masons who resigned the order in the furor of the Morgan murder allegations were not replaced by new recruits. Morgan's book was published by the burned-out printer, who restored his shop and printed the book the following year, 1827, under its extraordinary copyrighted title, *Illustrations of Masonry by one of the Fraternity who has devoted Thirty Years to the subject. "God said, Let there be Light, and there was Light."* Its revelation of the bloody oaths accelerated the events of the next few years, including the growth of the Anti-Masonic party. Among its unintended markets were Masters of Masonic lodges, who purchased the book to aid in staging ceremonies, since Freemasonry still maintained the rule of verbal communication only, and Morgan's book provided the first "guide book" to help administer the complex rituals of initiation. It is still published today, under the much shorter (and much more sensational) title of *Freemasonry Exposed*.[6]

---

[6]John J Robinson, *Born in Blood, The Lost Secrets of Freemasonry*, M Evans & Co, New York, 1989.

This extract is from *Tales of the New Babylon: Paris 1869–1875*, by Rupert Christiansen, and relates to the Franco-Prussian War 1870–1871.

29 APRIL [1871]

Over the previous week or so the Freemasons had taken a lead in making overtures of conciliation and peace between the Commune and Versailles – it was they who had negotiated the truce at Neuilly on 25 April.

Encouraged by the granting of that small concession, the Freemasons of Paris had called a meeting at the Théâtre du Châtelet on 26 April. They voted to march to the front line, where they would plant their banners on the ramparts and wait for the shooting to stop. A delegation went on to the Hôtel de Ville to inform them of this initiative.

Whose side were they on? There was some confusion over this question. Conspiracy theorists believed that the Internationale was behind Freemasonry or that Freemasonry was behind the Internationale, and it was certainly true that at least fifteen Masons sat on the Commune. But there were probably twice as many involved in the government of Versailles, and one can only assume that their agenda was sincerely pacific and disinterested.

The important Grand Orient lodge disassociated itself from a parade which would violate the Masonic code of secrecy and there was some argy-bargy about the ethics of Masonry being seen to take such an active and partisan political stand. Nevertheless, in golden sunshine, a magnificent procession assembled on the morning of 29 April. Led by a white banner inscribed in red "Love One Another", fifteen thousand Masons from sixty-five male lodges and one women's lodge paraded from the Place de la Bastille, down the rue de Rivoli, up the Champs Élysées to the Porte Maillot, chanting their ritual hymns and sporting their ritual robes and insignia, never before seen in public. A small balloon emblazoned with the Masonic triangle was launched and it was rumoured that irresistible magical powers passed down from the biblical King Solomon would be released into the ether.

Arriving at the ramparts as the Versaillais guns continued to fire, the Masons planted their glittering scarlet, gold and purple banners, interspersed with white flags. After more hymns and emanations, the shooting quietened (but not before bullets had pierced a banner and killed two Masons). A deputation went on to Courbevoie, where Thiers received the mellifluous injunctions with an indifference bordering on irritation. There could be no negotiations with the Commune. Criminals must be punished: Paris must surrender or face the consequences.[7]

So... what was Joseph Barnett saying and who was he speaking to?

The reference to Morganstone was made at the inquest into the death of Mary Jane Kelly, and Joseph Barnett was addressing the coroner, Dr Macdonald. Dr Macdonald understood Joseph Barnett perfectly:

"You have given your evidence very well."

It is conjectured here that Morganstone is an amalgamation of Morgan and stone: the stone that weighed Morgan down – and that the person alluded to by Joseph Barnett was Philip Davies Collier: a man not sympathetic to the Freemasons and, possibly, strongly opposed.

It is further conjectured here that Marie Thérèse Julien was a Freemason.

---

[7]Rupert Christiansen, *Paris Babylon: Grandeur, Decadence and Revolution 1869–75*, Pimlico, London, 2003. Also see *Tales of the new Babylon: Paris 1869–1875*, Sinclair-Stevenson, 1994.

A Man Named Joseph Flemming

> A man named Joseph Flemming passed as Marie's husband and frequently visited her. She was very fond of him.
>
> Joseph Barnett, 1888

Joseph Flemming lived in Bethnal Green Road. He was a mason's plasterer. And so, Joseph Barnett informed coroner, Dr Macdonald that he, in his guise as alter ego, Joseph Flemming, was a Master Mason.

Dr Macdonald understood perfectly:

> There is other evidence that I do not propose to call, for if we at once make public every fact brought forward in connection with this terrible murder the ends of justice might be retarded.

Joseph Barnett needed an alter ego to enable him to impart information about himself, but only to those possessing esoteric information. An outsider, not in possession of esoteric information, would assume that Joseph Flemming was an entity in his own right. Why Joseph chose the name Flemming is not clear. There was a Flemming Street (now Hare Walk) off the Kingsland Road, Haggerston, just half a mile north of Dorset Street. Was there a Masonic lodge on Flemming Street so that Flemming has an arcane meaning, the easier for Dr Macdonald to understand? Or did Joseph and Marie live on Flemming Street before they moved to Millers Court?

Barnett stated that he and Marie had three addresses immediately prior to removing to Millers Court: George Street, Paternoster Row and Brick Lane. No mention of Flemming Street. But there is only Joseph Barnett's word for these addresses and all of them are suspect since there is no reliable independent corroboration of Marie's presence in the East End until about March of the year 1888.

But perhaps, there is another reason for the choice of Flemming. Perhaps, just as Morgan was considered to be a bad mason, so Flemming was considered to be a good mason.

The Wedding – the Witnesses

The witnesses at the wedding of Philip Davies Collier and Marie Thérèse Julien were W J Collier and D S A Ballard.

W J Collier was obviously William James Collier, Philip's brother, then aged twenty-two years and ten months. This is the last time we will meet William James Collier. I have been unable to trace any record of him after the wedding. I believe that he went abroad where he married and produced children but this is not a certain fact. William James Collier will be considered again when we examine the last will and testament of Mary Rusher Collier.

The second witness was not so obvious, just who was D S A Ballard?

The Landlady

> Marie had stayed in a fashionable house in the West End of London.
>
> Joseph Barnett 1888

Aside from a beautiful and exotic name, Dinah Susanna Adelaide Ballard was something of a disappointment.

She had been born in Middlesex in the year 1831, daughter of a policeman, William Ballard. She had at least one brother and at least one sister, both of whom married; but Dinah remained single all her life.

The census for the year 1871 shows that Dinah resided at number 3, Chapel Place, Cavendish Square, with her father, William, then aged seventy-seven. They shared the premises with Harry, aged eight years and William, aged six years, both described as grandsons. In addition, the house provided accommodation for Elizabeth Carpenter, a servant aged twenty-seven years.

In the month of June in the year 1876, William Ballard died aged eighty-three years. In his last will and testament he left all his worldly goods to his dear daughter, Dinah Susanna Adelaide.

No doubt his death was a sad loss, but life had to go on and Dinah, finding herself without an intimate confidante and needing additional income, decided to let a room or rooms.

Philip and Marie were an attractive couple shortly to be married. It was decided then. Number 3, Chapel Place, would be the newly-weds first home.

In the year 1876, when Dinah was a witness to the wedding of Philip Davies Collier and Marie Thérèse Julien, she was aged forty-five years and she had less than five years left to live.

On 30 December 1880 afflicted with typhoid fever and a presentiment of her own mortality, Dinah drafted her last will and testament.

She died 14 January 1881, at number 3, Chapel Place, Cavendish Square. Present at the death was her nephew, John Donald, Jnr.

The census for the year 1881 records that James J Reynolds, a 55-year-old widower who was a retired pharmaceutical chemist, and described as a boarder, resided at number 3, Chapel Place.

Dinah had nominated James John Reynolds to be the executor of her will and she had set aside sufficient funds to cover her outstanding debts and her funeral expenses (about £500). The unexpired lease of number 3, Chapel Place, together with furniture, plate, books, engravings, pictures, china and clothes, she left to her beloved sister, Maria Alice Donald, who then resided at Raleigh House, Anerley, just twelve miles south of central London.

Dinah also left in the care of her beloved sister, her nephew, William James Ballard, son of their brother, James Ballard, with the wish that said nephew show her every kindness and consideration.

Of Philip Davies and Marie Thérèse, there was no sign.

(Chapel Place exists today as does the chapel itself, St Peter's Church, built in the year 1724.

In the year 1876, when Philip and Marie were newlyweds, there were ten residences along the eastern side of Chapel Place. The Trade Directory for the year 1880 records number 3 as a lodging house, managed by Miss Dinah Ballard.

In the year 1909 and again in the year 1937, D H Evans department store expanded their premises to the eastern border of Chapel Place. It seems probable that number 3 disappeared in 1909. Certainly none of the buildings that existed in 1876 survive today. The home of Dinah Susanna Adelaide Ballard is no more.)

Chapel, Chapel Place, today

James John Reynolds, boarder and executor of Dinah Susanna Adelaide Ballard's will was described as a retired pharmaceutical chemist.

So... who was James John Reynolds?

The Best Laid Schemes

James John Reynolds was born in the year 1826, in Bungay, Suffolk. On 5 November 1856, when he was just thirty years of age, he passed the Royal Pharmaceutical major examination which awarded him the status of pharmaceutical chemist. His address, at that time, was number 15, Hanover Street, just off Hanover Square. Certainly by 1862, James was resident at number 3, Hanover Street, where he operated a business with a man named John Lloyd Bullock, trading as "J L Bullock & J J Reynolds", pharmaceutical chemists and druggists. Bullock and Reynolds employed two assistants who lived at number 3 and, possibly, other assistants who resided elsewhere. The census for the year 1871 records this situation:

John L Bullock	Aged 59	Pharmaceutical chemist	
James J Reynolds	45	do	
George C Fox	23	do	Assistant
William James	35	do	do
Mary Butt		Servant	
Emma Challis		Servant	

In 1877–1878 James John Reynolds retired and he took up residence at number 3, Chapel Place, in rooms recently vacated by Philip Davies Collier and his wife. John Lloyd Bullock continued the business at number 3, Hanover Street, trading as "Bullock J L & Co".

James John Reynolds died at number 3, Chapel Place, in the year 1890. He was aged sixty-five years. (The building where first we met James John Reynolds; number 15, Hanover Street, is still there; having recently been vacated by Scandinavian Seaways (1998).

The building situated at number 3, Hanover Street, where once traded J L Bullock & J J Reynolds, is gone. The ground floor of the present number 3 is a bar called All Bar One. The higher levels are occupied by The Indonesia Tourist Promotion Office).

In the year 1841, The Pharmaceutical Society of Great Britain was founded and, a process whereby pharmacists could obtain evidence of their competence was introduced. There were two different examinations.

The minor exam awarded the most basic qualification and entitled the successful applicant to become an assistant to a pharmacist. The major examination was intended for established business – owning pharmacists who were, or aspired to be, members of the Society, though some non-proprietors did pass the major examination after first passing the minor examination.

The 1868 Pharmacy Act stipulated that the minor examination was to become the legal minimum requirement for all new entrants to the profession. In order to learn his trade, an aspiring pharmacist usually trained for several years with a practising pharmacist and supplemented this training with a course of study at a recognised school.

In 1870, the year William Lindsey Collier died, Philip Davies Collier was just eighteen years of age. He was obviously aware of the 1868 Pharmacy Act and the requirement to obtain a qualification should he aspire to own his own business. Undoubtedly, the death of his father caused a major reappraisal of his future and this would necessarily be tempered by concern for his mother's welfare. The immediate concern would be the sale of 149, Friar Street, since only William Lindsey was qualified to run the business. Then the family would need to be re-housed and there would be an urgent need to ensure adequate financial income for the future.

It seems likely that, whatever plans Philip Davies may have had at the beginning of the year 1870, they were put on hold following the death of his father.

It probably took about three years before the situation stabilised sufficiently for Philip Davies to review his future anew, after which time he decided that he would seek a placement with a pharmaceutical chemist in an organization of some stature. It would be of some advantage if this organisation was able to provide living accommodation.

It seems likely that, circa 1873, one or both of the assistants to J L Bullock & J J Reynolds qualified and departed from their employ, leaving a vacancy, or vacancies, at number 3, Hanover Street. Possibly through an advertisement in a trade magazine; possibly through a recommendation, it is suggested here that Philip Davies Collier applied for the post and was the successful applicant.

So, circa 1873, when Philip Davies Collier was just twenty-one years of age, he removed to London and to a great new beginning. The future was assured. He was a competent chemist and, in a few years, he would be a qualified chemist.

But the best laid schemes of mice and men...

Marie Thérèse Julien

Marie Thérèse Julien was born in the 11th arrondissement (today's 6th arrondissement) Paris, France, Thursday, 27 March in the year 1851.

Three days later, on Sunday, 30 March 1851, at the church of St Sulpice, Paris (the same church where her parents had married in the year 1847) Marie Thérèse Julien was baptised into the Holy Roman Catholic Faith. The certificate of baptism records that Marie Thérèse's godmother was her paternal grandmother, Anne Thérèse Bailly, a resident of Semur, Burgundy.

Her godfather was her uncle, by marriage to her mother's sister; a man named Honoré Julien Lepage, a resident of Paris but originating from a small village called Verte-le-Grand, some twenty miles south of the capital.

Marie Thérèse's proud parents recorded their address as rue Vieux Colombier, number 15. Paris, France. Almost certainly this is the address where Marie Thérèse Julien was born.

(Rue Vieux Colombier exists today. The road runs in an east–west line; the Place St Sulpice at its easternmost end. The great church of St Sulpice still dominates the square today and the building features in most modern guidebooks.)

Five hundred yards to the north-west of rue Vieux Colombier is the immense École Pratique de Médecine, the medical school for first and second year students.

Six hundred yards to the east of rue Vieux Colombier lies the Boulevard St Germain. On the south side of the boulevard is the École de Médecine with a second frontage on the Rue de l'École de Médecine.

Marie Thérèse's father was a man named Jean Etienne Julien and Jean Etienne had followed his own father's occupation, that of *sellier* (saddle/harness maker) though, certainly through the years 1847 to 1853, he followed the career of a merchant, running a dairy products store and working as a *crémier* (a milkman).

Birth certificate, Marie Thérèse Julien

In the year 1847 Jean Etienne, then aged twenty-two years (a minor under the then French law which stipulated twenty-five as the age of majority) married a woman aged thirty years, a woman named Marie Catherine Loeffler.[8] They married in the church of St Sulpice, 23 March 1847, and the marriage certificate records that immediately prior to the marriage Jean Etienne was residing with his brother, Adolphe, at rue de Coeur Volant, number 8, Paris (now named Grégoire de Tour) whilst Marie Catherine was residing at rue Vieux Colombier, number 19, Paris, just two doors from where the couple would be resident in the year 1851.

Jean Etienne Julien had been born in the year 1825, in Semur, Burgundy. He was the son of Claude Julien, *sellier*, and of Anne Thérèse Bailly, who was destined to become Marie Thérèse's godmother. It is known that Jean Etienne had one brother – Adolphe – though there may have been other siblings.

---

[8] Loeffler. There exists a variety of spellings of this name.

It is presumed here that the life of a *sellier* in Semur, circa 1845, was not exciting enough for the young Jean Etienne nor for his brother Adolphe, so the two sought their fortune in the city of enchantment – Paris – and there Jean Etienne found that life as a milkman was, at least initially, more attractive than life as a harness maker in Semur. It happened perhaps that when Jean Etienne was delivering the milk to number 19, rue Vieux Colombier, he met a lovely lady, a lady named Marie Catherine Loeffler.

Marie Catherine Loeffler was born in a tiny village a few miles north-west of Paris: Cormeilles-en-Vexin. Marie Catherine was the daughter of a man named Jean Louis Loeffler, *serrurier* (a locksmith), and of a woman named Marie Madeleine Finet.

Marie Madeleine and Jean Louis married circa 1814. Marie Madeleine gave birth to a child on Christmas Eve, in the year 1815, and they named the daughter Marie Madeleine Marguerite, but tragically she died a few months later.

Marie Catherine was the second child of the union. She was born 29 January, in the year 1817.

In April 1820, Marie Catherine was blessed with a brother. He was named after his father, Jean Louis. So far as can be ascertained, Jean Louis Loeffler survived to old age.

In 1825, a sister was born. She was named Louise Marguerite. Louise Marguerite would, at the age of twenty-five years in the church of St Sulpice, Paris, marry a man named Honoré Julien Lepage, a *menuiser* (carpenter) and the son of a *vigneron* (vine dresser/vine grower) from a village a few miles south of Paris – Vert-le-Grand. It was Honoré Julien Lepage who was destined to become the godfather of Marie Thérèse Julien and, even as Marie Thérèse was being baptised, her godfather was feeling a little anxious. His wife was expecting their first child. He was born just two weeks later. Marie Thérèse had a cousin – Ferdinand Julien Lepage.

It has not been ascertained how many siblings Marie Thérèse had. But she certainly had one. He was born 21 March 1853, at rue Vieux Colombier, number 5.

Just six days away from attaining the age of two years, Marie Thérèse Julien had acquired a brother. On 23 March 1853, the child was baptised into the Holy Roman Catholic faith at the church of St Sulpice, and, no doubt, Marie Thérèse clutched her mother's hand, overawed by the grandeur of the building and the solemnity of the occasion. The boy was named Joseph.

The godfather of Joseph was a man named Joseph Steinbauer, *sellier*, who resided a few doors away from the family Julien, at number 22, rue Vieux Colombier. His godmother was a woman named Josephine Elisa Scherer who resided at number 11.

In the year 1873, when Joseph Julien was aged twenty years, his birth certificate was reconstituted at the request of his cousin Ferdinand, who, at that time, resided with his family at rue Cardinet, number 1. The reconstituted birth certificate records that Joseph was, in 1873, 710 mm tall.

It is not, of course, possible to rebuild a person's life from scraps of paper, and the life of Marie Thérèse Julien is no exception. A social historian may conjure with the influences that prevailed but not the way in which a given individual might react to those influences.

It can be stated with certainty that Marie Thérèse was a Catholic girl born and raised into a Catholic family and it can be said, fairly safely, that the family were, at the least, moderately prosperous, and that Marie Thérèse enjoyed the benefit of a good education. It can be conjectured that Marie Thérèse came into contact with a large number of medical students given that she lived in close proximity to the schools of medicine.

The year of Marie's birth, 1851, is thought by many British historians to have been the high point of the British Empire, the year of the Great Exhibition. In France, the year 1851 was the year of the *coup d'état*.

In December of the year 1848, Louis Napoleon was elected President of the Second Republic but, by the *coup d'état* of 2 December 1851, he violently set aside the constitution and he assumed dictatorial powers. A year later he was raised, by the almost unanimous voice of the nation, to the status of emperor Napoleon III. It was the beginning of the second empire.

It was also the beginning of a long period of relative prosperity with France making great advances in the development of her natural resources and in manufacturing. Paris gradually assumed the role of the capital city of Europe – the City of Light – and thousands of visitors came to be entranced by its style and beauty. This was the atmosphere that graced the formative years of Marie Thérèse Julien. It was a period that reached its height in the year 1867, the year of the great Paris Exhibition, the year when Marie attained the age of sixteen. It is possible that this was the year she married a handsome Frenchman.

> She married when she was very young, about sixteen.
>
> Joseph Barnett, 1888.

But the Golden Age was dying. The light burned, briefly, ever brighter, the music louder, the dancing more frenetic, the visitors more louche, more debauched. Paris had become the new Babylon and, if financial embarrassment of the government caused unrest and discontent, few could hear the cries of the disaffected over the screams of delight of the pleasure seekers.

The band played on. The dancers twirled. The lights blazed. The party was almost over.

History would record the next act as… the Franco-Prussian War.

The Franco-Prussian War

> She married when very young, about sixteen but her husband was killed in some explosion, two or three years later.
>
> Joseph Barnett 1888

> She married a collier named Davies or Davis – Davies I think.
>
> Joseph Barnett, 1888

It is possible that when Joseph Barnett made these statements he was referring not to one marriage, but to two marriages i.e. that when Marie Thérèse Julien married Philip Davies Collier, she was a widow.

An earlier marriage has not been traced. The reason for concealing the existence of an earlier marriage isn't even guessed at. This possibility is expressed in the full awareness that, in the year 1876, Marie Thérèse described her status as "single".

In the nineteenth century, the German Empire comprised of a number of separate states. The largest, strongest – and most warlike – of these states was Prussia. Otto von Bismarck (later Prince and Chancellor of the German Empire) had a dream – a united Germany under Prussian domination. In order for this dream to materialise it was first necessary to expel Austria from the German Federation. The Prussian/Austrian war was over in a few weeks and Austria was forced to withdraw from German affairs. Prussia then annexed Hanover and Hesse-Cassel, incorporated Schleswig-Holstein, formed a Prussian Federation, then made treaties with Bavaria and other south German states.

In the year 1870, the Spanish expelled their shamelessly Bourbon Queen, Isabella, and the crown of Spain fell vacant. Spain offered the crown to a Hohenzollern (a principality of Prussia) prince, a gesture that was opposed by France, who considered that a political connexion between a united Germany and Spain would place them in an invidious position.

In the event, the Hohenzollern prince declined the crown, but the fact that the offer had been made at all indicated, to the French, that there existed a sinister Prussian intrigue. France decided to insist on an assurance from Prussia that the candidacy of the Hohenzollern prince not be renewed.

With this in mind, the French ambassador travelled to the spa town of Ems, where the Prussian King William was taking the waters. King William politely, but firmly, refused to guarantee that the Hohenzollern prince was permanently out of the running but he assured the French ambassador that, since the crown had been declined, it was an offer unlikely to be repeated and, if it was repeated, unlikely to be accepted. This was scarcely the iron-clad guarantee that the French ambassador required, but worse was to come.

Count Bismarck was not averse to a war with France, indeed he desired a conflict which would serve to unite the Germans in a common cause.

There was a bonus prize – the province of Alsace-Lorraine. Bismarck seized the opportunity to rub salt into the open French wound. He arranged for publication of the Ems interview but ensured that this was slanted in such a way as to infer that King William had deliberately insulted the French ambassador.

The published account had the desired effect. It was construed as a slap in the face that demanded satisfaction. French public opinion was outraged. Once again Bismarck seized the initiative, and he further provoked the situation by ordering mobilisation of the Prussian army.

Louis Charles Napoleon, later Napoleon III, was born 20 April 1808.

He lived, in common with the rest of the Bonaparte family, in the shadow of his illustrious uncle. In the year 1852 he became Emperor of France and the army was re-modelled on Napoleonic lines. Mindful of the Napoleonic traditions he was anxious that his army should emulate them. The first real opportunity came with the Crimean war where the army acquitted itself well.

In the Austrian campaign of 1859 the French army were victorious at Magenta and Solferino but the victories were costly in terms of money and human life.

A protracted anti-guerrilla struggle in Mexico (1863–67), ended in humiliating withdrawal and, by the year 1869, Napoleon III's popularity had waned perceptibly.

Desperate situations demand desperate measures, and Napoleon, aided and abetted by his bellicose advisers and his even more bellicose Spanish wife, Empress Eugenie (who asserted proudly, "This is my war"), responded to the Ems insult by declaring war on Prussia. The date was 19 July 1870.

(Marie Thérèse Julien was just nineteen years and four months of age. She had been married (presumed) two to three years.)

Albeit that Napoleon III had been provoked and then propelled into making a declaration of war, it was nonetheless a poorly considered move.

Bismarck had calculated, correctly, that the French army was lacking in leadership and its motivation and its effectiveness had been blunted by years of virtual inactivity. If that was not bad enough, the Prussians outnumbered and outgunned the French. But these were not realities that bothered either the government or the people of France who, blinded by rhetoric, anticipated an easy victory.

Notwithstanding the fact that the Germans were more quickly mobilised, the French drove out a weak German detachment in Saarbrucken, 2 August 1870, but failed to capitalise on their initial success. France would not smile again.

At Wissembourg the French were overwhelmed. At Froeschwiller and then again at Spicheren, the gallant but badly led and poorly disciplined French were smashed by the implacable fighting machine that was the Prussian army.

In despair, the Emperor retired into the Borny garrison and transferred overall command to Marshall Bazaine. He also took the precaution of sending his son, the Prince Imperial, to Belgium.

The German 2nd army reached the Moselle, threatening the roads leading to Paris and, after fighting a bitter retreat, the French under the command of Marshall Bazaine, were besieged in the Metz garrison.

At Beaumont the French ran in disarray and thousands drowned as they scrambled to cross the river Meuse.

The demoralised survivors that constituted the main French army were driven back on the Sedan citadel. The big guns of the Prussian army were trained against the walls of the fortress and, after three days of fighting, the French raised the white flag. 82,000 soldiers were taken prisoner. It was the blackest of black days. Nothing now stood between the Prussian army and Paris.

Paris was a fortified city and had been since the year 1840 – it was virtually impregnable. But that was in 1840. Since that time the defences had been allowed to deteriorate to a marked degree. In a state of near panic the authorities responded to the impending danger. Heavy guns were installed within the fortifications and armament output was placed on maximum. In anticipation of a siege, Paris was provisioned on a vast scale.

The people reacted to the news with fury and they rioted through the streets screaming, "Down with the Empire!" Napoleon's Spanish wife, Eugenie, no longer proclaiming "This is my war" was smuggled out of France en route to England.

The Second Empire succumbed to the will of the people. The Third Republic was joyously proclaimed. The new government was titled "The Government of Self-Defence".

The rest of Europe looked on, amazed by Prussian strength and astonished at the hollowness of French imperial power.

As the Prussians moved ever closer to the French capital, demoralised and wounded soldiers flooded into Paris to help man the defences.

The Government of Self-Defence elected to defend. To attack was an invitation to disaster. Let the Prussians attack and the French would meet them in the streets where the inexperience of the National Guard would not matter.

But Bismarck had no intention of risking his highly trained troops in a barroom brawl.

> "There is a Republic in Paris," he wrote to his son. "Whether it will last or how it will develop, we must wait and see. My desire is that we let the people stew in their own juice and that we make ourselves at home in the conquered departments until we can go

forward. If we do this too soon we shall prevent them from quarrelling among themselves. Internal peace cannot last long with this socialist crowd at the head of affairs..."

On 17th September, the Prussians began to encircle Paris. On 18th September, the last mail train left the beleaguered city and, on 19 September, 1870, the last remaining telegraph lines, to the west, were cut. The siege of Paris had begun.

(Marie Thérèse Julien was nineteen years and six months old when the German army completed their encirclement of Paris, and, almost certainly, residing in today's 6th arrondissement. It is possible that she had some medical training; impossible to verify since there exist no student enrolment records in respect of the period 1839 to 1921. If she did enrol as a student this would have been circa 1867, the year of her supposed marriage and, if she did become a nurse then her contribution at a time when ambulance stations were being set up all over Paris, would have been considerable.)

There was little military action during the early days of the siege, though the medical teams were kept busy tending to the thousands of wounded who had managed to return to the capital. All places of entertainment had been closed by order, and many of these were utilised by the revolutionary *Clubs Rouge*.

As early as the tenth day, shortage of food was being perceived as a problem and restaurants were suspected of selling horse meat masquerading as beef. Profiteering and hoarding were rife and there were many violent demonstrations by angry, hungry mobs. Bismarck would have been pleased to see that, already the people were quarrelling amongst themselves and that honesty, integrity and compassion were virtues that were being abandoned.

Meanwhile the French army fought to re-take Chatillon: a position they had ignominiously abandoned at the commencement of the siege, but they were beaten back with both sides sustaining heavy losses.

The hospitals overflowed. Private houses gave over rooms so that the injured might be better cared for. Meanwhile Strasbourg and Toul had capitulated, releasing another German army to further harass the capital.

On 5 October 1870, Prussian headquarters were established at Versailles, just ten miles from the beleaguered capital.

On 7 October 1870 a column of women marched on the Hotel de Ville and demanded to be put in charge of the ambulances so that more men night be made available for the defence of Paris. They also demanded the right to fight: to form a corps of Amazons. The latter idea was rejected.

On 21 October, Metz capitulated and veteran statesman, Adolphe Thiers, returned from his tour of the European capitals, with proposals, not for victory but for an armistice.

The Government of Self-Defence cowered in the Hotel de Ville while an angry mob screamed for their downfall and the election of a radical left wing party. The National Guard restored order and, two days later, after a vote by the people, the Government of Self-Defence narrowly won the day.

November signalled the beginning of one of the worst winters in living memory and the unhappy citizens of Paris added cold to the misery of hunger.

The beleaguered city, the once renowned City of Light, was now a dark, insanitary and dangerous place.

The revolutionary clubs gained new members every day and possibly, round about this time, Marie Thérèse Julien allied herself to a revolutionary group, possibly itself allied to the Freemasons.

The Government members who had committed themselves to war to the end, began to argue amongst themselves. The grim reality was that food stocks were nearly exhausted and a market, specialising in rat meat, was opened in the centre of Paris.

And then, news of a great victory. The French army of the south had drive the Prussians out of Orléans. It was the signal to commence a great military push.

During the night of Sunday, 27 November 1870, the forts around Paris commenced a bombardment of the Prussian lines and on Tuesday, 30 November 1870 the main French army crossed the Marne and quickly took the enemy positions located at Champigny and Brie. The German counter-attack inflicted massive damage on the French positions but the French clung on until nightfall brought relief. The first day of December was reserved for burying the dead and returning the injured to Paris.

It was a bitterly cold morning when the Germans launched their next onslaught but after eight hours of bloody fighting the

French had held their ground. Both sides suffered heavy casualties.

By 5 December 1870, a large medical encampment was set up to the right of the battlefield, where French men and women attempted to rescue as many of the wounded as possible. The women, from every class, many dressed in black with white aprons and Geneva armlets, comforted the wounded as best they could and, probably, one of these women was named Marie Thérèse Julien.

The great sortie had failed. Another 12,000 dead, mangled and mutilated French soldiers were returned to the French capital. In stupefaction, the starving citizens of Paris stood silently in the streets and gaped in bewilderment at the seemingly endless parade of bloody flesh.

The despairing population turned increasingly to drink, and drunkenness became another problem to add to the multitude. In desperation the government prepared a new sortie. As Christmas approached, troops launched an attack the length of the northern perimeter. The Prussians were waiting. The slaughter was terrible. Along the line, the French made a few small gains but, after three days, the increasingly mutinous army was marched back to Paris. On Christmas day the Seine was covered with ice floes. Men and women chopped down trees for fuel, and the Paris zoo became a butcher's shop: elephant was added to the menu, but now the population were dying from malnutrition.

But for the new year, the Prussians had plans to warm up the good citizens of Paris.

On 5 January 1871, the bombardment commenced. Officially the bombardment was haphazard, though the number of times hospitals, schools, churches, and buildings flying the flag of Geneva, were hit suggested a deliberate policy. The church of St Sulpice, where Marie Thérèse Julien, had been baptised, was hit several times. The main left wing party, the Commune, advocated revolution. The end was near. Paris was burning.

The final sortie was designed as a simultaneous three-pronged attack against the Prussian lines but heavy rain, which had turned the roads to quagmires, prevented a combined assault. The Prussians fell back from their own front line to fixed battery positions and pounded the advancing troops. The French rearguard, confused by fog and rain, poured murderous fire into the rear of their own front ranks inflicting heavy casualties.

The retreat back to Paris and a two-day ceasefire to recover the dead and wounded signalled the end.

In the last week of the war alone the number of non-combat deaths numbered nearly 5,000, and Paris stood on the brink of a humanitarian disaster.

On 23 January 1871, negotiations for peace were opened at Versailles. On 26 January 1871, at midnight, Paris troops, by agreement with the Prussians, fired the last shot of the war. The Treaty of Frankfurt, 27 February 1871, was negotiated to include not just Paris but the whole of France.

The terms included the surrender of Alsace and the Northern part of Lorraine: France to pay a war indemnity of five thousand million francs and to endure the ignominy of a Prussian victory parade through the streets of Paris and occupation of parts of the capital until such time as the preliminaries had been ratified.

On the morning of 1 March 1871, the Prussians had their victory parade though they restricted their celebrations to the less volatile areas. Ratification of the Treaty took place the same day. It was time for the bloody grand finale.

When Paris surrendered, following 135 days of siege, one party, the Commune, wanted France to continue the struggle in her unconquered territories. Thousands of disaffected Parisians allied themselves to the party, and they showed their disapproval by rioting. In spite of this the armistice was concluded and the Government of Self-Defence arranged for a National Assembly to be elected by Bordeaux, this Assembly to conclude the terms of the peace treaty.

To the consternation of the majority of Parisians, most of the National Assembly were royalists, not renowned for their working class sympathies.

The Assembly added fuel to the flames by imposing financial strictures which would be especially onerous to the middle classes and the poor. The most unpopular decree: to disarm the Paris National Guard and to stop its war time pay, was seen as a measure that would effectively ensure that the citizens of Paris were to be deprived of a say in their own future. A detachment of

French government troops was detailed to carry out the disarmament. The National Guard resisted. Shots were fired. Dead bodies lay in the streets. Paris was in revolt. It was 18 March 1871.

(On 27 March 1871, Marie Thérèse Julien celebrated her twentieth birthday.)

The Assembly, located at Versailles, but subject to Prussian regulations, sent in government troops to wrest back control of Paris from the Communards. The assault and subsequent bombardment of the city failed to impress the revolutionaries. More government troops were sent in and, under the eyes of the contemptuous Prussians, the French proceeded to destroy one another – and their capital city.

After five weeks of bloody fighting, the government troops forced their way into the city.

They fought their way through the streets, house by house, room by room, with total disregard as to whether they killed the innocent in the process.

As the Communards retreated they set fire to their own city until much of Paris was a blazing inferno. By 26 May 1871, when the last resistance had been extinguished, The Hotel de Ville, the Ministry of Finance, the Palais de Justice, (the building that housed the notarial archives) The Tuileries, had all been reduced to smouldering ruins.

(Marie Thérèse Julien would have been aware that the archives had been destroyed. Her marriage (assuming a marriage had taken place) was no longer a matter of record. This was her opportunity, if she so wished, to wipe the slate clean.)

Victory had been achieved and the bloodthirsty victors looked to exact vengeance against the surviving Communards. The gutters ran with blood, the prisons became abattoirs and the cemeteries were relegated to mass graveyards.

Many of those lucky enough to survive the carnage of the second siege of Paris, were transported or forced into exile.

One of the exiled could have been "the recently widowed" Marie Thérèse Julien. She would have been aged approximately twenty years and three months.

The Woman Who Never Was

A visitor to the Office of National Statistics, Myddleton Street, EC1 may, without charge, peruse the indices relating to births, deaths and marriages. These commence from the year 1837, when centralisation of these records were first augmented in respect of England and Wales.

In the section relating to deaths, he, or she, may refer to the binder relating to the last quarter of the year 1888 and, therein, find an entry under Kelly, Marie Jeanette.

For a charge of currently £7 that person may order a copy of the certificate of death, and approximately six days later will receive that document through the mail.

Headed "Certified Copy of an Entry of Death", the document records that, on 9 November 1888, at number 1 [sic] Millers Court, Christchurch, a female aged about twenty-five years was wilfully murdered against [sic] some person, or persons, unknown. Her occupation is described as "prostitute" and the cause of death given as, "severance of the right carotid artery". She is named as Marie Jeanette Kelly otherwise Davies. This information is supplied courtesy of the coroner for Middlesex, R Macdonald, the man who presided over the inquest into her death.

But there is no birth certificate for this woman for, apparently, she was born in Limerick, Ireland. Strangely, the authorities in Limerick had and have no record of her.

She had married a collier named Davis or Davies, in Wales, when she was very young, about sixteen, but there is no marriage certificate to record this event. It was rumoured that Marie had borne a son but there is no birth certificate in substantiation of this rumour.

Her husband died about three years after the marriage, in an explosion, but there is no death certificate to record this sad tragedy. She had a brother in the 2nd Battalion, Scots Guards, but no brother was ever traced.

Marie Jeanette Kelly's death certificate

She had a father, named John, and a mother, who, as far as could be ascertained, were both still alive, but they never claimed the body of their daughter.

There was talk of a relative on the London stage and a sister who sold materials in the market place. She had five or six brothers in addition to the one in the army, but they were never traced.

The "woman who never was" was buried Monday, 19 November 1888, at St Patrick's Catholic Cemetery, Langthorne Road, London, E11, and, on her coffin, was inscribed a name she never knew, Marie Jeanette Kelly.

In 1986, a memorial stone was erected to the memory of the "woman who never was", though this was later removed.

Today, the precise location of her grave is not known and the ground has been reclaimed. Someone has marked the approximate location with a marble vase, inscribed simply "Mary".

The question is: who *does* lie in the grave of the "woman who never was"?

Emily Julia Julien

Emily Julia Julien was born at number 29, Cheltenham Place, Brighton, 29 March 1859. (Almost all of the houses in Cheltenham Place, including number 29 stand today.)

(Emily Julia would have been twenty-nine years and nearly eight months of age in November 1888.)

Her father was named James Arthur Julien, which, of course, immediately raises suspicions. If James Arthur was the brother of Jean Etienne, why isn't James Arthur named Jacques Arthur? That question can be answered, perhaps a little too easily, by assuming that Jacques Arthur found it more convenient to anglicise his name.

James Arthur's occupation was, in the year 1859, that of hairdresser, journeyman. Emily Julia's mother was named Emily Julien née Colley.

A check of the census record for the year 1861 revealed only that there was nobody by the name of Julien residing at 29, Cheltenham Place but a check through the register of births indicated another Julien born in Brighton: a child named James Arthur Julien.

James Arthur Julien was born 15 March 1862, at number 55, Richmond Buildings, St Peter's, Brighton (the whole street – close to St Peter's church – disappeared in the 1960s).

The details of James Arthur's parentage, including the occupation of the father, are identical to the details on Emily Julia's birth certificate, save that the mother has decided that her maiden name is not Colley but Marchant. There is no obvious explanation for this anomaly.

A check of the census record for the year 1861 revealed only that there was nobody by the name of Julien residing at 55, Richmond Buildings. A check of all of the entries in respect of St Peter's, Brighton failed to trace anyone by the name of Julien (substantial sections of microfilm are indecipherable).

There is no record of the marriage of James Arthur Julien and Emily Colley/Marchant which suggests that either they married in France or that they did not marry at all.

There is no record of the death of James Arthur Julien nor of Emily Julien which suggests that they returned to France.

There is no record of a marriage nor of a death in respect of either of the children, James Arthur and Emily Julia.

The question is – was Emily Julia Julien the cousin of Marie Thérèse Julien, and did Emily Julia stay in or return to, England, to be slaughtered in Millers Court?

The Victim – an Alternative Cousin German

When Joseph Barnett said that he had left room number 13, Millers Court, because Marie had allowed a prostitute named Julia to share the room, it is just possible that Joseph Barnett did not say "Julia" but instead, said "Julien": "She invited a prostitute named Julia in (Julien) to share our room". (I am paraphrasing but, almost certainly, paraphrasing that which has already been paraphrased.)

Certainly crude but no cruder than Joseph Barnett's other devices and, if so, we are seeking a woman with the surname "Julien", any Christian name possible; but, in order to be a first cousin of Marie Thérèse Julien on the spear side, i.e. the male side of the family, she would necessarily have to be the child of a brother of Jean Etienne Julien.

At this point in time only one brother is known – Adolphe Julien – and a marriage has not been traced.

Messrs Laurie & Marner

> Her father's name was John and he was a gaffer in some iron works in Carmarthenshire or Caernarvonshire.
>
> Joseph Barnett, 1888

It is presumed here, but certainly not proven, that Jean Etienne Julien brought his family to London some time early in the 1870s. It has been established that Marie Thérèse Julien was living at number 3, Chapel Place during at least part of the year 1876 and it is presumed that it was in the vicinity of Market Place, off Oxford Street, that the family, Julien, first set up their home.

Chief amongst Jean Etienne's priorities would be the availability of suitable employment and Jean was, by profession, a coach maker.

On the south side of Oxford Street, at number 313, almost opposite to Chapel Place, was the renowned carriage manufactory of Messrs Laurie & Marner.

The premeses stood on a site which was formerly the garden of a townhouse which had its frontage on Tenterden Street. The townhouse became the Royal Academy of Music, and the grounds, which covered an area of 1½ acres, served as an extension to Messrs Laurie & Marner's existing business, which was sited 400 yards further west on Oxford Street and which had been established since the year 1820.

It was still a thriving company, certainly in the year 1878 and, no doubt, skilled tradesmen were much in demand.

The owner of the townhouse was Lord Caernarvon.

Laurie & Marner, 313, Oxford Street, was totally destroyed by fire in the year 1866. It was rebuilt shortly thereafter.

The Worshipful Company of Coach makers and Coach Harness makers state that their records were destroyed by enemy action in 1940, so that they do not have a picture of the rebuilt premises. I have therefore been unable to ascertain if the new structure was, in fact, a construction made from iron.

The site is presently occupied by Tesco. The ornate building next door was once a public house named Noah's Ark.

Marie Thérèse Julien (After the War)

By the year 1873 (the precise year is unknown) the family Julien had removed to a new home and Jean Etienne had resumed the life of a *sellier*. In the year 1876, on her marriage certificate, Marie Thérèse gave her father's occupation as coach maker *(carrossier)*. The family's new address was number 21, rue Bayard, Paris (today's 8th arrondissement).

This is a résumé of the situation taken from the land registry of 1876 and 1890:

> The building was owned by a man named Hetzel, who did not live on the premises, but in the suburbs, at Levallois. He is listed as the owner in both 1876 and 1890.
>
> The building is described exactly the same way in both years:
>
> House – single door. Composed of a building on the street and courtyard, double in depth with cellars below the ground floor and three upper floors. Of light construction.
>
> Three casement windows on the street front. Another building at the back of the courtyard behind: double in depth, with a ground floor and upper floors.
>
> Worker housing.
>
> A cafe is listed as occupying the ground floor on the street side.

Number 21, rue Bayard, Paris, exists today. It is probably, substantially, the same building that existed in the nineteenth century. (An upper floor was added circa 2001.)

Whether the move was made before, after or during the Franco-Prussian war cannot be ascertained, so to what extent it was regarded as "home" by Marie Thérèse is unclear. It is known that the birth certificate of her brother, Joseph Julien, was reconstituted in the year 1873 at the request of his cousin, Ferdinand Lepage, and on that document he gave number 21, rue Bayard as the address of the family Julien.

Sometime after the Franco-Prussian war, Marie Thérèse Julien removed to London, either alone or with her family. When she arrived and where she stayed cannot be ascertained: neither can her *raison d'être* be established.

What is known, positively, is that circa 1875 she met a man named Philip Davies Collier and, having agreed to marry him, she wrote to her mother at number 21, rue Bayard, Paris, and requested that her birth certificate be reconstituted, presumably that the marriage might be better enabled. Marie Catherine Loeffler duly complied with this request and, in the month of September 1876, the reconstituted document was produced and forwarded to London. On the document of reconstitution, Marie Catherine Loeffler gave her occupation as *cuisinière* (cook) – probably in the cafe at 21, rue Bayard.

As we know, Marie Thérèse Julien and Philip Davies Collier married 7 October in the year 1876, and they set up home at number 3, Chapel Place, Cavendish Square. But not for long. Within a short period of time Marie Thérèse fell pregnant with child.

Circa May of the year 1877, Philip Davies and Marie Thérèse made a fateful decision. They would remove to Paris. They would stay with her parents at number 21, rue Bayard, at least until the child was born.

Was this a joint decision, entirely agreeable to them both – or was it the result of subtle manoeuvring by Marie Thérèse?

The impression gained is that Philip Davies had embraced Marie Thérèse's religion; would do anything to please her, was putty in her hands – but perhaps this is unjust. Whatever the answer, Philip Davies had embraced a foreign religion (his parents had married in an Independent chapel – suggesting a rejection of formal religion) a foreign country; was about to become the father of a foreign child, and he had forsaken advancement in his chosen career, whilst Marie Thérèse had made little, if any, visible sacrifice. This is not a criticism: merely an observation which may not be relevant. Whatever the truth, if Philip Davies Collier had not actually burned all his boats, they were certainly on fire.

The land registry records that the family Collier occupied apartment number 8, second to the right of the landing, on the second floor of the building, facing the street, number 21, rue Bayard, Paris.

The family Julien occupied the same apartment, which is listed as having heat. They also rented space in the back building, apartment number 38, on the fourth floor: the second apartment to the left of the landing, facing the courtyard, also listed as having heat.

On October 4 1877, at 21, rue Bayard, Paris, Marie Thérèse Julien/Collier gave birth to a child: a boy named William – presumably the name Ernest (Etienne – see the last will and testament of Mary Rusher Collier) was added when the child was baptised. I have been unable to trace a record of this baptism, assuming that it took place.

Some time after the birth of William, Philip and Marie moved to the south of France; to Menton, which is situated to the east of Nice and is the last town before the Italian border.

During the nineteenth century Menton was much in favour with the British; the climate considered efficacious, particularly to those suffering from tuberculosis, and many houses and hotels were built to accommodate the influx of afflicted visitors. The crowded cemetery bears silent witness to those who discovered that the climate was not as beneficial as advertised.

Philip Davies Collier perhaps saw a business opportunity in Menton and certainly he practised his trade as a chemist, though there is no record that he owned a business (his lack of qualifications might have hampered him in France as they would have done in England).

On 28 December 1881, Marie Thérèse gave birth to a son. Philip and Marie named their new child, Guillaume (known to be William J – believed to be William James, possibly William Jean/John, but not proven).

Certainly William Ernest (aged four years) was still alive and would remain so for some considerable time to come, so it seems odd that they are both named William, but possibly justified by naming one William, the other, Guillaume.

On 30 December 1881, Philip registered this birth with the British consulate in Mentone (the English spelling of Menton). Philip had not registered the birth of William Ernest with the British consulate. Possibly, at this juncture, Philip envisaged a return to England at some future date. There is no address on either the French certificate of birth or the British certificate of birth. I have been unable to trace a record that William J was baptised into the Catholic faith.

On 16 October 1883, Marie Thérèse gave birth to a girl and this child was named Marie Louise. The very next day, 17 October 1883, Philip registered the birth with the British consulate. There is no address on either the French certificate of birth or the British certificate of birth. I have been unable to trace a record that Marie Louise was baptised into the Catholic faith.

Given the fact that Menton was/is not a large town and has few churches, the conclusion is that either the research is faulty, or else no baptisms took place, which latter explanation leads to the question: why not?

Joseph Barnett stated that Marie had been disowned by her parents. Why? Was religion, or rejection of religion, a factor?

Summary

The 1901 census records that William J Collier, aged nineteen years, born in Mentone, is living with his grandmother, Mary Rusher Collier, in Reading. William J is a clerk in a biscuit factory (almost certainly "Huntley & Palmer", an illustrious Reading company).

The birth certificate of Marie Louise is cross-referenced with the record of her death.

Marie Louise never married and, as far as can be known, never bore children. She lived a magnificent ninety-six years and died 30 August 1980, at number 2, rue Kleber, Lavallois-Perret (Hauts de Seine). Her actual address is given as number 115, rue Chaptal, Lavallois-Perret (Hauts de Seine).

Marie Thérèse's mother, Marie Catherine Julien, nee Loeffler, died Wednesday, 24 October 1888, just six days before Joseph Barnett departed from room number 13, Millers Court.

I have been unable to trace the burial of Marie Catherine Loeffler in any of the Paris cemeteries and, possibly, her earthly remains were returned to Cormeilles-en-Vexin – where there are no extant records for the 1800s.

Jean Etienne Julien left 21, rue Bayard, following the death of his wife in the year 1888 – his name is not recorded on the land registry for the year 1890. I have been unable to trace a record of his death.

There is no record of Marie Thérèse Julien and Philip Davies Collier living in Menton following the birth of Marie Louise, and there is no record of the death of Marie Thérèse Julien in Menton at this, or any other time. Some time after October 1883, they departed from the town. Officially we will not meet Marie Thérèse Julien again.

Philip Davies Collier we will meet in London, in 1901, but there is strong circumstantial evidence that he was in London in 1888, and, probably, a good deal earlier.

> Mary Kelly came to the East End of London about 1884. She said that her parents had disowned/discarded her. Her father came to London searching for her but she avoided making contact with him.
>
> Joseph Barnett, 1888

21, rue Bayard, Paris, 1998

The Second Time Around

On Sunday, 22 January 1901, at Osborne House on the Isle of Wight, Queen Victoria died. She was aged eighty-one years. The Victorian era was ended. The Edwardian age had begun.

On Saturday, 28 September 1901, almost exactly twenty-five years after he had sworn his earthly devotion to Marie Thérèse Julien: Philip Davies Collier stood at the altar with another woman: a woman named Annie Agnes Nowers.

The ceremony took place at the established Church of St Paul, in the Parish of Penge. And so, Philip Davies Collier had forsaken the Catholic Church he had so ardently embraced for the love of a beautiful French woman, that long ago October day in the year 1876.

He gave his address as 124, Ledbury Road, London, W11, and his age as forty-eight years. Annie Agnes gave her address as 35, Lullington Road, Penge. Her status she gave as "spinster", her age as "full" (she was forty-six). The marriage was witnessed by Louise J Nowers and Mary Anne Nowers.

Philip's bride was the daughter of James Henry Nowers, Clerk in Holy Orders (deceased).

Philip gave his status as "widower".

So... Marie Thérèse Julien had gone to her grave.

(Ledbury Road is situated one mile from Paddington Station, with its direct services to Reading and it is just over two miles to the west of Philip's old address, Chapel Place. Most of the fine houses that line both sides of Ledbury Road still stand today. Number 124 has not survived.)

The Last Will and Testament of Mary Rusher Collier

Mary Rusher Collier departed from 153, Oxford Road, Reading, circa 1884–85. She lived, for a time, at number 10, Ayrton Villas, Oxford Road, Reading.

I have speculated, but to no avail, as to whether the *disappearance* of William James or possibly traumatic events in the life of Philip Davies were, in some way, connected with Mary Rusher's decision to move house – but probably not.

It was during the latter part of the year 1897 that Mary Rusher Collier moved to 124, Caversham Road, Reading (the house stands today) and there she resided with her faithful friend and companion, Eliza Anderson.

On 24 August in the year 1909 (a codicil was added 30 August 1913) Mary Rusher Collier prepared her will. This document (reproduced here) provokes more questions than it gives answers.

Mary Rusher Collier had three known grandchildren but her will revealed the existence of two more grandchildren. The known grandchildren are:

William Collier
(presumed William Ernest, as specified in the will)
William Collier
(known to be William J from the 1901 census, presumed William James)
Marie Louise Collier

These three are, indisputably, the children of Philip Davies Collier and Marie Thérèse Julien.

Two more grandchildren was something of a revelation. Whose children were John Philip Collier and Mary Florence Charlton?

William James Collier (the second-born son) had been absent for some time and he was now officially transferred to the missing list. But these grandchildren had to be his progeny or the progeny of Philip Davies Collier and/or John Osborne Collier. But how were they to be apportioned?

THIS IS THE LAST WILL AND TESTAMENT of me MARY RUSHER COLLIER of Caversham Road Reading in the County of Berks Widow I revoke all former Wills and testamentary dispositions made by me I appoint my son Philip Davies Collier and John Holland Jeffs of "Grenville" Marlborough Avenue Reading Solicitors Managing Clerk EXECUTORS and TRUSTEES of this my Will I give the following legacies free of duty To Ellen Matilda Richardson now residing at Stony Creek Gippsland Victoria Australia Fifty pounds To each of my grandchildren John Philip Collier Mary Florence Charlton and William Ernest Collier One hundred pounds To my old servant and friend Eliza Anderson Fifty pounds and all my wearing apparel and such of the furniture in her bedroom as at the time of my death shall not be hers To my sister Susan the china tea service that belonged to our Mother To each of my Executors who shall prove my Will Tenpounds for his trouble I devise and bequeath all the rest residue and remainder of my estate and effects both real and personal unto the said Philip Davies Collier and John Holland Jeffs upon trust to sell convert and get in the same with power to postpone such sale and conversion indefinitely without being responsible for loss and out of the proceeds thereof to pay my funeral and testamentary expenses and debts and the legacies bequeathed by this my Will and the duty on such legacies and subject thereto to stand possessed thereof In trust for my said sons Philip Davies Collier and John Osborne Collier as tenants in common in equal shares absolutely I declare that if either of my said sons shall die in my lifetime leaving issue living at my death such issue being male and attaining the age of Twenty one years or being female and attaining that age or marrying shall take by substitution and if more than one in equal shares the share which his or her parent would have taken under the trusts in that behalf hereinbefore contained had he survived me and attained a vested interest Provided always and I declare that the sum which I have advanced by way of loan to my said son John Osborne Collier and any other sum or sums which I may hereafter advance to him or for his benefit or so much thereof as may be owing to me at my decease and the interest thereon shall not be charged or claimed as a debt owing to me from him or his representatives but every such sum (whether legally constituting a debt or not) with interest thereon from my decease at the rate of Four pounds per cent per annum (but not any interest thereon prior to my decease) shall be brought into account in the way of hotchpot in the division of my residuary estate as against the said John Osborne Collier and his children or other the person or persons interested in his share of my residuary estate under the trusts hereinbefore declared I desire that my funeral may be conducted as quietly and inexpensively as is consistent with propriety IN WITNESS whereof I hereto set my hand this twenty fourth day of August One thousand nine hundred and nine - MARY RUSHER COLLIER - Signed by the said Mary Rusher Collier as her last Will and Testament

M R Collier's will

in the presence of us both present at the same time who in her presence and in the presence of each other hereto subscribe our names as witnesses - H CRUTCHFIELD SIDNEY SPYER Clerks to Messrs Blandy & Chambers Solicitors Reading

I MARY RUSHER COLLIER of Caversham Road Reading in the County of Berks Widow declare this to be a Codicil to my Will which bears date the twenty fourth day of August One thousand nine hundred and nine I hereby revoke the legacies given in my said Will to Ellen Matilda Richardson John Philip Collier Mary Florence Charlton and William Ernest Collier respectively and in lieu thereof I give the following legacies free of duty to the said Ellen Matilda Richardson Twenty five pounds and to the said John Philip Collier Mary Florence Charlton and William Ernest Collier Fifty pounds each And in all other respects I confirm my said Will AS WITNESS my hand this Thirtieth day of August One thousand nine hundred and thirteen MARY RUSHER COLLIER - Signed by the above named Testatrix as a Codicil to her said Will in the joint presence of us who in her presence and in the presence of each other have hereunto subscribed our names as witnesses - J HOLLAND JEFFS - SIDNEY SPYER Clerks to Messrs Blandy & Chambers Solicitors Reading

On the 6th day of January 1916 Probate of this Will and Codicil was granted to Philip Davies Collier John Holland Jepp the executors 2

M R Collier's will (cont.)

A search through the register of births for the years 1876 to 1909 failed to unearth a record of birth in respect of either of these grandchildren.

A search through the register of deaths for the period 1913 (when Mary Rusher Collier added a codicil to her will) to 1985 failed to find a record of death in respect of any of the grandchildren. A search through the marriage register for the period 1892 to 1909 failed to uncover the marriage of Mary Florence Collier to a man named Charlton. It was time to consider the youngest son.

On May 29 in the year 1879, in the Parish Church, Grey Friars 64, Friar Street, Reading, John Osborne Collier married a woman named Isabel Jemima Grover.

John Osborne gave his occupation as bookseller. Both he and Isabel Jemima gave their age as "full" (they were both twenty-three) and their address as Great Knolly Street, Reading.

George Grover, builder, and the father of Isabel Jemimah, lived at number 55, Great Knolly Street so, probably, the newly-weds resided with the bride's parents.

On 9 August in the year 1881, John Osborne and Isabel Jemimah were blessed with a son. The birth certificate records that the family were living at Castle Hill, New Windsor, Berkshire, and that John Osborne was a bookseller's manager. The happy couple named their first, and only child, Philip Osborne – Philip Osborne Collier. So Mary Rusher Collier had just acquired an additional grandchild, bringing the known total to six.

But Philip Osborne Collier was not named in the will of Mary Rusher Collier. Mary Rusher Collier had overlooked him. Or that is how it first appeared. Later it became obvious that, in fact, Philip Osborne was the favoured grandchild and, as time went by, it became clear that he was the *English* grandchild.

On 8 May in the year 1909, the English grandchild, Philip Osborne Collier, a photographer, married a woman named Ellen Blanche Louise Pike. Philip Osborne was aged twenty-seven years and Ellen Blanche Louise was aged twenty-eight years. Ellen Blanche Louise gave her address as 11, Cardigan Road, Reading, but the happy couple resided (all their long lives) at number 13, Thames Bank, Reading; a house just around the corner from where lived Mary Rusher Collier. It was therefore likely that this wedding had caused Mary Rusher Collier, just three months later, to make out her will, superseding all other wills. Almost certainly she advanced her favourite grandchild sufficient money to purchase, or at least to make a down payment on the house, 13, Thames Bank, conditional upon him receiving no further award in her will: though he may have been the recipient of further, privileged largesse.

(From private information, coupled with the absence of any official record, it is absolutely certain that John Osborne and Isabel Jemimah had no other children.)

All of this was not particularly good news. It left two grandchildren unaccounted for and only two possible fathers – Philip Davies Collier and/or William James Collier.

The conclusion is that the missing grandchildren are either the children of Philip Davies Collier and Marie Thérèse Julien or, perhaps more likely, the children of William James Collier and "wife". If that is so then William James Collier emigrated to a foreign shore; married and sired at least two children.

The Dying Days

The Great War had just entered its second year when on 21 November 1915, Mary Rusher Collier passed away. She was aged eighty-five years.

Four days later, at two o'clock on the afternoon of 25 November 1915, the mourners congregated in the little terraced house at 124, Caversham Road, from whence the funeral procession proceeded to Reading cemetery, Division 30 – unconsecrated ground – and there at three o'clock, the body of Mary Rusher Collier, née Davies was laid to rest. Her earthly remains were buried in brick grave number 4743, close to the grave where her husband, William Lindsey Collier, had been interred over forty-five years earlier, 8 August 1870. Mary Rusher Collier had been a widow for more than half of her life.

Henceforth the house at number 124, Caversham Road, would be occupied by John Osborne Collier and his wife Isabel Jemimah. But, as the Great War staggered into its bloody fourth year, on 28 December 1917, Isabel Jemimah Collier, aged sixty-one years, died – and John Osborne was left alone. But not for too long.

On 26 June 1920, John Osborne Collier, aged sixty-four years, married 26-year-old Daisy Emma Allen. (One could speculate that the shortage of eligible men, following the appalling casualties of The Great War, played some part in Daisy Emma's decision to marry the aged John Osborne, who himself was sufficiently abashed to prune five years off his age. The marriage certificate records his age as a youthful fifty-nine years!)

Daisy Emma Allen had been an employee of John Osborne Collier's son, Philip Osborne (a photographer), and the marriage created a rift between father and son that would never be healed. This difficult situation must have been compounded by the fact that their respective addresses were only separated by 300 yards. And so it was that the family connection was broken forever and, sadly, no further information could be obtained from the forebears of the family Collier.

Philip Davies Collier viewed the second marriage of his younger brother with equanimity, if not approval, but his own marriage to Annie Agnes had run its course, and certainly by the year 1923 – possibly a good deal earlier – Philip Davies Collier, removed to his spiritual home: *la belle France*.

In the year 1923, Philip Davies Collier bought a house. His new and last address was number 15, rue Henri Regnault, Suresnes. (Henri Regnault was a popular young artist, tragically killed in the Franco-Prussian war – and mourned heartbreakingly by his sweetheart.)

Suresnes is a suburb of Paris situated at the western edge of the Bois de Boulogne. Philip's house was probably new in 1923 for there are no previous owners listed. His neighbour, at number 17, was Alexandre Mongault who had lived there since the year 1918; and at number 13 resided Antoine Alexis Bargot who had lived at that address since the year 1917.

The census for the year 1931 records that Philip Davies Collier lived at number 15, rue Henri Regnault, Suresnes, and that the property also provided accommodation for his housekeeper: Marie Fabre, born 1877, in Grandsagnes (Aveyron), unmarried.

How often Philip Davies Collier made trips back to England cannot be ascertained but he was certainly back in Reading, Berks, 8 August 1925, when he and his brother, John Osborne, travelled to their family solicitor, "Blandy & Blandy", situated at number 1, Friar Street (Blandy & Blandy still occupy the same address today).

It was at the office of Blandy & Blandy that Philip Davies Collier prepared his last will and testament. It is a document (reproduced here) that is brief to the point of being terse.

Philip Davies Collier bequeathed all his worldly goods to his brother, John Osborne. There is no mention of his wife, Annie Agnes, who was certainly still alive at this time and, perhaps more significantly, no mention of his children. Certainly Marie Louise was still alive and it seems likely that so too were William Ernest and William "James". Even if Marie Louise was the only survivor then Philip Davies Collier either considered her sufficiently well

OFFICE COPY
VALID ONLY IF BEARING
IMPRESSED COURT SEAL

THIS is the LAST WILL and TESTAMENT of me PHILIP DAVIES COLLIER of Number 15 Rue Henri Regnault Suresnes in the Republic of France Chemist I APPOINT my Brother John Osborne Collier and my friend John Victor Jeffs of Reading in the County of Berks Bank Official Executors of this my Will and I give to the said John Victor Jeffs the sum of TEN POUNDS free of duty as an acknowledgment for his trouble I GIVE all the residue of my real and personal estate to my said Brother absolutely IN WITNESS whereof I have hereunto set my hand this *eighth* day of *August* One thousand nine hundred and twenty five.

Philip Davies Collier

SIGNED by the above-named Philip Davies Collier as his Will in our joint presence and by us in his presence.

Albt. J. Stevens) Clerk to
John W. Brookes) Messrs Blandy
& Blandy
Solicitors
1 Friar Street
Reading

P D Collier's will

provided for, or else she was out of favour. It is interesting to speculate; how much bitterness, how much disappointment, how much pain is concealed behind these omissions?

On 11 June 1931, Annie Agnes Collier, née Nowers, the woman who had consented to be the wife of Philip Davies Collier thirty years earlier, died. She was aged seventy-six years. Her address was given as number 54, St George's Park Avenue, Westcliff-on-Sea, Essex though she died at 777, London Road, Westcliff-on-Sea, Essex – presumed to be a nursing home.

Annie Agnes Collier had neglected to prepare a will so that her estate was subject to letters of administration. The document is dated 1 December 1931. Philip Davies Collier gave as his address, his late wife's address, 54, St George's Park Avenue, Westcliff-on-Sea, Essex. The estate, valued at £1,425 gross, was, however, to be shared with a woman named Emma Taylor, wife of Arthur Taylor of Braunton, Devon.

The world did a few more revolutions. On 30 January 1933, Adolf Hitler was proclaimed chancellor of Germany.

If Philip Davies Collier heeded this momentous event at all, he did not have long to ponder its implications. On 12 August 1933, at number 15, rue Henri Regnault, a man who had started out life in the year 1852; who had seen the world change out of all recognition to the world in which he was born, died at the age of eighty-one years. The story that had begun in the 1820s with William and Mary was nearly done.

Philip Davies Collier was buried 16 August 1933, in the Voltaire Cemetery, Suresnes, in a "free plot": a euphemism for a pauper's grave. (In his will, Philip Davies Collier left the sum of £1,445 but he seems not to have provided any money for his funeral expenses and one gains the impression that, like the rest of the family Collier (Mary Rusher Collier had been at pains to stipulate in her will that she be buried with a minimum of fuss and expense), he cared little or nothing for how his earthly body be disposed of.)

269
C O L L I E R
Philip Davies

Death certificate, P D Collier

Le douze aout mil neuf cent trente trois a vingt trois heures est décédé en son domicile 15 rue Henri Regnault, Philip Davies C O L L I E R, sans profession, né à Reading (Angleterre), le neuf avril mil huit cent cinquante deux, fils de William Lindsay COLLIER et de Mary RUSHER COLLIER Davies, décédés. Veuf de ...... sans renseignements connus du déclarant Dressé, le treize aout mil neuf cent trentetrois à dix heures, sur la déclaration de Ernest CHAILLOU, employé, trente quatre ans, domicilié à Suresnes, 29 rue du Mont Valérien, qui lecture faite a signé avec Nous Alexandre JOYEUX, adjoint au Maire de Suresnes, officier de l'état civil par délégation./.

On 19 September 1938, at The Royal Berkshire Hospital, Reading, John Osborne Collier breathed his last. Although aged eighty-two when he died and, almost certainly aware that he was terminally ill, John Osborne Collier had neglected to make provision for his young wife – herself now a creaking forty-four years of age – for John Osborne Collier had neglected to make a will. It seems a fairly spiteful omission and perhaps says something for their "happy" relationship. John Osborne Collier's estate was therefore subject to letters of administration. There are two people recorded on this document – the young (now middle aged) wife, and the son who loathed the wife, Philip Osborne Collier. Poor, sad, "misunderstood" Daisy Emma would have to fight for her share of the £78 net.

But life rolled on, and the world took very little notice of a dynasty that was nearly extinct.

On 18 February 1961 Ellen Blanche Louise Collier, née Pike, aged eighty years, died at her home, number 13, Thames Side, Reading, Berks.

On 22 February 1979, the English grandchild, Philip Osborne Collier, aged a magnificent ninety-eight years, died at his home, number 13, Thames Side, Reading, Berks.

Philip Osborne and Ellen Blanche Louise had conceived a daughter who is probably still alive today. She no longer bears the surname Collier and knows nothing about the Collier side of her family. If there exists today a Collier connection, it is probably a French connection.

Somewhere in France today exist, possibly, the grandchildren, maybe the great grandchildren, and, optimistically, the great great grandchildren: the descendents of a Collier named Davies and a woman named Marie, a woman named Marie, but known to the world as Mary Jane Kelly.

It would be somehow comforting, to consider that Philip Davies Collier still lies peacefully in his grave. But, sadly, this is not so. The "free plot" was only free for a period of five years.

In the year 1938, as Neville Chamberlain waved a piece of paper and proclaimed "Peace in our time," the earthly remains of Philip Davies Collier were disinterred and unceremoniously consigned to the general ossuary of the Voltaire cemetery. His bones lie there today – jumbled and confused with all the other anonymous bones: all with their own interesting story.

But what a wondrous tale the chattering teeth in the empty skull of Philip Davies Collier could tell.

15, rue Henri Regnault, Suresnes

Checklist – Did Marie Thérèse Collier masquerade as Mary Jane Kelly?

The only real barrier to Marie Thérèse Collier being Mary Jane Kelly is her age.

Joseph Barnett was not specific, but thought her age, in 1888, to be twenty-five years. He had known her for over one year (he said) but did not volunteer her date of birth, though he had a wealth of quite inconsequential life details.

Marie Thérèse Collier was, in fact, thirty-seven or thirty-eight years old in the year 1888.

She did not marry at age sixteen but at twenty-five, so that Joseph Barnett, having reduced her age in order to maintain her life experience, reduced the age when she married (or there was an earlier marriage).

Another possibility is that because the real victim of the Millers Court murder really was aged twenty-five to thirty, and would be subject to forensic examination, Joseph Barnett deemed it prudent to give the age of the victim, not the age of Mary Jane.

It should be emphasised that we only have Joseph Barnett's estimate of Mary Jane's age and this estimate was made after her death, and would hardly be questioned.

> She was known as Mary but her real name was Marie.
> Yes.

> She came from Limerick (Llymaryke).
> Yes.

> She married a Collier.
> Yes.

> Named Davis or Davies.
> Yes.

Her father's name was John (Jean).
Yes.

She once lived in a fashionable house in the West End of London.
Yes. 3, Chapel Place, Cavendish Square.

She made many trips to Paris and drove about in a carriage.
Yes. She was born in Paris. Her father was a Parisian coach maker.

She had a son, aged in the year 1888, six or seven years.
Yes. William J. Born Menton, 28 December 1881.

She had an aunt.
She certainly had, at the very least, one aunt: Louise Marguerite Lepage née Loeffler.

She had six or seven brothers and one sister.
France does not have a centralised system for recording births. Only one brother, named Joseph, has been traced. This does not preclude the possibility of there being other siblings.

She had a female cousin.
Only one cousin, Ferdinand Lepage, has been traced. Should Julia happen to be Ferdinand's sister, then the body that lies in Leytonstone Catholic cemetery is that of Julia Lepage.

She had a brother named Henry, and Henry, in the year 1888, was serving in the 2nd Battalion Scots Guards then based in Ireland and Henry was known amongst his comrades as Jonto (or Johnto).
No. The police tried to trace this brother following the murder of Mary Jane Kelly, without success. I have examined the roster in respect of the 2nd Battalion Scots Guards (which reposes in the public records office, Kew) and there is listed no one by the name Julien (or, of course, Kelly).

I assume this strangely worded statement has arcane meaning.

Why did Joseph Barnett give Marie the second name of Jeanette?

Thérèse was impossible to use without running the very real risk of revealing her true identity. He constructed Jeanette from her father's name: Jean Etienne.

The Wales connection is a fiction designed to lend credence to the fact that Marie married a collier. The Ireland connection is a fiction created to support the fact that Marie came from Limerick.

Life… and Death

Joseph Barnett – the Anatomy of a Life

> Be an opener of doors to such as come after you,
> and do not leave the universe a blind alley.
>
> Ralph Waldo Emerson
> born 25 May 1803

John Barnett was born in Ireland in the year 1817. Catharine O'Brien was born in Ireland in the year 1821.

There is no known record of when or where they married, if indeed such event ever took place, but they probably wed in their hometown or village, in Ireland, circa 1844.

Catharine and John had received little or no schooling and they were certainly illiterate, evidenced by the fact that they both signed official documents with their mark: an "X". They were thus condemned to a lifetime of unremitting toil and hardship.

If life was hard it was about to take a turn for the worse for, in the year 1846, all of Ireland was devastated by the failure of the potato crop, leading to a famine that would cause death by starvation of over a million souls.

In a desperate attempt to avoid the same fate, a further million people boarded anything that would float, and they fled across the Atlantic, to America. Others went in the opposite direction, to England. And so it was that John Barnett and Catharine Barnett, née O'Brien, arrived in England, circa 1847.

Where they arrived and how they survived those desperate early days is not recorded. Probably they headed straight to London, armed only with a pathetic bundle of belongings and a few coins. The East End catered exclusively to the wretched and the starving and John and Catharine added their misery to the sum of misery.

Catharine Barnett gave birth to her "presumed first" child (an earlier child could have been a victim of the Irish famine) at Chalk, Kent, 8 August in the year 1849. The Barnetts had their first son. They named him Denis.

(It seems likely that Catharine found temporary refuge in Chalk where she could have her child away from the London slums, though the census return for the year 1861, in contradiction of the birth certificate, records that Denis was born in Aldgate in the City of London.)

John Barnett was the informant and he gave his wife's maiden name as "Bryan". John Barnett gave as his occupation "labourer".

In 1850–51 Catharine Barnett gave birth to a second son. The proud parents named their second child, Daniel.

(A birth certificate cannot be traced. The census return for the year 1861 records that Daniel was born in Aldgate, City of London, but this document has already proven itself unreliable, due, no doubt, to the census officer taking the line of least resistance.)

It is possible that Catharine returned for a brief while to Ireland, and that Daniel was born there, else John and Catharine were strangely inconsistent in registering the births of their children. (The registration of Births, Deaths, and Marriages was first introduced in July 1837, but was not made compulsory until the year 1874.)

The Barnetts were living at number 4, Crown Court, Whitechapel, when on 29 September 1853, Catharine gave birth to a daughter. The couple named their child Catharine. Catharine Barnett was the informant. She gave her husband's occupation as "Labourer in the fish market, Billingsgate". She gave her maiden name as "O'Brien".

On Monday, 24 May 1858, Queen Victoria celebrated her thirty-ninth birthday and, on the following day, Tuesday, 25 May 1858, Catharine Barnett gave birth to a child who would become the "King of Murder". He was born under the sign of Gemini and thirty years after his birth, he would be living in room number 13, Millers Court, with the "Queen of Murder": a woman he named Marie Jeanette Kelly. He would style himself Jack the Ripper. John and Catharine named their fourth child, Joseph.

Joseph was born at number 4, Hairbrain Court, Whitechapel. Catharine Barnett was the informant. She gave her husband's occupation as "dock labourer" and she gave her maiden name as "Hayes". There is no obvious reason for this anomaly save that

Catharine was illiterate and registrars have been known to make mistakes. (Perhaps Catharine became confused and gave her mother's maiden name. It is of course possible that it is "Hayes" that is correct and "Bryan/O'Brien" that is incorrect – but this is less likely.)

In May–June of the year 1860, Catharine gave birth to her last child: a son. The couple named him John. The census return for 7 April 1861, records that John was aged ten months and that he was born in Aldgate, which places his date of birth as June 1860. The same census document records that the Barnett family were residing at number 2, Cartwright Street.

It is presumed that all of the Barnett children attended school locally and the Ordnance Survey Map for the year 1873 records that there were a number of such establishments within easy distance of the Barnett's home. The family lived in one room with all the privations that that entailed, and in an area of desperate poverty, poor sanitation and virulent disease.

In July 1864 as the American Civil War entered its final phase, John Barnett contracted pleurisy. John died on American Independence Day, 4 July 1864, at number 8, Waltons Court, Cartwright Street. He was aged forty-seven years. Joseph was aged six.

At nearly fifteen years of age, the eldest son, Denis, was probably already at work whilst Daniel, aged thirteen was on the threshold of leaving school.

It was a desperate time for a family already hard pressed and Catharine Barnett would have to shoulder the main burden. How she fared cannot be known for the census return for the year 1871 records that the family resided at 24½, Great Pearl Street and the name of the mother, Catharine Barnett, is conspicuous by its absence.

The last record of Catharine was in July 1864, when she was named as the informant on her husband's death certificate. Where she went and when cannot be ascertained but the absence of a death certificate suggests that she returned to Ireland (for a holiday) where she died. It seems improbable that she abandoned the family she had been loyal to for so long.

(The fact that Catharine Barnett is not recorded on the census for the year 1871 is not proof of her being in permanent absentia. It is possible that she was away for only a short time, which happened to coincide with the date of the census – 3 March.

There is a death certificate for a Catherine Barnett, aged sixty, recorded at number 1, Vine Court, Whitechapel Road, 25 January 1881, the wife of Daniel Barnett from Cork, who could have been John Barnett's brother: given the coincidence that John and Catharine named their second-born son, Daniel – but this can only be surmise.)

Joseph Barnett was an intelligent boy and, perhaps encouraged by a mother and father who were both illiterate, he developed a fascination for words and their meanings. He would twist them into shapes and designs simply for pleasure, and perhaps the habit became something of a compulsion.

He had been taught to keep himself as clean and presentable as circumstances allowed (a reporter at the inquest into the death of Mary Jane Kelly described Joseph Barnett as "very presentable for one of his class") and he would do so all his life, developing an abhorrence of the filth and disease he saw all around him, though he maintained an allegiance to the East End and its people that would never leave him. If he could find a way, he would improve their lot.

His father's death in 1864 and his mother's death (presumed) when Joseph was twelve or younger, must have been traumatic and the vagaries of fate and the casual way God ended a life must have made a deep impression on his young mind. People lived in misery and died in despair, but if God was a merciful God then it could only mean that He regarded earthly life as necessary for a greater understanding of the universe, but ultimately unimportant: and that only the soul was worthy of salvation.

(Hairbrain Court, where Joseph Barnett was born; Crown Court, where Catharine Barnett was born; and Waltons Court, Cartwright Street, where John Barnett lived and died were all situated within the same small area (Cartwright Street is there today though there are no buildings pre-1900), just 150 yards to the east of the Royal Mint which is itself sited diagonally opposite the Tower of London. The area is immediately to the north of St Katherine's Dock. St Katherine's is today a trendy marina of bars and restaurants but, when John Barnett, and later his sons, worked there, it was a place where desperate men fought for the privilege of working for slave wages.

Dock Street where, 4 October 1936, Oswald Moseley and his blackshirts were dissuaded by the police from entering into a violent confrontation with a hostile crowd, still has buildings which would be familiar to Joseph Barnett (though many are now dilapidated and empty) and, just eighty yards east from where Hairbrain Court once stood (100 yards to the rear of the Crown and Seven Stars public house – with its frontage on Royal Mint Street) stands the Peabody Estate. On the wall of this building a plaque records that seventy-eight people died there in an air raid, 8 September in the year 1940.)

It cannot be ascertained how many times the depleted family moved house following the death of the stalwart, and sadly missed, patriarch, John Barnett, but their number reduced by a further digit, 23 March 1869, when the nineteen-year-old Denis Barnett married nineteen-year-old local girl, Mary Ann Garrett. In the parish church, St Matthews, Bethnal Green, the entranced pair gazed lovingly into each other's eyes.

Denis Barnett signed his name. Mary Ann Garrett appended her mark: an "X". Denis Barnett gave his address as number 3, Pearl Street, and he described himself as a "general dealer". Mary Ann gave her address as number 53, Tyssen Street. (On the marriage certificate the name of Denis's father is shown as John Barnett: his occupation as "general dealer". The explanation for this is probably that, since Denis was a minor, he needed parental permission to marry and a friend volunteered to pose as the father of the groom.)

In the happy years following their blissful union, Denis and Mary were blessed with two sons, Dennis and John, before they decided to move south of the river, to Bermondsey.

Connubial bliss notwithstanding, circumstances did not improve for the beleaguered remnants of the family Barnett for, as previously stated, in April 1871, Daniel, Catharine, Joseph and young John, were residing at number 24½ Great Pearl Street, situated a mile north of Royal Mint Street and strategically positioned in an area soon to be condemned, by the medical officer for health, as unfit for human habitation. (The street was immediately behind the Royal Cambridge Music Hall.)

At that particular moment in time, Catharine Barnett was aged seventeen years and the census for the year 1871 does not indicate that she had a job, suggesting, probably, that she had a full time occupation organising the Barnett household and attending to the thirteen-year-old Joseph and the nine-year-old John, both of whom were attending school. That Catharine Barnett must have had some free time is evidenced by the fact that 20 August 1871, aged nearly eighteen years, she wed a local brewery driver: the aptly named Joseph Beer. Joseph Beer appended his signature to the marriage certificate. Catharine Barnett signed her name with her mark: an "X". The ceremony took place at the parish church of St John the Baptist, Hoxton. The happy couple gave their address as number 10, Cottage Street. (Cottage Street still exists – off Poplar High Street and overlooking the New Billingsgate Market.) Catharine Barnett was the last member of the immediate family to marry. Daniel, Joseph and John would never do so.

Taken from the census of the year 1881: Joseph Beer, a carman aged thirty years, together with his wife Catharine aged twenty-seven years, were living at 21 Splidts Street (now Forbes Street – one side of Forbes Street is lined with old warehouses which just might date from 1881 but there are only new houses and flats on the other side. The 1881 number 21 has long ago disappeared) with daughters Catharine, aged seven years, and Elizabeth, aged five years. Mr and Mrs Beer will, in the next few years, be removing to 21, Portpool Lane, Gray's Inn Road (there are no nineteenth-century houses in Portpool Lane today though there are many Georgian houses along the Gray's Inn Road) where they will give temporary refuge, at different times, to Joseph Barnett and brother, Daniel.

Precisely when Joseph Barnett left school cannot be ascertained but it was probably in the year 1871 when he was thirteen years of age. His brother Daniel and, almost certainly, Denis, were then working as porters at Billingsgate fish market: Joseph completed the trio. Only John, then aged twelve years, was still at school but he would have been considered independent enough to fend for himself until Daniel or Joseph returned home from work.

In the year 1878 it became mandatory for all Billingsgate porters to be licensed by the Corporation of the City of London, and all four of the Barnett brothers received their licence on the 1 July of that year.

Joseph Barnett's licence (number 853) records that he was 5'7" tall, aged twenty years, with a fair complexion.

The licence also records three addresses:

4, Osbourne Street, Whitechapel (deleted)
St Thomas Chambers, 1, Heneage Street, Spitalfields (deleted)
4, North east Passage, Wellclose Square

Daniel Barnett's Licence, (number 213) records that he was 5'4½" tall, aged twenty-six years and fair.

The licence also records addresses:

6, Goulston Buildings, Bermondsey
9, Aldery Road
14, Goulston Buildings
21, Portpool Lane, Holborn (with his sister and brother-in-law)

Denis Barnett's licence (number 528) records that he was 5'6½" tall, aged thirty years, and fair.

The licence records just one address:

8, Goulston Buildings, Bermondsey New Road

John Barnett's licence (number 564) records that he was 5'4" tall, aged eighteen years, and fair.

The licence records just one address:

5, Goldsmiths Buildings, Bermondsey New Road

Precisely when Joseph Barnett became a Freemason is not freely available information (I have not thought to enquire) neither is it known how long it took him to reach the exalted status of Master Mason, but certainly he embraced Freemasonry and he envisaged the society as a stepping stone to improving the conditions of the general populace. It would mean a fight and a fight would mean victims, but they were expendable for the greater good, and the ends would justify the means. The war would be declared. The battlefield would be the streets. The weapons and the tactics were, as yet, unknown.

It has been said that Joseph Barnett was known, to at least some of his friends, as "Danny" (Daniel was his own brother's name) though why (assuming it to be true) is not clear. But Daniel is Hebrew for "The Judge of God" and perhaps it was a name given to him by his fellow Freemasons. In any event it was apt enough as events would show.

In the year 1881, Joseph Barnett, aged twenty-two, describing himself as a general labourer, was living at number 1, Horatio Street, Bethnal Green.

A visitor, on the day of the census, was his younger brother, John, then aged twenty and describing himself as a fish porter (presumably Joseph was in temporary absentia from Billingsgate). (There were something like 6,000 licensed fish porters at Billingsgate market, though at anyone time there were only about 2,000 jobs, so that possession of a licence was not of itself a guarantee of employment.)

(The house where Joseph Barnett once lived is gone – the site where once it stood, is now a mini-market. Joseph would, no doubt, have been familiar with the building on the opposite corner: a public house named The Marksman.)

It is interesting to encounter Joseph Barnett at this particular point in time: just seven years before he became Jack the Ripper.

Number 1, Horatio Street, Bethnal Green, gave shelter to nine souls, in addition to Joseph Barnett. Listed here, they are:

Frederick Wegart	aged 69 – a shoemaker	– born Germany
Elizabeth Wegart	aged 63 – his wife	– born not known
George Bailey	aged 28 – general dealer	– born City of London
Mary A Bailey	aged 26 – his wife	– born St Luke's
James Bailey	aged 5 – their son	– born Shoreditch
Lizzie Bailey	aged 3 – their daughter	– born Shoreditch
Alfred Bailey	aged 1 – their son	– born Shoreditch
Thomas Healey	aged 65 – cooper/unemployed	– born not known
Matilda Healey	aged 72 – his wife	– born Burton-on-Trent

The census for the year 1891 (5 April) records that John Barnett, general labourer, aged thirty years, was residing in a common lodging house at number 46, Hanbury Street, whilst his brother Daniel, fish porter, aged forty-four years, was a resident of Victoria Home, number 1, Commercial Street. (I have not been able to locate Joseph in the 1891 census.)

On 8 April in the year 1902, John Barnett, aged forty-two years, described as a dock labourer, died in the work house infirmary, Raine Street, St George's-in-the-East. Up until the time of his demise, John had resided at number 2, Mayfield Buildings, Princes Square, Cable Street, St George's-in-the-East. The cause of his death was given as bulbar paralysis – apoplectic form – coma. The informant was Marcus A Bowlam – resident medical officer. (Bulbar paralysis pertains to the medulla oblongata – a truncated cone of nerve tissue anterior to the cerebellum which *inter alia* controls respiration and circulation.)

In the year 1906, Joseph and his brother, Daniel, were living at number 18, New Gravel Lane, Shadwell. (In December of the year 1811, number 81, New Gravel Lane – The Kings Arms – was the site selected by the infamous Ratcliffe Highway murderer/s to kill the publican, his wife, their granddaughter and a servant: an outrage which had been preceded a few days earlier by the killing of Timothy Marr, his wife Celia, their baby, and a servant lad, at number 29, Ratcliffe Highway.)

There is a number 18, Garnet Street today (New Gravel Lane was renamed Garnet Street in 1939) but the house and the location are new.

On 22 December 1906, Daniel Barnett died. He was aged fifty-six years. The cause of his death was given as morbus cordis (heart disease). On Christmas Eve, a tired, grey haired, 48-year-old Joseph Barnett travelled to the General Register Office and there he registered the death of his dearly beloved brother. Christmas celebrations, 1906, together with the New Year celebrations which ushered in 1907, must have been somewhat subdued.

Following the death of Daniel in 1906, in August 1907, Joseph Barnett was issued with a new Billingsgate porter's licence, number 739. His age is shown as forty-nine years; his eyes: blue;

his hair: grey. His height has increased by half an inch; he is now 5'7½" tall (new boots perhaps).

Number 60 Red Lion Street 1922

In the same year he moved to number 60, Red Lion Street, Shadwell, just two doors away from the Old George public house. The accommodation was not particularly to his liking though he liked the area and, in the year 1908, he moved around the corner, to number 1, Tench Street.

Sometime around this period Joseph Barnett met a woman, though probably he had been acquainted with her for some time since she resided at Goulston Buildings, New Road, Bermondsey, an address which appears on the porter's licence of two of his brothers.

Her name was Louisa Denis. Louisa was a widow and, in the year 1901, she resided at number 1, Goulston Buildings with her eldest son Alfred and her four other children, Louise sixteen, Susan thirteen, Rose twelve and William eight.

After 1901 Joseph and Louisa married, or rather they lived together and Louisa claimed to be Joseph's wife and, certainly, Louisa Denis changed her name to Louisa Barnett.

Her eldest son, Alfred, was destined to be present at the death of Jack the Ripper and his name appears on the death certificate.

Philip Davies Collier... and Violet

Such information as could be gleaned from the census for the year 1901 has been incorporated into the text of this book – with this exception.

The census for the year 1901 (April) revealed that Philip Davies Collier resided at an address with which we are already familiar, 124, Ledbury Road, Paddington – a house let as apartments by a Mrs Louisa Doswell, who herself resided on the premises.

In September of this year Philip Davies Collier will marry Annie Agnes Nowers. As might be supposed (at least in this *enlightened* age) Philip is not residing at number 124 by himself. But it is not with Annie Agnes with whom he resides – she is resident at number 35, Lullington Road, Penge, masquerading, incidentally, as just thirty-five years of age.

Philip Davies Collier, aged forty-eight years, a widowed chemist born in Reading, Berks, is living with a twelve-year-old girl – a twelve-year-old girl named Violet, who Philip claims is his daughter, so, naturally she is called Violet Collier – and, Violet Collier, Philip states, was born in Bunwell, Norfolk. (Bunwell, Norfolk, is a small village today, and was even smaller in the year 1891.)

But, even allowing a plus or minus of five years, there is no record of the birth of this girl. So who was Violet and why does Philip state that she is his daughter?

It took only thirty minutes to look at the 1891 census for the entire population of Bunwell. Despite the fact that there were very few inhabitants, there were, as fate would have it, two girls named Violet, and they were both aged two years.

One was named Violet Chandler, and Violet Chandler was quickly eliminated by reason of the fact that Violet Chandler was also listed in the 1901 census, still residing in Bunwell.

The other two-year-old Violet was named Violet Cannon and Violet Cannon was not listed in the census year 1901.

So... who was Violet Cannon?

Selina Ellen Sturman

Violet Cannon was the daughter of Selina Ellen Cannon, née Sturman.

Selina Ellen Sturman was born in Bunwell, Norfolk, in the year 1867. She was the second child of Levi and Harriet Sturman. Levi was a farm labourer though, in the parlance of the day, he described himself as "a gentleman".

Selina was raised in Bunwell (Low Common) with her older brother, David and her two younger sisters, Hannah and Esther. Circa 1885, when she was aged about eighteen years (presumed – it could have been a lot earlier) Selina went to London and arrived eventually, in Paddington.

Possibly she obtained work as a dental receptionist. What is certain is that she met a dentist; a mature man named John Goodfellow Cannon and on 19 March in the year 1888, (roughly at the same time that Joseph and Marie moved into room number 13, Millers Court) Selina Ellen Sturman, aged twenty-one years, married widower, John Goodfellow Cannon at Paddington register office. John gave his age as forty-two years though in all probability he was older than that. John's profession is shown as "M. D. D. D. S."

(The Dental Council, situated in Wimpole Street, have no record of him though they emphasise that this is not unusual since it did not become compulsory to register until the Dentist Act of 1921. Up till that time a blacksmith (and sundry other tradesmen) might legally administer comfort to those suffering from toothache.)

Both Selina and John gave their address as number 2, Titchborne Street, Paddington.

(Titchborne Street has been totally erased. It was sited off Edgware Road roughly opposite to Crawford Place and just 800 yards from the little chapel where Philip Davies Collier and Marie Thérèse Julien had married in the year 1876. A block of flats cover the area.)

Circa September 1888 Selina found that she was pregnant with child and circa November 1888 (at the time of the Millers Court murder) she returned to Bunwell to stay with her parents. On 26 March 1889, Selina gave birth to a girl and she named the child Violet Grace Essie.

When she registered the birth Selina gave her address as number 15, Old Quebec Street, Hyde Park, London.

(The street is there today. The site where once stood number 15, is buried under The Cumberland Hotel.)

The father's name is shown as John Goodfellow Cannon. His profession is given as "American dentist". The word "American" is gratuitous. There is nowhere on the form that requires nationality to be given. The insertion of this superfluous information sounds as if Selina is in anticipation of being challenged and is preparing a defence.

Selina was still in Bunwell in May 1889 when she registered the birth but shortly after this date she returned with Violet to Paddington and the welcoming arms of John Goodfellow. Whilst she had been away, John had been busy obtaining better accommodation for his family.

This accommodation was located next to Marylebone Station: the address, number 7, Dorchester Place, Blandford Square.

(Blandford Square exists today. The present buildings are comparatively recent. There is no sign of Dorchester Place.)

On 30 October 1890, at number 7, Dorchester Place, Blandford Square, Marylebone, Selina Ellen Cannon gave birth to a female child and she named this child Gladys Elizabeth May. The event was marred by the fact that, in the interim, John Goodfellow Cannon had died.

Selina found herself in a dilemma and, immediately following the birth of Gladys, she, together with her two children, returned to Bunwell.

(The census for the year 1891 records that Selina E Cannon, aged twenty-three years, a widow, and her daughters, Violet aged two years and Gladys aged five months, are residing in Bunwell with Selina's parents, Levi aged fifty-seven years and Harriet aged fifty-two years.)

In her distress over the death of John Goodfellow, Selina had neglected to register the birth of her second child, and this oversight was remedied by means of her making a written declaration. This declaration was dated 2 January 1891, and the registration was effected 12 January 1891.

On the birth certificate for Gladys, Selina records that the father of her child is John Goodfellow Cannon (deceased). His occupation she records as, "Dr of Dental S".

Despite the fact that the demise of John Goodfellow Cannon can be pinpointed with some accuracy, there exists no official record of his death.

On 3 October 1891, Gladys Elizabeth May Cannon, aged just eleven months died at Bunwell. Cause of death, tuberculosis, whooping cough and convulsions. Harriet Sturman was present at the death. The whereabouts of Selina is not recorded.

There is no record of Selina's death or of a remarriage prior to 1901 so why does Philip Davies Collier have custody of Violet – and why does he say he is her father?

Whatever the answer, 3 May in the year 1910, Violet Grace Essie Cannon married stockbroker's clerk, Charles Daniel Chapman at Strand Registry Office, London. Violet gave her address as number 9, Clifton Hill, St Johns Wood. Her father's name she gave as John Goodfellow Cannon (deceased). His occupation is given simply as "dentist".

It is probable that John Goodfellow Cannon (dentist) and Philip Davies Collier (chemist) were acquainted, and likely that Philip enjoyed a close relationship with Mrs Cannon.

It is, of course, possible that John Goodfellow Cannon was Philip Davies Collier's alter ego.

And if Philip Davies Collier really was Violet Cannon's father then he was with Selina in London, probably Paddington, June–July 1888, which would suggest that Philip and Marie had left France sometime soon after October 1883 and returned to England – and had gone their separate ways.

Repent – for the End is Nigh

Sometime during or after the year 1908, Joseph Barnett vacated number 1, Tench Street, Wapping. On 24 November 1910, he read in the newspapers, that Doctor Hawley Harvey Crippen had been hanged, at Pentonville prison, for the murder of the good doctor's faithless wife and, perhaps, he rubbed his neck.

In April of the year 1912, he was shocked to hear that the *Titanic* had hit an iceberg and had sunk.

But eleven years and a World War pass before we meet him again officially. (His name doesn't appear in the index in respect of the 1901 census and I was unable to locate him in the census of 1891.)

Certainly by the year 1919, Joseph Barnett, aged sixty-one years, was "married". He was "married" to a woman named Louisa Denis and he was back in Red Lion Street, this time at number 106, just 150 yards from his old address, number 60, Red Lion Street, which was itself situated just two doors away from number 64, The Old George public house. Joseph and Louisa shared number 106 with Louisa's son, Alfred.

It seems probable that around this time, Joseph Barnett, in common with the majority of the population, became enamoured of the cinema and, probably, he enjoyed the antics of Charlie Chaplin, The Keystone Cops, Mabel Normand, Fattie Arbuckle, Buster Keaton, etc.

Following the Great War in the year 1919, the law was changed to give the vote to any male who met a six-month residential requirement and to any female over thirty years who was a householder or who was married to the householder. There is no record of the marriage of Joseph Barnett to the widow, Louisa Denis, which means that she was his common-law wife.

Alfred Denis is the only other known resident of 106, Red Lion Street. Almost certainly there were others who resided at the same address but, because they were not entitled to vote, they are not shown on the register (possibly one or more of Louisa's other four children).

Red Lion Street was once named Anchor and Hope Alley (the infamous "hanging" Judge Jeffreys was apprehended in a nearby public house in the year 1688). Today the northern tributary-renamed Reardon Street – continues as far as Tench Street. Number 106 was just a few yards to the north of St Peters Mission School, itself built in the year 1871, which still stands today and which would have been a familiar sight to Joseph and Louisa.

Opposite to where once stood number 106, a blue plaque adorns the wall. It records the legend:

> William Bligh RN FRS, who transplanted breadfruit from Tahiti to the West Indies, lived in a house on this site, 1785–1790.

Thereafter Reardon Street becomes a paved footpath (named Reardon Path), which initially runs along the frontage of a block of flats and allows access to same. Where once stood number 60 is now a grassed area in front of the flats. Reardon Path ends at Wapping High Street.

On 20 August in the year 1920, at 48a Lower Road, Rotherhithe (presumed to be St Olaves Union Infirmary) Denis Barnett, former fish porter, aged seventy-one years (the death certificate records seventy-three years) died. The cause of his death was given as chronic bronchitis – myocardial degeneration. Up until the time of his demise Denis was residing at number 18, Larnaca Street, Bermondsey. (The street no longer exists.) The informant was John Barnett, son of Denis, and John's address is given as 7, Earl Road, Bermondsey.

On 28 February 1922, at Archway House, Archway Road, Upper Holloway, Catharine Beer, née Barnett, widow of Joseph Beer, coal carman, died. Catharine was aged sixty-eight years. The cause of her death was given as bronchitis. Catharine's last known address (1901) was number 5, Beauchamp Street, just 200 yards from Portpool Lane, Holborn. The informant was her daughter, Mrs Kate Millichamp, of 68, Cumming St, Clerkenwell.

Joseph Barnett was the last survivor of the children of John and Catharine Barnett – a family that had begun in the year 1849.

In 1922 Joseph Barnett first listened to a new fangled invention called the wireless. The British Broadcasting Corporation was born. The world was getting smaller.

On 1 June 1926, a child named Norma Jeane Mortenson was born. She would become famous as the queen of the silver screen – Marilyn Monroe. On 23 August 1926, the king of the silent screen – Rudolph Valentino – died at the age of just thirty-one years.

At some time, notwithstanding that Joseph Barnett was the possessor of a porter's licence, he forsook Billingsgate and resumed work as a dock labourer. But the damp and the cold were hazardous to health and this, coupled with advancing age, contributed to both he and Louisa contracting the most prevalent illness of the British climate – bronchitis. It is probable that Joseph and perhaps Louisa had had previous bouts of bronchitis and had recovered during the summer months. This time there would be no recovery.

It began just like an ordinary cold. It developed into a dry cough which made the chest and throat sore and painful. That was in late September; then came October. Joseph and Louisa could scarcely breath. The slightest exertion exhausted them. They coughed and wheezed, heaving up thick yellow matter. There was acute pain in their respective backs and their joints hurt. They fought for each bloody, painful breath.

In late October they were separated. Louisa was taken in by friends (or relatives) who resided at number 3, Raine Street, just around the corner from Red Lion Street and nearly next door to the infirmary where John Barnett had died in the year 1902. It was there that bronchitis became bronchial pneumonia. On Wednesday, 3 November 1926, Louisa Barnett was certified dead from broncho-pneumonia. J Carver, resident of number 3, Raine Street, was the informant. The hearse called at this address on the precise thirty-eighth anniversary of the Millers Court murder – 9 November 1926 – and from there it travelled the three miles to the East London Cemetery, Plaistow. There, courtesy of the parish, Louisa Barnett, aged seventy years, was laid to rest in a pauper's grave. There is no marker.

Joseph Barnett stayed on at 106, Red Lion Street, tended by Dr Collins and the stalwart Alfred Denis. But it was all to no avail. On Monday, 29 November 1926, at number 106, Red Lion Street, Wapping, Joseph Barnett, aged sixty-eight years, was pronounced dead. The cause of his demise was given as bronchitis – oedema (excessive accumulation of fluid) of the lungs. No post-mortem. The informant was A Denis.

On 3 December in the year 1926, the hearse stopped outside number 106, Red Lion Street. The coffin containing the body of Joseph Barnett was carried from the house in sight of the tower of the church of St George's-in-the-East. The masts of the ships in the dock, reared and waved a sad, final farewell. It was a funeral fit for a king – a King of Murder.

The hearse proceeded to the gates of the East London Cemetery and Liz Stride stirred in her grave. She remembered Joseph Barnett. Thirty-eight years earlier he and another man had dragged her into Dutfields Yard and cut her throat. (Elizabeth Stride is the only Jack the Ripper victim buried in the East London Cemetery.)

Joseph Barnett was buried, courtesy of the parish, Friday, 3 December 1926, in a pauper's grave. There is no marker: no guard of honour, no eternal flame. Just grass and a few trees.

Exactly how Jack the Ripper would have wanted it.

A few months later, in 1927, John Logie Baird pioneered the Baird Televisor.

In the years 1928–1929, the north side of Dorset Street, which included the Horn of Plenty, the Blue Coat Boy, the Britannia and Millers Court, was demolished to make room for an extension to Spitalfields Market.

In the year 1929, a book was published. Written by Leonard Matters, it was entitled, *The Mystery of Jack the Ripper.*

In the year 1930 Mary Ann Barnett, née Garrett died. It was the end of a generation – the end of an era.

Ten years later, in 1940, Goering's Luftwaffe was busy pounding the haunts of Joseph Barnett to blazing rubble. Had he lived to see it, he would have been aged eighty-two years.

It is interesting to reflect that today there might be people alive to whom Joseph Barnett was once a familiar figure. To be sure, they were young then; only children and he would have been an old man, but they saw him and some of them certainly spoke to him, and perhaps they danced and sang in the little recreation ground that is still there, at the bottom of Reardon Street, today. And maybe they skipped and chanted a little rhyme with funny words: funny words that made them laugh – Jack the Ripper stole a kipper, hid it in his father's slipper.

And maybe he smiled.

How could they understand how it had been.

CERTIFIED COPY OF AN ENTRY OF DEATH

GIVEN AT THE GENERAL REGISTER OFFICE

Application Number: 1004515

REGISTRATION DISTRICT Stepney

1926 DEATH in the Sub-district of St George in the East in the County of London

No	When and where died	Name and surname	Sex	Age	Occupation	Cause of death	Signature, description and residence of informant	When registered	Signature of registrar
	Twenty Ninth November 1926 11 Road 54 Leman Street	Joseph Barnett	Male	65 years	Dock Labourer	(1) Bronchitis Oedema of lungs P.M. certified by Dr E.J. Ludgin	A. Davis Present at the Death 106 Red Lion Street	1926	Herbert Marks Registrar Holborn Sub-district

CERTIFIED to be a true copy of an entry in the certified copy of a Register of Deaths in the District above mentioned.

Given at the GENERAL REGISTER OFFICE, under the Seal of the said Office, the 15th day of October 1995

DXZ 300625

See note overleaf

CAUTION:- It is an offence to falsify a certificate or to make or knowingly use a false certificate or a copy of a false certificate intending it to be accepted as genuine to the prejudice of any person or to possess a certificate knowing it to be false without lawful authority.

Death certificate, Joseph Barnett

Jack the Ripper's Dead

And this is where the story ends – at least for the time being.

Others will find the record of death of Marie Thérèse Julien. I surmise that she died, somewhere in France, circa 1896.

The real victim of the Millers Court murder should be comparatively easy to trace (assuming, of course, that she is not Emily Julia Julien) since I have only scratched at the surface of Marie Thérèse Julien's antecedents.

> *Jack the Ripper's dead*
> *He's lying on his bed*
> *He cut his throat with*
> *Sunlight soap*
> *Jack the Ripper's dead.*

Printed in the United Kingdom
by Lightning Source UK Ltd.
109918UKS00001B/22-45